DAILY LIFE SERIES 18
DAILY LIFE IN VENICE
in the time of Casanova

Only the following titles in this series
are available from Praeger Publishers:

DAILY LIFE IN SPAIN IN THE GOLDEN AGE
DAILY LIFE IN JAPAN AT THE TIME OF THE SAMURAI
DAILY LIFE IN VENICE IN THE TIME OF CASANOVA
DAILY LIFE OF FRENCH ARTISTS IN THE 19TH CENTURY

MAURICE ANDRIEUX

DAILY LIFE IN VENICE IN THE TIME OF CASANOVA

Translated by Mary Fitton

PRAEGER PUBLISHERS

New York · Washington

BOOKS THAT MATTER

Published in the United States of America in 1972 by
Praeger Publishers, Inc., 111 Fourth Avenue, New York,
N.Y. 10003

© 1969 by Hachette
Translation © 1972 by George Allen & Unwin Ltd.

Library of Congress Catalog Card Number: 76-134525

Printed in Great Britain

CONTENTS

ILLUSTRATIONS

Illustrations 10, 11, 13, 19 and 20 are supplied by the Mansell Collection, and the remainder by the *Radio Times*, Hulton Picture Library.

INTRODUCTION

The Most Serene Republic had known her time of world-wide glory in the fifteenth century. Then, as the palaces, churches and campanili rose in the silvery light at the edge of the lagoon, she was in truth the *Dominante*, firm against the Holy Roman Emperor, against kings and Turks and Greeks and Genoese, planting her banners in cities and islands. The East was full of her forts and trading-posts, and Venetian money was the only current coin. There was no one to compete with her. Five thousand ships passed on the sea to fetch the gold, the scarlet dye, her pearls and rich tissues and the trophies she so constantly set up – the four horses from Byzantium, the pillars from St Jean d'Acre, the stone lions from Piraeus. In those days her people had a noble spirit and brave hearts and she gave example to every state in Europe. The mere name of Venice conjured visions of victory and legend, of glorious painting and magnificent festival.

Then, one day, it all stopped. She was suddenly an anachronism, more or less a ghost. The charm and the mystique remained, but now the spell depended on past history for, despite the readjustments she managed to make, and though she roused herself now and again with some inspiring show of civic or martial quality, her decline was continuous after the new route to the Indies was discovered. She was no longer the focal point of commerce, no longer ruled the sea. She was relegated, in the phrase of Montesquieu, to a corner of the universe. In 1508, forsaken and more than half-way to ruin, she had to face Pope Julius II, the Emperor Maximilian, Louis XII of France and Ferdinand of Aragon in their formidable League of Cambrai. From that struggle Venice emerged wasted, mangled and in no shape to oppose the huge and rapidly increasing power of the Ottoman Empire. Drawn unwillingly into Charles V's war against the Turks, she lost fourteen of her islands in the

Greek Archipelago by the Treaty of Constantinople in 1540. The Sultan took Cyprus from her in 1571 and Candia in 1645. The final blow came with the Peace of Passarowitz in 1718, when she was stripped of her last maritime outpost, her possessions in the Morea.

But in spite of these curtailments her territory was still considerable – the Veneto, Brescia and Bergamo on the mainland, and the coastal areas of Istria and Dalmatia. Yet, though theoretically she ruled these *terra ferma* provinces, they lived their daily lives in independence. Only the scattering of islets in the lagoon with their lovely names – La Grazia and the rest – were truly part of Venice, and even some of these had attained a degree of freedom; Murano, for instance, had its own Great Council and its Golden Book. Venice, in fact, was now the isolated city of Venice, nothing more.

So, at the opening of the period with which we have to deal, her history was written. She was a mere name, figuring as an odd survival, a sort of lapsed property, with no policy beyond that of perpetual shuffling. Aware of her weakness, her sole desire was to avoid trouble and she met the humiliations that are heaped upon the weak when all notion of resistance leaves them. It was only for the sake of what she had been that foreign powers condescended to keep their embassies open. Official instructions to one of the French ambassadors indicate that his establishment, for one, was regarded as futile and maintained for pure tradition. 'As things are,' wrote the Foreign Minister, 'the possible influence of Venice in Europe can obviously afford the King no political reason for continuing the embassy. His Majesty, however, has no cause to complain of the conduct of the Venetians . . . and no wish to alter what he and his predecessors have always done. . . .' The ambassadors whom Venice on her side sent out to foreign capitals were looked down upon, in the sorry words of one of the Senate's own secretaries, as 'envoys from a puppet-show', and he added, 'in every court they kick us about because they know they can then get anything they want out of us'. The Doge Paolo Renier at the end of the century drew up a bitter reckoning of decay for Venice: 'We have no more army, no more fleet, no more allies. We are the sport of destiny and accident.'

And yet, deserted by fortune, relegated by her own torpor to the margin of events, consumed with cowardice, no longer mistress of the galleys that sailed triumphing over the sea to impose the might of the winged lion far and wide, she was still Venice, under a different guise. With courage and honour gone, she turned to pleasure as her last resort and remained dazzling on her deathbed, clinging to life with pride unrelinquished, fascinating, desirable as never before. Her days were a pageant of rapture and fantasy. As a political cipher she was yet the home of wealth inexhaustible and unparalleled luxury. Hypnotized by the thought of former glory, she strove to recapture it by sheer magnificence and went on dazzling the world with her beauty and charm and a glittering splendour of fêtes and ceremonies. She set up shop as a merchant of delights and the foreigners, more numerous than ever before, came flocking as though to an assignation, drawn spellbound to the promising, marvellous city where pleasure was an article of faith and poetry the law of common day.

Talleyrand's famous saying about the *douceur de vivre* suits Venice of the eighteenth century better than any other place or time. Life attained its ultimate refinement here, its most exquisite modification. The whole Venetian *Settecento* appears like one grand festival, all enjoyment and comfortable lack of moral stress, as Venice in her mortal danger laughed and sang. After three centuries of splendid and unchallenged power she did not wish to think of her approaching end, though it weighed upon her sorely. *Après nous le déluge* might have been her motto. She presented a sublime spectacle, heavy with drama and incredibly moving, a magic ballet in which a city that was once an empire went down in a blaze of light and a concord of music with an inward anguish only to be guessed at under the seeming gaiety. Venice, sinking to her grave, never found life sweeter than in those last hours, nor lived it more gorgeously. 'Like the sun setting over the water, she cast on all she was leaving an unforgettable farewell light.'[1]

And so we find that the most typical Venetian of this period is neither Doge nor gallant sea-captain nor merchant-prince; none of the over-life-size figures whom the Serenissima had so often bred to work her fortune or her glory. He is in fact a brazen adventurer, apt alike for skulduggery and the practice of high-flown philosophic doctrines. At one time or another he had played the fiddle in a theatre orchestra and acted as a government informer. Giacomo Casanova, self-styled Chevalier de Seingalt, and as such accepted by a posterity equally baffled on several other points about him, was a human compound of the attractions and corruptions of the Venice he knew and whose symbol he may claim to be.[2] And if this scapegrace is admitted to preside over our studies we need not therefore take his celebrated Memoirs for true history. 'Recollection is a form of embroidery', it is said, yet, despite the exaggerations and the disguised characters, their picture of society is by no means inaccurate. This really is what one might have seen, at the height and heart of Venetian life, anywhere between San Marco and the now-demolished church of San Geminiano at the other end of the square.

Nevertheless, Casanova slanders the society of Venice in silently ignoring such virtue as it still retained. For all that it had become the general resort of idler and debauchee, a whirligig of festival, there could yet be discerned behind the extravaganza a sober commons and a thrifty middle class, folk still capable of withstanding the forces that were pulling their nation out of the mainstream of events. Here the comedies of Goldoni are a useful counterpoise, for they show Venetian life on a very different moral basis.

Furthermore, this period had an intellectual vitality that endured to the last. Never before had there been so many brilliant men in Venice. A nineteenth-century historian, Samuele Romanin, names over two hundred of them adorning art and letters in the final fifty years of the Republic, men who, if they include no towering genius, at least founded the only truly national school of painting and the only national drama. Music they served with devotion; they treated learning and philosophy as important but unforbidding subjects, and they made of Venice the great centre of gazettes, those lucid broadsheets with their gay, witty articles, the platform for a band of poets skilled in every grace of the lisping, soft Venetian dialect. And they all, musicans, painters, poets and journalists, expressed the same lighthearted spirit of their time and of their city, the voluptuous life, the airy fantasy and irresistible charm.

Certainly a happy state of mind is apparent in every word they wrote, and Stendhal thought that Venice between 1740 and 1796 must have been the happiest place on earth, 'freer than anywhere of the idiocies of feudalism and superstition that still beset the rest of Europe'. Germany was busy forging her unity, England in acquiring her colonial empire, France with political theorising. Venice had nothing to bother about but pleasure and no ambition left save to act as the capital of joy and wellbeing. The only trade she

did was in tunes and arias. She was all song and laughter, sole remaining devotee of the sunny side of life. The ugly side she had
forgotten so completely that in 1797 she extended her neck to a little
Corsican general, uncomprehendingly, and let him wring it.

CHAPTER ONE

VENETIAN SETTING

I. THE BACKGROUND

Anyone trying to describe the life and habits of a town 200 years ago will usually find it very difficult to form a picture of what it can have looked like. But of Venice the enquiring historian has an unimpeded view. As she was when Casanova lived here, so we see her today, immobile through the centuries because of the way she was built and the site she was built on. That unvarying and familiar scene, that 'geometry of stone between the sky and water' recorded by artist and cameraman, has hardly changed since Canaletto, the Guardi brothers and Bellotto were painting it in all its aspects, princely or popular. Campi have been widened and canals filled in from time to time, but it has been spared what have been called the 'pompous, ghastly, monumental cemeteries' that constitute the residential districts of a modern town.[3] Venice is still her old, peculiar self, constructed according to the laws of the stage and against the laws of nature; a place with water where the ground should be, where the usual distinctions between in and out of doors do not apply and where illusion and reality are one.

She is the creation of her inhabitants, her every street a monument to resident determination. The founders of other cities had at least the soil to start with; Venetians made their own. It was not for the fun of the thing, as Goethe reminds us, that people took refuge in this watery plain, an awkward retreat for which only a seer would have foretold a glorious destiny. They were seeking safety here because they had to. And yet the miracle happened and the far-fetched conception, the marine city, is unique – alone, so Goethe thought, in being itself 'a whole new world; not the country, for you never see a tree, nor the town, for its quiet is unbroken save for the splash of a gondolier's oar'. A Frenchman on his travels at about the same time wrote, 'I am just now at Venice, that is, in the middle of the sea on a great stone boat held at anchor by art and nature for over thirteen centuries'.

At the period we are considering Venice seemed, more than nowadays, to float on the lagoon. From whatever direction you came she lay there in a forest of masts through which, little by little, the stately buildings were revealed as they lifted out of the water. Sea-going ships rode in the Grand Canal where the crowding boats and gondolas went endlessly to and fro and buyers thronged about the merchandise heaped up in quayside *fondachi*. And the Grand Canal is still the heart of Venice, though the craft have lost some of their ornamental value in our progressive days. Every house is a palace on the banks, and the spectacle, unaltered since the days of the Doges, is such as no other town can offer. There is notable architecture on great highways elsewhere in the world, but here it has a special magic in conjunction with lagoon and sky; here the varying, beautiful façades are mirrored in the water, where the reflected palaces are often lovelier still. The diversity of noble buildings, each the creation of its own time and fashion, melts into a whole. There is every architectural ingredient in the mixture, Lombard, Saracenic, Gothic and, last in succession, the baroque, but the eye will catch no discord. These mansions constitute a sort of Golden Book of Venice. They are devoted to exalting, in their own way, the life of lordly splendour, and it is the way of poetry, delicacy and grace. No massive towers or keeps, no crenellations save for ornament. Instead, the light arcades are open to the blue sky, the walls are alive with fresco painting or glittering with mosaic. They are carved with shields and roses, flecked with gold. With their stone flowers and fretted stone carving, they are houses to embrace life, not to guard against it.

It is the shifting, subtle light of Venice that blends all this magnificence into an enchanted opera scene. Sometimes it may create a filtered, gleaming, quivering atmosphere, shot through with misty filaments like swathes of silk or mother-of-pearl transparencies; at others, everything will leap and glow in a dazzle of sanguine and red-gold. By limpid first light or the gorgeous blaze of sunset there is nothing to be seen but marble, sky and water; the world might have risen from a mirage. It is the kind of shore one lands on in a dream.

Every city has its special central point, and the more powerful the city the more imposing this will be. In Padua it is the Palazzo della Ragione, in Florence the Palazzo Vecchio, and here the Piazza di San Marco and its annexe the Piazzetta frame the stately arms of Venice in token of the might of the Republic. There at the threshold, facing the lagoon that flashes and reflects behind them, stand the two tall granite columns that came from the Eastern lands. On one a handsome St Theodore tramples a crocodile; on the other is the scowling lion of St Mark, wings spread and claws displayed.[4] Between these columns the gallows were set up for criminals of note and as late as the eighteenth century people would avoid coming ashore there. One heard of terrible things happening to famous men who had been storm-driven to the unlucky landing stage.[5]

But no superstition about this baleful reach of the shore troubled the boatmen who watched there for custom, the tattered beggars and the *facchini* waiting to swarm round as the gondolas touched nearby; they were concentrating exclusively on jobs or charity or tips. Together with them, those with time to spare came to enjoy a ceaseless, entertaining spectacle of boats of every kind and pattern. Indeed, so long had the fascinated Venetians flocked to this attraction that their assiduous behinds had worn the steps to curves around the columns.

Close at hand, an insubstantial pageant of painted arches, colonnades and balconies, is the palace of the Doge.[6] Had this been Siena, Florence, Ferrara or anywhere else in Italy, prince or government would have lived in lofty palaces behind a strength of stone, ready with keep and drawbridge in case of disagreeable emergencies. But the form of the Venetian government, and the spirit that pervaded it, served as guarantees against popular revolt. Here free rein was safely given to the taste for ornament and arabesque, an oriental habitation could be built for ruler and counsellors, raised like a victor's trophy by the united genius of the Republic at the height of her greatness. The huge rectangular mass of rose-coloured marble rests on two arcaded storeys, and the stylistic outrage is the very image of the city on its wooden piles – the power and the grace upon the frail foundations. It is also, under another aspect, the symbol of authority as that was conceived at Venice, for beneath and above the Arabian Nights palace were the prisons of the state. The Senate, deliberating among the brilliant frescoes of Veroness and Tintoretto, had the dreadful subterranean dungeons under its feet and the cells of the Piombi, with their unenviable reputation, overhead. The government, aptly summed up as a mixture of terror and voluptuous appeal, was housed appropriately in what was both a museum and a gaol. The duality comes out in detail after detail, and even in the torture-chamber the plastic arts were not forgotten; there was elegant carving on the Ponte dei Sospiri which condemned men crossed to execution, and the iron helmet for crushing a suspect's head had a sombre beauty of its own.

The Doge's palace and the Old Library face one another in grandeur across the Piazzetta, whose former name was the Broglio, meaning 'intrigue' in Italian. Here the nobles would meet to discuss their devious designs, and from describing their purpose in walking about together the word was applied to the place they walked in, and finally to the square itself. But only part of the Piazzetta, varying with the season and the time of day, was their exclusive territory. In the winter and on warm mornings the patricians gathered under the colonnades of the ducal palace and on the area in front of it, about a third of the square; their afternoon strolling was sheltered from the sun on the opposite side and beneath the first arches of the Procuratie.[7]

The side they were not occupying was left free for the middle and lower sort, who were firmly forbidden to stray over, even with the most respectful of intentions. Young patricians might appear on the Broglio only when old enough to sit in the Grand Council, when their elders would introduce them with all due solemnity. The noble who lost his place on the Council was barred from the Broglio as well. On the Broglio one could follow the canvassing for state appointments. There the negotiations went on, with the whole gamut of cunning, sharp practice and manoeuvre displayed to an incredible degree, involving, as the Président de Brosses observed, *les dessous des cartes admirables* – some very specialized knowledge indeed. Tactics of Machiavellian subtlety were, moreover, combined with spaniel-like bearing towards anyone with a vote to cast. Before a voter, candidates bowed to the ground till their wigs brushed the pavement and people of the most exalted ancestry would disguise their usual scorn and humbly kiss the robes of patricians inferior to them in the hierarchy.

The Piazzetta forms as it were an ante-room at right angles to the Piazza di San Marco, across one end of which there stands the church that Venice fabricated to astonish Christendom. St Mark's basilica is among the greatest and most splendid of all religious buildings, a poem of stone and light, a living part of the city and a living illustration of her history. Clearly it could be no other than the church of a sea people. From across the water it suggests, as it did to the writer Edgar Quinet a century ago, 'some consecrated ship coming under full sail to land, loaded with relics and sacred vessels from Byzantium'. The eastern look is so pronounced that it has been called a transplanted Hagia Sophia. The furniture, the very walls, were spoils of holy warfare. But the Venetians in re-creating the Byzantine forms at home adapted them with such freedom to the light and colouring of their city that everywhere rules are broken, styles intermingled and the normal expectations of the eye deceived. Diversity, contrast and extra adornment, three things which, according to Taine, inspire all architects with horror, here make delicate harmony.

Outside, the bulging domes rise one above another and the arcades have a light and airy grace; but inside, St Mark's is a miracle of splendour. It is one stupendous reliquary, and the loot, as much as the art, of Venice contributed to its richness. Gold is the keynote; gold alive and breathing; responsive to the light, vivid as long as daytime lasts. It shines on roof and columns, glows along the naves and illumines every pillar. A superb Persian tapestry of mosaic covers more than 4,000 square yards, underfoot there gleams a wealth of precious marble. When these coloured surfaces take the play of light the whole scene transcends reality and becomes, as Gabriel Faure describes it, 'a sort of phantasmagoria'.

St Mark's has not changed since the eighteenth century, but it was not then open to all comers. For long it had been the preserve of the Doge and the great officers of state and its atmosphere was still that of a private enclosure, discouraging the presence of the generality, who were invited as a favour on important feast-days only. The fact that it was not then the seat of the bishop also em-phasised this feeling, for until 1807 the cathedral was, for no very obvious reason, at San Pietro in Castello, at the city's eastern limit. A stone's throw from San Marco, straight as a mast, the tall Cam-panile reared into the sky, visible from far away as a sign of the majesty of the Republic, with the flowering stone of Sansovino's elegant Loggetta at its foot.

The Piazza di San Marco is, together with the Piazzetta, the only true piazza in Venice, though the term is applied to dozens of small and very small squares which hardly qualify. In the eighteenth century, even more than today, it was the heart of the town, the grand centre for loafing and gossip; magnet, too, of the pleasure-seeker, meeting-place for company of every kind, the more and the less desirable, and customary rendezvous of lovers. 'There no constant check was kept upon fidelity,' as a chronicler once put it, 'and it could be very favourable for love.' And then, as now, it was as much pigeon territory as promenade; and still its pigeons disport themselves by thousands, flying in the faces of the passers-by, bowing and cooing at the ears of statues, 'as though delivering heavenly messages', and still they come plummeting from the top of the roofs, wings folded, chasing their own shadows. They were doing all these things two hundred years ago, though nothing but the noon gun from San Giorgio Maggiore disturbed them in those days.

The disappearance of San Geminiano from the far end opposite St Mark's has, however, made the square look different. Napoleon, with his demanding passion for symmetry, ordered the beautiful church to be pulled down in 1807, though the Fabbrica Nuova with which he replaced it harmonises very well with the older Procuratie and their triple galleries. This Piazza is worthy, as he said, of having the sky for a canopy; penned in its arcades, hedged with superb buildings, it is indeed incomparable.

The long line of cafés under the arches all round was even then the great attraction. There were over two hundred cafés in Venice, but the best known were all here under their various names and signs, allegorical, artless or high-sounding: the Queen of the Sea, perhaps, the Liberality, the Matter of Fact, the Coach of Fortune, the General, the Three Wise Men. Several saints, such as Antony and Lawrence, were included, and one Holy Trinity. Most popular seems to have been the Venice Triumphant which is open still, rechristened Florian's after Floriano Francesco, its proprietor in 1720. Coffee-houses did not go in for gilding and looking-glass on a lavish scale. The décor was if anything rather shabby and, except in the depth of winter, customers stayed outside. Weather permitting, they sat under the arcades in the Piazza, where tables and chairs awaited them, so that the tiniest café might easily have five hundred patrons on the pavement. People then, however, were not allowed to impede free passage and would never have believed the extent of the modern overflow into the square.

The owners made use of occasional ingenuities to keep on the right side of the law. Café furniture, for instance, was supposed to be cleared away by midnight, but we learn from a police report for March 24, 1772, that poultry-coops left in a neighbouring market were then set out instead. The *sbirri*, or constables, must have been lax, for most regulations were treated very casually and infringements, denounced to the Inquisitors of State, would be ignored unless there had been scenes of open scandal or talk prejudicial to the dignity of government. In defiance of what were called the 'most revered' official commands, the café pavements seethed with activity the whole day long and well into the night. Night, for that matter, never fell in the Piazza, which seemed to a contemporary 'a dazzle of everlasting day'. The customers at their coffee were pestered meanwhile by an unceasing crowd of candied-fruit sellers and urchin beggars, ragged and dishevelled; by fortune-tellers and pretty flower-girls who were difficult to get rid of. And when Carnival came round the Piazza, as we shall see, was the centre of delights innumerable.

Such were the show-places, but there was another Venice where the ordinary people lived their ordinary lives and coped with the troubles and pleasures of their lot. The busiest quarter was Rialto, with its famous bridge spanning the canal in a high single arch that let the ships go through whatever the state of the tide. On it were twenty-four houses, 'narrow as knife-blades'. heavily roofed with lead.

Leading to Rialto from the Piazza was the Merceria, a street paved with squares of Istrian marble, and the only one where any such improvement was attempted. To reach it you went under the clock whose claim to mark only the happy hours – *horas non numero nisi serenas*, it says – may remind us that the Venetians plumed themselves on a remarkably individual attitude to time in any case. Mechanical bronze giants told all the hours God sent with their heavy hammer-blows, hours shown on the great clock-face with phases of the moon and signs of the Zodiac. An infinity of shops in the Merceria sold everything you could think of, from cooked food to fine lace and precious stones, and there alone in Venice the trades were intermingled. Shops were usually separately grouped, with each trade giving its name and character to its own particular street. Thus bakery after bakery lined the Panetteria, and beside the

23

Grand Canal the Pescheria could show every fish the sea or the lagoon produced. Near the Rialto bridge the Erberia was the province of the greengrocers as it is today, though oranges were sold in a special market known as the Maranzaria.

What we should call local trade was the affair of itinerant vendors, operating quite illegally and barely tolerated by the police. On the other hand, you could take a snack or a drink, or even buy a bottle, almost anywhere. No district was without its coffee-shops and water-shops with liquids of every kind on sale, nor the *malvasie* which dealt not only in malmsey but in Greek wines generally. All these establishments partitioned off their premises for the benefit of couples wishing to enjoy each other's company undisturbed, and the *malvasie* especially had a lurid reputation; the authorities were informed that many of them had become 'veritable brothels.' The water-shops, though better conducted, lent themselves to scandal of another kind, for they were usually in the little squares before the parish churches. This meant that women going in to pray had to pass between the tables and benches just outside the door, and *en route* afforded particularly fine occasion for the gentlemen seated there to launch complimentary remarks, gestures of invitation and witticisms of an indelicate nature.

Each of the seventy-two parishes of Venice had also its *magazzen*, a kind of bar-depository where wine was sold and cooked meat could be bought and consumed on the spot. These places would accept articles in pawn, though one-third of the sum advanced had to be taken in a very poor brew known as borrower's wine. They stayed open all night and had rooms fitted up 'for purposes of debauch'. Patronised entirely by the lower classes, they were centres of ill-repute, frequent disorder and never-ending uproar.

The city was cut, as it is today, into a multitude of island blocks by a bewildering complex of narrow canals, several of which have filled in since and are now streets. If the Président de Brosses came back to Venice he would be somewhat less justified in complaining that he 'could not take a step without putting his feet in the water'; and certainly less ready with criticism of the 'appalling stench'.[8] 'Obviously,' he says, 'things have to smell of whatever it is they smell of, and obviously canals will reek in summertime, but this really is too much.' In his day, unprotected by the sanitary regulations of a watchful town council, they were assuredly dirtier and more odorous than now, though no less picturesque for that. For it is still what people throw in – and despite the rules they still throw in a great deal – that adds the rainbow dyes which, all stippled together, give their artist's-palette look to the canals. Waterways that would be dismal anywhere else are here a pleasure to the eye. The light colours the surface and leaps up, reflected, on every side. 'It throws soft tones of green and gold on the canals,' someone once wrote, 'and the grand Venetian marriage-feast of sea and sky can be watched from any of the *calli* as easily as on the shining width of the Grand Canal, that Champs Elysées of the water-god.'

One might infer from the Président's unflattering report that the canals were stagnant, but even in his time they were nothing of the kind. The unseen currents have always run at night through the dark arteries of Venice, washing the crumbing walls and slimy steps. Regularly the cleansing tide comes in that has been likened to a sort of youthfulness injected into the veins of the city from the sea. The *acqua alta*, the sharp equinoctial rise in water-level, was presumably less disturbing then than nowadays, when ground-floors are often flooded and business comes to a halt. The houses have settled by now a little further on to the wooden posts beneath, but then, too, the Piazza could disappear under sheets of liquid mud.

Strangely enough, the aquatic city has not a single natural spring. 'Set at the water's edge,' wrote Edgar Quinet, 'she might have been Palmyra in the desert', and the two wells in the ducal courtyard have something of an oasis air about them. Fresh water for the reservoirs came by boat from Fusina on the Brenta canal. The well-heads in the little squares are mere ornamental features, hollowed-out capitals stolen from Greek churches and brought home by returning voyagers in the good old days.

In time some of the canals were provided with double quays, like those of Amsterdam, but the sea lapped the housefronts in the eighteenth century. The water-lanes came up to the walls on either side and only a few of them left an inch or two for walking. But one could walk, as we can today, on the islands in the watery maze. The streets, or *calli*, were variously named according to width and importance – a street might be a *strada*, *salizada*, *ruga* or *rughetta* – and so idiosyncratic are their wanderings that it seems indeed incredible that any of them lead to anything, so 'self-contained and self-sufficient' are they.[9] And where there were a few feet to spare the miniature *campi* would open out before the churches, each like a theatre scene, harbouring the sun.

25

Every house could be reached by land and water in the criss-cross of pathways and canals. A gondola could take you anywhere, of course, but thanks to the multiplicity of bridges you could also go anywhere without their aid. Anyone was free to build a bridge for his personal convenience or with the object of collecting a toll from other people; he only had to satisfy the officials of the Piovego[10] that his arches left sufficient clearance for the boats. There were almost 500 bridges, not all of stone, as they are today, and many without parapets. Fortunately the users were cautious and agile and seem not to have fallen in too often, but getting from one place to another on foot was always a complicated undertaking. There was no such thing as a direct route in the whole of Venice; she was a labyrinth then and a labyrinth she remains.

In the innermost *calli*, high-walled and narrow, plunged in the familiar twilight all day long, it was easy to walk, as now, unimpeded by anything on wheels, but the scene was livelier. In the terrific bustle you could have your knives sharpened, your cat castrated, buy flowers or drinking-water, hear a violin or oblige a beggar. The poorer classes lived in relatively cramped conditions and liked the open air in any case. The street was their theatre and nursery-school, their workshop and scullery. The women peeled the vegetables and did the washing there, and it was part of the business world as well, for though true shops were restricted to the recognised sites, hawkers by the dozen went up and down the *calli*, rousing the echoes with persistent cries. A basket let down by a cord put the purchaser in touch with ground-level or canal, and dotted about at convenient spots were makeshift and unlicensed stalls, with awnings like coloured sails, where shrewd dealers sold watermelon, pumpkins, grapes, stewed pears, preserved fruit and sweet potatoes in season, and grilled fish the whole year round. In the heat of the day the *acqaioli* would offer the much-prized treat of water 'chilled like ice' with a splash of alcohol, to which real connoisseurs added a drop of aniseed for its tempting opal tint.

And among it all you could do what you liked, and do it at your own pace, for there was a universal, comfortable consideration for others. The contemporary Count Giuseppe Gorani records that people 'rarely stopped to peer into each other's faces, nor was one ever stared at in the street'. Any crowd that gathered would be listening to some water-borne barrel-organ, most popular of entertainments, whose sound the gondoliers themselves would go out of their way to follow. Indeed, criticism of the barrel-organ seemed to come only from the cage-birds of which every household had a large collection, sometimes in a room set aside as a sort of Noah's Ark. Canaries, tropical sparrows and turtle-doves sang in rivalry when they heard the tunes, though the rest of the menagerie, rabbits and guineapigs, took no more notice than did the serene and meditative cats who lived in colonies in odd corners, safe from playing children. The common people made much of cats and lavished friendly attentions on them. One theory is that the Venetians recognised in the cat their own characteristics – scepticism and amiability, detachment from the world's affairs, irony and a refusal to take anything seriously except love.[11] But practical reasons matched the emotional involvement, for the canals were swarming with rats, and who knows if Venice, without those guardian cats, would stand today upon her wooden underpinnings?

The streets were as filthy as all Italian streets were at that time. Refuse dumped by the bucketful could have rotted there for ever had the inhabitants of the nearby islands not needed manure and collected it occasionally. A cleansing service did exist, but as two men were expected to see to a whole district with the aid of a single boat, their visits were few and far between. For lack of sewers, moreover, these men heaped the garbage up wherever the fancy took them, often beside the churches and sometimes in the heart of the commercial quarter near the Grand Canal. Here, we are told, 'the noble merchant in his loggia could negotiate only with his nose in a pocket-handkerchief'.[12] Some unorthodox assistance came from the pigs that were left to grub about in freedom for St Antony's sake, these animals being his emblem, perhaps in memory of kindly service during his life in the desert. Travellers without exception marvelled at the dirt, and Goethe especially thought it inexcusable in a town 'as perfectly situated for cleanliness as anywhere in Holland'.

Public lighting was little better organised, although at night the Piazza and the nearby shopping streets were bright as day. Shops and windows in the Merceria were lit up until a late hour and the gaming-houses and resorts of pleasure until dawn, but before streetlighting was introduced in 1732 the narrow alleys were all in pitch darkness. Carlo Goldoni, back in Venice in 1737 after a long absence, tells how delighted he was to see the new lamp-standards, 'so charming, so useful', where he could remember people groping through the gloom. But it is to be feared that the joy of homecoming ran away with him, for impartial and official records say that what roused his enthusiasm was a collection of farthing rushlights, set too far apart to give more than an apology for illumination.[13] Nor did they alter the fact that only Venetians with a flawless knowledge of local topography could venture after dark into the maze of streets. For strangers there was instituted a guide-service known as the *codega*, with lantern-bearers to take them back to their houses, or forth to the night's enjoyment.

These circumstances, together with the Venetian way of staying indoors, grandly aloof from all events outside, might well have left an open field for criminals; and yet this town, so entirely apt for ambush and surprise, was known to be remarkably secure. On this the local chroniclers and foreign visitors are universally agreed. There is a truly touching chorus in praise of the gentle native character and the resultant safety of the late-night stroll. The French traveller Lalande[14] for one is most careful for the reputation of Venice and states categorically that the streets were free of peril. The Président de Brosses, too, says there are not four murders a year, 'and most of those committed by strangers'. We may perhaps wonder, nevertheless, whether these informants were not, in their innocence, aiding official propaganda whose natural object was to lure the incomer. Since medieval times all Europe had been drawn to the water-city. Commerce and the tourist trade had been her mainsprings of prosperity and the tourist trade had taken a very long lead by the eighteenth century. The perpetual throng of visitors – over 30,000 in the six months of Carnival – brought considerable revenue to a town of 135,000 inhabitants. Most of these guests were rich, and prepared to spend liberally during their stay; it was therefore important to keep them happy and confident, and the careful Signory took especial pains to see that people were not aware of any of the risks they might in fact encounter. Things were not, to be sure, so dramatic as in other parts of Italy, where in the States of the Church, for instance, 11,000 murders occurred in slightly less than ten years when Clement XII was Pope in the 1730s. But the archives of the State Inquisitors, in their orderly files, certainly record death sentences passed in Venice while the Président was there in the summer of 1739. In those few weeks there are seventeen of them, all for killing, and the motive is always robbery; and many non-fatal assaults and serious affrays are heard of at the same date. These facts provide a more realistic picture of supposedly tranquil nights by the lagoon.

There were other disturbances, too, besides quarrelling and fighting and the despoiling of inoffensive passers-by, for all the wild young men loved upsetting solid citizens in the dark hours. Casanova, who had been a wild young man himself, lists the favourite diversions pursued in little bands by his fellow delinquents. Not all were innocent jokes. The effect was relatively limited when they roused an unsuspecting midwife with urgent pleas to attend some lady who was not even pregnant; or hastened a priest away with the viaticum to some good man sleeping happily by his wife. But when it came to a gang of them in a campanile ringing the bells as for a fire-alarm, they could set a whole parish by the ears, as men leapt out of bed, women dashed to the windows and the entire locality was given over to chaos and alarm.

As the population increased, so more and more houses rose along the streets and canals, huddling ever more closely together and growing taller and taller in quest of light and air. They paddled in the gleaming water with their roofs in the sun, walls painted red above and green below. They were crowned by the peculiar Verétian chimney-pots, like bells hung upside down, whose design was said to be French, though it gave the roofscape the look of a Turkish graveyard, full of stone turbans. In addition to street-doors and boat-doors, every house had other discreet, convenient entrances, most useful for dishonest serving-men, procuresses and those engaged in clandestine love-affairs.

The houses of old Venice were like ships with coloured sails and flower-strewn decks. They had a poetic, heart-lifting character, too often lost as the passion for change has played havoc with the place. In those that have escaped the indiscriminate whitewashing can be recognised a style of architecture unique as the city is unique – waterfront building, but without monotony. The merchant ships brought home the feeling and forms of the Orient, and Venice, seizing upon the most diverse styles, had made a wonderful blend of them; and since all her borrowings came by sea, she was, in this sense, sea-born like Aphrodite. The house-walls were covered at the foot in delicate green moss, so the gondolas slid between hangings of velvety green, flecked by the foam of the wake dissolving as they passed. In those days there were more of the wooden balconies, resembling Arab lattices, running the length of every floor, bright with flowers and leafy plants and overhanging vines. On every roof rose the traditional *altana* where the family met to enjoy the cool of evening and discuss the happenings of the day. And here in the sunshine the women staged their transformation scenes, dyeing and drying their hair until the jettiest locks took on the famous red-gold tint of true Venetian blonde.

The humblest *altana* was invariably a roof-garden, with small shrubs and the luxuriant flowers that grow here as nowhere else, so thick and soft and fresh in the damp air, looking, as George Sand later wrote, as langorous as any Venetian ladies. Few people had gardens and these balconies and *altane* were almost the only places where they could sit outside and have some taste of the countrified surroundings that they loved. Theirs was a compact city; or, as a French observer put it, 'very full up'.

A handful of the noble palaces had famous gardens, though these were noteworthy not for the amount of space they occupied but for the statuary, the stone vases, columns or sarcophagi they contained. Palazzo Gradenigo and Palazzo Cappello, where Napoleon lodged for the short amount of time he needed to destroy the Serenissima, were much admired for the magnificent marble groups that stood among beds of verbena and rare plants expensively imported from the East. There were other, hidden pleasaunces, the only clue to their whereabouts a glimpse of cypress-trees just topping the walls of tortuous streets, but though a local optimist at the beginning of the eighteenth century thought there must be one for every day of the year, a couple of paces would take you from end to end of most of them. If a patrician wanted a real garden he had to follow the fashion and make one over on Giudecca, which became the pleasure-island of Venice, a perfect background for carefree picnics and splendid hospitality.

In conclusion, we may note that the ordinary houses were generally comfortable and not without some touch of elegance. The Venetian did not live in a hovel. Having turned his back on an expatriate career on the high seas he was determined to have everything handsome about him at home. We know from Francesco Sansovino[15] that table-silver and fine pewter dishes were used in quite modest households. Rooms were floored with splendid parquet in various colours, and cleaned and polished scrupulously.

Beds of walnut wood were spread with coverlets, decorative copper plaques hung on the walls. Cupboards and chests with patterns of bright marquetry-work (try buying them in an antique shop today!) completed what would be more than adequate furnishing in many a middle-class home in modern times. In Venice you did not have to be rich to appreciate good shape and sound material.

II GOVERNMENT

The first Doge was elected in 697 and over the next five hundred years Venice forged the remarkable polity that assured her the kingdom, the power and the glory in her golden centuries. A series of what were on the surface mere adjustments of detail, but which in fact were radical reforms, had established the aristocratic nature of her institutions, and these the world long regarded as a model of wise government. It never tried to copy them, all the same; the attempt to do so would have been foolish and unsuccessful, for they sprang from a civic structure and an ingrained attitude that were unique. Opulent Venice, with her trader's wealth, put her faith in earthly treasure, took that faith to all extremes, provided the perfect system for its protection, and unfalteringly made it work.

She chose to function as an oligarchical republic in which the people were a purely passive element and professional politicians unknown. The oligarchy consisted of the great merchants who, with their personal interest in its smooth working, banded together to run the state like a business house. All the care and cost were on their shoulders, but they had no power to abuse their own prerogatives. These fundamental principles were so applied that no one of the governing class could evade his responsibility, while faction and intrigue were foiled by processes of election complicated beyond belief. Short terms of office and shared authority at every level effectively discouraged dreams of despotism. At no time did one man hold the slightest authority alone. Always there were groups of men, advising, deciding, acting on decisions. On such a basis all the wheels went round to the maximum benefit of a governmental ideal which, unexciting as it might seem, made Venice, despite her secret courts, a land of law and general liberty.

The Serenissima was the only Italian state in the eighteenth century with a system surviving directly from the Middle Ages, unchanged in spirit by minor adaptations. Such continuity was all the more remarkable in a republic, but what happens in most republics had never happened here – no opposition had ever crystallised. In gradually taking over the whole machinery of state the upper classes never ceased their efforts to merit the people's trust; and the people, easy-going and sweet-tempered, for all they had been such wonderful military material, were content with a soft life, and shows and holidays. They were 'the best folk in the world', according to Montesquieu. The class struggle with its passions and violence passed them by. They were not in the least upset at having no political rights. So far as they were concerned their pleasant servitude was liberty, and they longed for nothing else.

It was not merely a happy-go-lucky attitude, however, that exiled them so cheerfully from public affairs. On a more exalted plane, all classes were united by a feeling of solidarity that was born with Venice herself and kept alive by her peculiar circumstances. By dint of courage and energy a nation of heroes had overcome apparently unsurmountable difficulties, raised their magic city from the sea and made her ever more beautiful as time went by. She was their common masterpiece, regarded by everyone with pride and joy and, most of all, with love. A touching filial piety welded the people together. Everything was judged by the good it would do the Republic, and no one therefore dreamed of criticising its theories of government.

There existed also a very special natural characteristic that made for stability. Venetians simply hated change. What had always been was held in honour, automatically. It made not the slightest difference to their reverential respect that the circumstances from which a custom arose were lost and forgotten; the need to keep up the tradition was a successful argument in any debate and could produce absurd results. Lalande, for instance, has a sad and telling example of blind devotion to the little weaknesses of the past. In his day – which was also Casanova's – there was a Venetian noble with an important charge in the Public Works department who adopted the unheard-of course of paying over to the Treasury certain moneys which his predecessors had, by general consent, put into their own pockets. This was considered extremely bad form. The man was trying to give his fellow citizens a lesson; worse, he was going against an ancient usage. So he was sent off to govern a very obscure village, which is the moral of the story.[16]

But in the eighteenth century the government of Venice, that

1　The Rialto Bridge (from an old print)

2 Interior of the Doge's Palace

3 Piazza S. Marco, by (?) Canaletto

settled miracle of politics, was showing obvious signs of maladjust-
ment in the modern world. So many things had changed. The city
had lost her power, the faith was gone out of Venetian religion, her
laws were empty dictates, moral standards had declined. All this
had been going on for a long time, but the Republic, lapped in ease
and lack of urgency, had done nothing to alter either her way of
thinking or her rules and regulations. Stability had become rigidity,
so that all her past advantages were now defects, open to the justified criticism of the *philosophes* and their new school of thought in
France. But she was still indifferent to novelty, ever more isolated
and driven in upon herself, thinking only to preserve her customs,
laws and outward forms, all of them now meaningless. The ranks
of the patriciate, open to merit in the victorious days, were henceforth fixed and limited. No one, however suitable, was to hold high
office unless he were a noble, and the path to nobility was closed;
the state in consequence lost much valuable talent and sacrificed
the progressive impetus that comes from competition. In her council chambers the assumptions of a bygone age were still as truths
revealed from heaven. The wind of change simply never blew there.

The Venetians in their fallen estate were beyond requiring any
consolation save that of outward splendour and the brilliance of
their great festivities. The energy that once went into conquest or
huge commercial undertakings was now employed in the narrow
sphere of super-exaggerated ceremonial and the government, to
protect its dignity and what was left of its prestige, became more of a
riddle than ever. What it talked about and what it actually did
were wrapped in utter secrecy.

In theory, the Doge was head of the Republic. He, with his six
counsellors and the three chiefs of the *Quarantia Criminale*, or supreme
court of justice, together constituted the Serenissima Signoria, the
Signory of Venice, a group of ten who stood for the entire state.
The Doge was the leading representative among them, nothing
more, and the only one who held office for life. His slender authority
was assigned him by his colleagues, and nothing but his ceremonial
duties now marked him from the rest.

The Great Council, made up of the whole patriciate, chose him
after a series of intricate preliminary elections and this process,
tedious though it may seem, should at least be glanced at. The
assembled Council would send the youngest member present over

B

to St Mark's, where he briefly prayed and afterwards returned to the palace with the first small boy he happened to encounter. This child then acted as *ballotino*, drawing the ballot-balls from an urn to indicate who should vote at the various stages. The urn to begin with contained as many balls as there were members of the Council, but only forty-one were marked 'Elector'. Successive draws reduced the number of electors to thirty, then to nine. This first group of nine – there were others yet to come – chose, by a majority of seven, twenty-five. From these, nine were again chosen by lot. The new nine then nominated forty-five who, after recourse to the urn, elected, not the Doge (they had not finished ballotting) but the forty-one who were to go into conclave and choose the head of the Republic.

It was a combination of sheer chance and balanced judgement, a clear demonstration of the care with which the nomination of great dignitaries was guarded from intrigue and undue influence. Every vacant office was filled by a similar process – election, blended with the luck of the draw.

The conclave itself was modelled on that of the Sacred College at Rome. Shut up in the ducal palace, its members deliberated in secret, cut off from the outside world, They were traditionally supplied with anything they asked for and all were traditionally treated alike, so the provisioning was sometimes inappropriate. If a bored counsellor yearned for Aesop's fables to brighten his seclusion, each of his forty companions received a copy too. Should a pious counsellor request a rosary, then rosaries arrived for all, not excepting any freethinkers who happened to be among them. In this way the assembly ended up with a clutter of useless objects wafted to it at the whim of individual members, or in answer to someone's strictly, if not intimately, personal needs. The considerable expense involved developed into scandalous waste as the century wore on. The thirteen-day conclave of 1709 cost only 59,325 lire, but eighty years later, when the same number of men sat for half as long, the bills came to precisely 378,387 lire, which was six times as much.[17]

After a varying but always large number of lengthy sessions – every name put forward entailed forty speeches for or against – the conclave finally selected some illustrious or at any rate revered elder, often best described as 'a noble ruin, still on his feet'. Advanced age, especially if supplemented by infirmity, was in fact a trump card for any candidate. The Maggior Consiglio, like the

College of Cardinals, preferred its throne to be empty at frequent intervals.

After his election the new Doge was conducted in pomp to St Mark's, where he saluted the people from the pulpit to the left of the choir, swore fealty to the state and received his mantle and the standard of the Republic. Then, carried in triumph by hulking workmen from the Arsenal, he entered the palace up the marble Scala dei Giganti, between the colossal statues of Mars and Neptune. There at the top he was given first the *berretta*, or linen cap, then the ducal *corno* which was his chief badge of office. The golden *corno* was so precious that the Procuratori kept it in the basilica under lock and key, ready for ceremonial occasions. As it was placed on the ruler's head all the guns and bells and cheering stopped and in the solemn silence a single voice proclaimed the Doge.

He next went to the Sala del Piovego, where he signed the record of his election and encountered the first of his many mortifications. For mingled with the shower of official compliments there came other traditional voices with brusque and sometimes brutal warnings as to proper conduct. Lord of the Republic he might be, but they reminded him all the same that where he now stood his body would lie for three days while strict judges weighed his every act as sovereign, and they bade him remember how his posthumous fame would suffer if the verdict went against him. With these admonitions ringing in his ears the Doge at last withdrew to the private apartments, there to live in great outward luxury, hedged about with reverence, a cipher in the grip of tyrant formality.

He was treated in all things as a ruling monarch. His robes and his retinue were the wonder of the crowds at fêtes and state occasions. Then his emblem-studded tunic shone with gold and silver and he wore his pointed crown, the *corno*, that was removed only for the elevation of the Host at Mass or in greeting to a royal prince. He went on his way preceded by attendants with lighted candles, by musicians sounding silver trumpets, and by the eight bright-coloured standards with the arms of Venice. His chair of cloth of gold, his umbrella-like state canopy and scabbarded sword were borne by officers in gorgeous uniforms, and behind came the long file of great dignitaries and senators in gala array.

The Doge in state presided over the deliberations of the government and displayed the utmost magnificence for visiting kings or their ambassadors.[18] Five times a year, dressed in a purple robe, he

35

gave a sumptuous feast to the leading officials and their wives, and the banqueting-hall of the palace, built in the seventeenth century to accommodate several hundred guests, was thrown open to the public. Pressed against the walls, they enjoyed their purely visual share of the carouse.

It was well worth seeing. The tables shone with light and colour. Set on the fine lace were triumphal arches in glistening dyed wax, a treasury of gold plate, golden centrepieces, figured candlesticks, with allegorical groups at intervals in wonderfully wrought glass illustrating the victories and epics of the Serenissima. The plates were all of silver, yet – a paltry touch – every item had to be accounted for at the end of the meal, and we hear of a distinguished company having to wait about for over an hour when one small dish was missing. Twelve courses were the rule, each played in to the sound of oboe, violin and harpsichord, whose soft strains alternated with resonant operatic tenor voices singing the newest arias. Dignity was forgotten over the dessert, when diners took to throwing sugared almonds and such-like ammunition round the room. Some were poor marksmen, and wigs were knocked awry, goblets and windows shattered.[19]

The Doge in past ages had been in truth a sovereign prince, leading and hiring armies, making alliances and administering justice without reference to any other person. But the encroaching nobles had taken away his prerogatives one by one and only the show of royalty remained; he was nothing now but the symbol of national greatness. And this deliberate transformation of the ruler into a living lay-figure was as cunning an expedient as the French traveller Misson, who was no fool, said it was.[20]

'The Doge is the Image or Representative of the Republick, whose pleasure it is to reflect its Glory upon him, as it were to ease it self of the trouble of it; yet appropriating to it self all the Honours he receives. And those Honours to which the Quality of Doge entitles him, are not paid to him who is invested with it, but that they may be immediately transferr'd to the State, which seems to have only set him up for that purpose.'

This explains why care was taken that such honours should belong to the office rather than to the man. It was long since his likeness had appeared on the coinage, where the kneeling figure in the ducal robes bore no resemblance to the occupant of the throne himself. So much did the nobles dread the rise of individual mastery that the Doge's portrait was to be glimpsed only in those few churches specially authorised to hang it, out of the way in a dark corner.

The Duke of Venice, then, in his confined and faceless life, was a mere gilded personification of the state. He had no function but appearance and no power to speak of. He signed the laws, he was the ostensible fount of justice and sat at the head of every council table, but he was blocked at every turn with such consummate skill that any opinion he might venture served usually to generate support for the other side. His only rights were petty things like nominating the canons of San Marco, allotting minor posts about the palace and handing out little awards for literary merit. The Senate governed in his name and left him nothing to do but proclaim decrees on its behalf.

A further check on his freedom came from the six advisers who formed his Privy Council. They were primarily watchdogs to ensure his absolute subservience and controlled his every action. He could neither give audience nor read political dispatches or private letters unless they were there. Word by word, they prompted or dictated his replies to delegations and ambassadors. And towards the counsellors the Republic was as distrustful as towards the Doge himself. They counselled for no longer than eight months at a time, retiring in turn every four months and never including more than one member from the same district or family.

Subject as he was to many irksome duties laid down by law and inescapable, the Doge had also to put up with the deliberate humiliations traditional even on formal occasions. There was, for instance, the man who followed him about with a broad-bladed sword to remind everyone of the beheading of the Doge Marino Falier after an attempted *coup d'etat* in 1355, and when the anniversary of the execution was celebrated at San Vitale a priest walked behind the Doge with a phial of red liquid to represent the traitor's blood. He was never allowed to forget the renouncement of all personal power in his election oath, and the state was cruelly frank about it. He was under the law like any private citizen, although he was the leading magistrate, and more exposed than most to the attentions of the Council of Ten. Even the prerogative of mercy was denied him and any intervention of his could only have made things worse for a convicted prisoner. In the rare case of some decision's being reached on his advice, even though the Savii[21] approved and it was ratified by one of the Councils, it could still be held up by the *avogadori* acting, rather as does a Public Prosecutor, in the interests of the state. Any imprudent word of the Doge was solemnly disavowed by the Senate. When he presided at the equivalent of a Cabinet meeting he was heard for form's sake, along with everybody else, but his speeches never carried special weight.

Misson sums up the position admirably. ' 'Tis plain then, that if in any case Gold and Purple are but glaring Pageants, and if the Grandeurs of the World are but Chimera's and stately Yokes; the Doge of *Venice* is an Eminent Instance of these Truths.' One remembers to what solitude he was condemned, and how this was perhaps the most striking aspect of his situation. Any of his family in government posts had to resign on his accession. He was allowed no contact save with the officials who supervised and directed his private life, and without whose leave he could not even move about; if he had to take the waters it was the Great Council that concerned itself with his cure, settled how long it was to last, and sent a delegation to keep an eye on the proceedings. The first citizen, surrounded on all sides by honours directed rather to the state than to himself, was the least free and most restricted man in Venice. He lived immured in a luxurious palace in an intolerable servitude from which he could not even resign, and so escape. And when death cancelled his election at last, there was not a day's official mourning for him. He received an impressive funeral and was immediately forgotten.

Not least among the unpleasant features of his function was the ruinous expense. A new Doge must at once relinquish any property he might own beyond the immediate boundaries of Venetian territory, and this was enough to make the prospective dignity an alarming one to the wealthiest families, who still had business and possessions in the colonies of the Republic. The ban applied, too, to all private trading interests. The Doge might accept no gifts; he merely touched with his hand the rich presents that came in token of respect from foreign princes. At his death, as we have already noted, a commission enquired, *praesente cadavere*, into whether he had transgressed these iron rules, ready to deny him the last honours had he done so. But it was a laughable threat, for they invariably found the Doge to have been poor, if not actually penniless. In this period alone Marco Foscarini died bankrupt in 1763 and Paolo Renier, immensely rich at the beginning of his reign, was 6,000,000 ducats in debt when it ended in 1789. It is hard to see what else could have happened. With a Civil List barely sufficient to pay a handful of servants, the crushing, inevitable cost had to be met from a Doge's personal fortune.

And yet the office was sought after most eagerly. The 'Chinese Spy'[22] could write, 'The Doge of Venice is little more than a famous painting, but it is incredible how the nobles love to sit for that likeness in a ducal cap. They intrigue over the copy-portrait as though it were original.' And indeed, for all its burden and slavery, the function never lost its glamour. A Doge traditionally commanded deference and respect, as well as being particularly esteemed in his rôle of old man bowing to the harsh requirements of the state.

His wife was not, in the eighteenth century, the hieratic idol she had been in former days. In the ceremonies of the past she was as important as he, wearing cloth of gold and a mantle lined with ermine, with 235 nobly-born girls attending her in white satin. But her public honours had been gradually reduced and finally abolished. After 1656 she was not even crowned. Her gorgeous robes and jewels remained, but from 1745 onwards she might no longer wear her little headdress, a version of the ducal *corno*, though a Dogaressa must still be of high birth and blameless reputation. The Procurator Andrea Tron, for all his great deserving, lost his chance of the throne because of the behaviour of his wife, the beautiful Caterina Dolfin. She was one of the most beguiling women of her time, but far too frank and free, and the poor man's career suffered.[23]

There were surprises, nevertheless, when ballotting was held, and the century produced one non-aristocratic consort, the wife of Paolo Renier. Because of her obscure extraction and dubious background (rumour had it she had danced the tight-rope at Constantinople), the state ignored her and her official place was filled by her husband's niece. In these difficult circumstances she retained her dignity and Goethe found her 'a woman of noble aspect and austere expression'.

By a curious reversal, the Republic at its last gasp restored the Dogaressa to her former pomp in 1797. The ceremonial etiquette relating to her was overhauled, allowing her richer robes, more gondolas, extra pages; and the state in its wisdom even decided that she merited a really good funeral.

The foundation and basis of the whole polity was the Great Council, from which all power derived. Having passed the executive function, in clearly defined terms, to its offspring the Senate, this Maggior or Gran Consiglio remained as the legislative body and director of affairs. It made the laws and controlled all public office by appointing all magistrates, from the Doge downwards. Those few nominations reserved to the Senate – ambassadors and army commanders – had to be approved and confirmed in the other House. Political life, in short, depended wholly on this sovereign assembly, the soul and mouthpiece of the nation, and its exclusive use of the Venetian dialect served to emphasise this national character. It met in the palace, in the great chamber looking on to the Riva degli Schiavoni and into the Piazzetta, with the heroes and glories of Venice painted blazing on the walls by Tintoretto, Bassano and Veronese.

All the patricians, vowed as they were from infancy to the service of the state, belonged to the Maggior Consiglio. Whatever their abilities, membership at the age of twenty was automatic so long as their families were entered in the Golden Book, which was carefully gone through every year. There were 206 noble families, comprising about 1,500 males. In 1714 there were 1,731, but the muster had fallen to 962 by 1769. Owing to illness and to voluntary absence there were seldom more than 600 present at any sitting of the Council and sometimes only half that number, too few to form a quorum. The assembly would then cut through the rules, deciding the proceed with business, 'for this occasion only'.

Voting for the many magistracies, even though some of them were honorary and none was permanent, was as complicated as that for a Doge, and sittings were perforce frequent. A long series of eliminations produced four candidates for any given office and there was an extended performance with lots and ballot-balls before three of these were discarded. The system was further slowed down by the rule that, after an abortive session, the next meeting must preserve the workings of pure chance by going through the whole thing again from the beginning. This was supposed to prevent the formation of parties in favour of those who had done well in the preliminary rounds.

But corruption crept in, despite these safety measures. Plots and projects flourished, webs of conspiracy were woven and heights of Machiavellianism scaled that left the Président de Brosses, who was not an ingenuous man, quite flabbergasted. And the dark deeds hatched in secrecy on the Broglio or whispered in the ante-rooms, could certainly be deduced among the uproar of the council chamber, where political rivalry came into the open. Many were the hopeful but vain attempts to obtain tranquillity of debate, for the vengeful remarks of defeated candidates failed to match the Republic's picture of itself as a model of brotherly love. No details of the voting were made known, nor were members permitted to leave their seats to communicate with one another during the count. This was a rule aimed at securing a free vote, but they sidestepped it by coughing and sneezing and taking snuff in a system of secret signals, and even managed to vote twice if they were really clever.[24]

Demonstrations by the public were forbidden, but the Procuratori responsible for good order in the Chamber were posted at a distance and would have found it difficult to intervene in case of need. Their base was the lovely little Loggetta built by Sansovino below the Campanile in the sixteenth century. They had a guard, recruited from the Arsenal, and this was supposed to warn and protect the House should disturbance threaten. But who was to protect it against its own, self-generated storms? As debate grew boisterous the presence of the guard in the ante-chambers did no more than restrain noble members from actual violence, though their verbal exchanges were heated enough when important votes came up. Charles de Brosses attended a sitting of the Maggior Consiglio and likens it to a sort of devils' sabbat. Nor will it come as a surprise to any student of latter-day political gatherings to learn that its excesses were constantly being condemned as 'thoroughly out of keeping with the proper gravity of so illustrious an assembly'.

The Great Council delegated to the Senate all political, economic and military authority. It was the Senate that negotiated treaties, made peace and war at will and appointed ambassadors.[25] It proposed to the Great Council the names of the *avogadori*, the magistrates who represented the state in the law courts; fixed and assessed the taxes and administered public funds. The government of the Serenissima was in its hands. Before the Senate, at state ceremonies, the naked sword was borne in token of power.

One hundred and twenty senators were ballotted for annually in the Great Council. Half of these served as full-time senators for the ensuing year, while attendance for the others was limited to certain set, though very numerous, occasions. But there was no other difference between them and none received either pay or expenses.

To these elected members were added first the Doge, who sat at the head of their meetings, then his six counsellors, the chiefs of the Quarantia Criminale, the Council of Ten, the *avogadori*, the *Savii* and various others, making some eighty *ex-officio* members. In addition, and although the qualifying age was forty, the Senate admitted fifty young men at twenty-five years old in order to educate them for the part they would later play in the public service. Of these, however, only twenty might join in the debates.

Thus about 250 people would gather in the Sala dei Pregadi in the palace on Thursdays and Saturdays.[26] This room was decorated with portraits of famous Doges and pictures of great events in the annals of Venice, and has kept its character in spite of restorations.

Business was conducted more decorously in the Senate than among the hurly-burly of the Great Council. Here noise was practically unknown, argument was calm and the penalty for untimely interruption could be two months in prison. Anyone with something to say had to wait his turn, but had a free hand when it came, so that the Senate was a shrine of oratory and polished speech-making. Wily members had been known to seize the heaven-sent opportunity to deliver themselves, with much auxiliary gesture and highly-charged eloquence, of some remarkable flights of rhetoric; in 1761 the Procurator Morosini actually died as a result of speaking for eight hours at a stretch. And as a rule, though more moderately, senators liked to make the most of their talents, for a speaker's reputation spread round the city far beyond his immediate audience. Lalande says that a brilliant debate was always discussed at the *conversazioni* 'that night and next day, even among the ladies, who often talk of politics'. The applause of the man in the street and the approval of the salons were considered well-earned recompense, for the Senate itself was bound to preserve its impassivity. Not the most admired orator who sat there was ever encouraged or congratulated at the time; such a departure would have been contrary to law and custom.

Though the Republic winked at slackness on the part of the Great Council, it would excuse no absence from the Senate. To miss a sitting was to incur severe penalties. However, since it was enough to be there for the vital moment of voting, senators would leave a few of their number gravely dissecting the problems of the hour and troop out of their spectacular meeting-house to stroll in the corridors and ante-chambers. Here they wandered round in groups, chatting of this and that on topics far removed from state affairs, until the signal came and they all dashed back to vote. Their procedures of choice, for such offices as the Maggior Consiglio had resigned to them, were a little less devious than those of the other House, but the principle was the same – a progressive shortening of the list of candidates by alternate votes and lucky dips, until the final name was taken from the urn.

The Senate, then, was the essential government. It knew every-thing that happened in Venice, down to the merest trivialities, but it had lost the right to initiate discussion and might consider only the carefully annotated measures submitted to it by the Consulta. This body was chosen by, but independent of, the Senate. What the Consulta laid before it the Senate could not alter. It could only agree or disagree, though the disagreement was of a special kind. It never said no, nor gave an out-and-out refusal, but merely accepted 'for correction' anything that failed to meet with its approval. The matter was then indefinitely delayed and the rejection wrapped up in polite formalities that deceived no one.

The Consulta, or Consiglio degli Savii, handled day-to-day affairs, and since it acted by means of its proposals to the Senate, that body had permanent and absolute control. Save for its peculiar make-up, the Consulta was not unlike a Cabinet, though the com-parison is not exact. There were twenty-six members: the Doge and his six counsellors, the three *capi* or heads of the Quarantia Criminale, the six Savii Grandi, the five Savii di Terra Ferma and the five Savii agli Ordini. Only the Savii Grandi had any truly active rôle, and they were not all equally important. The Savii di Terra Ferma, relic of the days of colonial power, were now a minor board responsible for 'the proper administration of conquered territory', for shipping and military finance.[27] Nevertheless, they gave advice on everything that came under discussion, though they did not always vote. The Savii agli Ordini, or Little Sages as they were sometimes called, were young nobles chosen by the Great Sages to act as assistants or attachés, and showed their seniors a respect reflected in a ceremonial that verged on veneration. Their short six months' educational interlude was intended purely as an introduction to the management of the public weal and established,

43

as it were, a nursery from which the Republic could fill its leading offices later on.

Executive power belonged to the Savii Grandi, who also served for six months and were chosen from among the greatest persons in the state. They alone were what we should recognise as ministers. They had no special individual departments, but discussed all political business before bringing it to the attention of the Senate. Each in turn acted at the head of affairs for a week as the Savio di Settimana, receiving all petitions, memorials and dispatches. These he brought before his colleagues, who usually did what he advised and approved anything he might have decided in emergency. All this meant that the Savio di Settimana was for his brief eight days the mightiest man in Venice, and more or less Prime Minister.

The main corporate duty of the Consiglio degli Savii, or Pieno Collegio as it was also known, was to keep up friendly contact with the foreign ambassadors, despite the fact that it hardly ever saw them. Diplomatic notes were solemnly and publicly handed over to a secretary, who bore them to the Collegio in a neighbouring room and returned directly with the news that the matter 'was to be considered'. After a day or two another secretary went to tell the ambassador concerned how his request or his suggestion had fared. The Republic was determined never to risk putting pen to paper even on the least controversial topics and its answers always came by word of mouth.

So many, so various and often so complex were the matters studied by the Consulta for submission to the Senate that the help was necessary of a large corps of specialists, experts and secretaries, men of experience to shoulder the technical work. These secretaries understood all the problems and shared all the secrets and had a great art of summing-up at speed. The précis they produced would save the Savii from toiling through the files, afford them a wider view and keep them fully informed.

Although the Serenissima reserved office and authority of every kind for the patricians – so that tremendous aristocrats were to be found directing such lowly activities as the inspection of its slaughter-houses, and pleased with their employment – it had long realised that talent could appear in any class and should not be shut out. And so, while politics remained the preserve of the nobility, admini-strative posts were held by those of less than noble rank, and this body of citizens became in time a forcing-ground of gifted men.

These opportunities were open to anyone who had attended the College of Secretaries and who was by birth a *cittadino*. There was no difficulty about joining the *cittadino* class – all that was necessary was long residence or a Venetian wife – and to it the Republic had given emphatic proof of recognition and esteem, making one of its members the Grand Chancellor, with precedence over the nobles. He had nothing to do beyond care for and keep the Chancery papers, but the dignity was enormous. In procession he walked with the Procurators of St Mark beside the Doge. His election was a national festa with illuminations, and free drink for all the gondoliers, and the panegyric at his costly funeral was delivered by one of the chief dignitaries of the state.

But after this one concession the *cittadini* were kept firmly within bounds. They might hold high office, accompany ambassadors abroad, help in their tasks and even themselves represent their country in the lesser reaches of diplomacy; it was for ever impossible for them to join the ranks of the nobility.

An inevitable drawback was the way in which these fine civil servants proliferated as their calibre, fidelity and devotion led the government to give them ever more, and more difficult, things to do. The whole conciliar idea, based on the non-importance of the individual, seemed designed to create more jobs. In the end there were three men for every job, with nothing decided save by unanimous vote or, in special and strictly limited cases, by a majority of two to one. As a result the government of Venice, so anxious for the public good, in many ways so thrifty and adroit, began to suffer from an overplus of administrative machinery. All these superfluous people and the pay they drew placed a dangerous burden on the finances.

Parallel with the Great Council and the Senate there was another power in the Republic, one whose name calls up a dark and fearful picture – that of the Council of Ten, which was at once a political body and a court of law. It had been created at the beginning of the fourteenth century as the result of an unsuccessful conspiracy that determined the government to reduce the number of those responsible for the public safety. At first temporary, the Council of Ten was made permanent, after several extensions, in 1346. Since then it had continually consolidated and increased its power to become the real ruler and mainstay of the oligarchy by means of undeniable dictatorship. There were no limits to its jurisdiction as a court and its decrees had equal force with those of the Maggior Consiglio. It was the more dreadful for being answerable to no one, whatever and whomever it was judging; and the stronger for the presence of its three Inquisitors, trustees of its authority and its instruments of absolute rule. The Ten were always old men, too old to be swayed by passion or temptation, men for whom reasons of state were the whole of the law.[28] Holders of unrestricted power, they and their Inquisitors watched over all that ever happened and such was the healthy respect that they inspired that the distant sight of the special red lantern on their approaching gondola was enough to scatter any crowd and calm all sign of violence.

Their repressive methods, or what were imagined to be so (evidence taken in secret, sentences never published, executions carried out, it was said, in impenetrable mystery), terrified the thought of opposition out of people's heads. Politics and state affairs were forbidden territory, and that was that. Venetians who valued their freedom simply never discussed them. Goudar's invented mandarin, Sin-ho-ai from Pekin, advised the stranger to 'leave his tongue at Fusina and come on to Venice without it. Here they bury babblers alive in a leaden tomb, a man who talks once is condemned to everlasting silence. There are those who for uttering a single word have disappeared for thirty years.' All this was much exaggerated, as we shall see, but it was nevertheless true that no wrong act or unacceptable opinion escaped the implacable Ten. They picked the cases they wished to hear and judged them absolutely. Offences against morals and the management of gaming-rooms were as much their province as was high treason. Intention, even presumed intention, was punished as severely as guilt itself. What was Casanova's crime when he was thrown into the Piombi and condemned to five years' imprisonment? He never knew the whys and wherefores of the sentence. Was it for atheism, or for being a cynic, or for living on his wits? As a matter of fact he was there on mere suspicion of having recourse to the Cabbala and the rites of the Rosy Cross; no crime was involved, but it was ideas, states of mind, the Ten were there to punish.[29]

By logical conclusion, therefore, nothing fell outside their province. There were nobles who gave ear to the subversive notions blown in from abroad, from France especially: they must of course be strictly watched. The middle and lower orders, politically non-existent though they were, had nevertheless to be controlled – their conduct and their talk could well affect the security of Venice. The Inquisitors needed to know everything, the private manners and morals o every citizen.

A noteworthy organisation of spies and informers helped them to the knowledge. It may be that Italians are guileful by nature and born private detectives, but certainly there was never any shortage in Venice of men who wanted to be useful, or earn some extra money, or simply fill in time. On the inner porch of the Doge's palace you may see the carved stone mask of a lion, the *bocca di leone*, and here, as into a letterbox, might be put written denunciations of any questionable incident, whether seen or merely suspected. The Inquisitors claimed to take note only of such *denunzie secrete* as were signed, but there is plenty of evidence that this was not always so, and an anonymous informer could identify himself by means of a scrap of paper torn from his denunciation and so collect the reward for interesting or usable accusations.

But most of their intelligence the Ten would gather from the innumerable reports of the agents who were known, by way of sweetening their unenviable reputation, as *confidenti*. To Casanova they were 'vile tools', but that was before 1776, when he had joined their ranks under the pseudonym 'Antonio Pratolino'. He would never see fifty again; he had spent every penny he had and women were no longer quite so eager for his ageing attentions. Frowned on as he was by authority, he decided to turn informer before being informed against, wrote a very humble letter offering his services and became a *confidente*.[30] He was not an ideal choice for the work and met with poor success. They made him wait five years for an official appointment and took it away again in 1782 because he was not sending in enough news. It was then that, 'with heavy step and downcast eye', he left his native city, never to return.

But other spies had more to show. There were clever, cultivated men among them, and some who were barely literate. Some were decayed aristocrats, others the lowest of the low, and they spun a unique web of political espionage that enmeshed the whole community. Each was put to work where he could do his best and they trailed the Venetians to café, theatre and church. Indoors and out they pried. No aspect of life and no single person went unobserved, for the slightest and least important thing that anybody did was sure to affect the public interest somehow or other. Worming their way at every level of society they kept the Inquisitors in touch with all

47

they saw or heard, so that deeds, words and even thoughts might be duly dealt with. Under a regime that would arrest a man on simple, vague suspicion and whose repressive spirit readily assumed him guilty once arrested, it is easy to see how the *confidenti* and their activities menaced the liberty of quite inoffensive people. Their reports in the State Archives are a valuable source of material, filling several hundred boxes.[31] There are set out the private opinions, and business, the customs and vices. Methods of enquiry are revealed as cynical, sometimes naïve, and often bogged down in footling detail. Thus Gian Battista Manuzzi reports on April 6, 1757, that, further to instructions, he has checked on N.H. Ser Marin Zorzi[32] and learned from the neighbours that the gentleman in question is in the habit of having a joint cooked on a Friday, to say nothing of a Saturday, which is just as bad. People living near his *casino* in the *corte* Contarina could hear it roasting on the spit.

But particulars of this kind were exactly what the Ten wanted to know, and demonstrate how widely their net was cast. Anyone, however innocent, upon whose words and deeds they required information, had a spy clinging to him like a leech. It is interesting to follow such an agent as he trails, for what dark reason it is difficult to fathom, a nobleman of Venice, and to learn from his notes not only the minutiae of detection, but the peaceable way the patricians passed their time. How busy they must have been, unoccupied, the whole day through! Gerolamo Mazzucato writes, on June 2, 1791:

'Obedient ot the commands with which Your Excellencies honoured Zuane Tolomei and myself, I kept the Noble Gentleman Pietro Giacomo Foscarini under faithful observation throughout yesterday, the first of the month. He never left the house. Towards noon, a boy from the San Giulian café came, rang the bell and had a word or two with the servant, then went off again. About the twenty-fourth hour the gentleman came out and had an ice at the Della Nave in the Calle Larga. He stayed there until two, chatting a little with many of the customers, but said nothing of importance. He then went home, changed and came out again. Went to the Piazza, walked about for a few minutes and visited Stefani's coffee-house in the Frezzeria and fell to discussing the recent events in France with some of the people there. They left one by one and he stayed on alone. Ordered a coffee.

Around three-thirty walked a little in the Piazza. Home at midnight, and I saw no one enter until about the eighth hour. All this I beg to submit to Your Excellencies, humbly kissing your robes.'

Foscarini was again faithfully observed on June 30th.

'He stayed at home all day and nobody, so far as I could see, came to the house. At about the twenty-fourth hour he went to the Della Nave. Ordered a coffee. Stayed half an hour or so, but spoke to no one. Went to the Vecchie Procuratie, to the snuff-merchant's, for an ounce of snuff. Walked in the Merceria for perhaps fifteen minutes, and then home. About one o'clock came out again; to the Delle Rive, the café under the Padaglione. There till two, spoke to no one. Then to the tailor on the San Moisè bridge, and spent half an hour talking to the owner. Owner and he came out together and proceeded to the Piazza, where they strolled until nearly three, talking. Parted. The Noble Gentleman went to the Della Nave and met some people there. Said little, drank a barley-water and left at four-thirty. Back to Piazza, walked under Vecchie Procuratie and greeted someone I did not recognise. Went to the Arco Celeste, said very little and nobody addressed him. Strolled once more until five o'clock or so; back home. I saw no one enter the house until round about seven. [Some clue to the curious time-sequence may be found in note p. 68].

Others, as well as the Venetians, were subjected to this close invigilation and the foibles of foreign visitors were noted with care. Here, for instance, are the doings of two young Frenchmen as reported by the *confidente* Giuseppe Gioacchini:

'Monsiú Vrí [the spelling of the *confidenti* is of course variable] lodging at the Tre Vele, left the Filarmonici academy at seven o'clock with another French friend. They went to the Corte delle Colonne, and then to the Calle dei Zendai, looking for harlots, but without success. They returned, therefore, to the Piazza and finally found a prostitute under the arcades of the Vecchie Procuratie, took her to a courtyard across the Ponte dei Dai and left her there half an hour later. Apparently a disappointing encounter, for she seemed displeased'.

Informers were past masters in the art of seeing without being seen and no thought that they were under observation would have occurred to these young men. But the foreigner had scarcely set foot on Venetian soil before the Inquisitori heard why he had come, how long he meant to stay, what money he had, who his family were and what, if any, politics he professed. Nobody would bother him, not a single question was asked, and he would presume himself unknown to the authorities until the day came that he wanted something of them. It was then he realised that his every action since arrival had been noted, hour by hour, with disconcerting exactitude, and all without the smallest interference in anything he did. Even Montesquieu, so immersed in the study of comparative legal systems as to be impervious to the sybaritic charm of life in Venice, was left free to bombard anyone he could find with questions on the government, and jot down the answers undisturbed. The Ten knew what he was up to and, seeing no great harm in it, held their hand. His hurried departure was caused in the end by an unkind practical joke on the part of a chance aquaintance who sent a seedy-looking messenger to say that his enquiries had aroused suspicion – those in power would soon impound his papers and clap him into gaol. The horrified philosopher at once forgot his airy scepticism ('there is nothing fearsome about the fearsome Council of Ten, its decrees go unobeyed'), burned the compromising memoranda, hurled the ashes into the Grand Canal and never stopped running until he got to Rome.[33]

Official ears listened yet more attentively to the utterance of the Venetians themselves, who spent their time trying to keep out of trouble. As one of the *confidenti* said, 'those present lowered their voices and evaded the subject' when any topic was publicly mentioned that could possibly interest the supreme authority. It was indeed the wisest thing to do. The man so foolish as to be drawn into saying what he thought of the secret motives behind this or that decision of the Ten would pay for his frankness soon and dearly.

Watch and ward were similarly kept on stage plays, and not even ballet was exempt. The documents repeatedly show the care the government took to eradicate anything that might suggest a thought of reform or provoke an unsuitable idea. Thus we have an adverse report on the ballet *Coriolanus* given at the San Benedetto theatre in 1776. It points out the temerity of the hero and his contempt for orders sent him by the Senate, things apt to disturb 'that

amenable spirit which Your Excellencies so ardently desire to fos-
ter in all proper submission, that your sacred and ever-wise commands may not only be observed, but observed without demur'.
How pleasant to see that this profession of entire fidelity to inquisitorial mandate bears the signature, Giacomo Casanova.

But in many departments the sacred commands were hardly
accorded the ready deference the adventurer-turned-spy was re-
commending, and in what Montesquieu calls *la représentation cor-
porelle* they were defied absolutely. Venetian housekeeping, and more
especially Venetian dress, had always been the object of official
regulation, and on December 18, 1776, the Council of Ten was still
emphasising the vital importance of a good moral tone, and in-
veighing against domestic luxury and cost as all too likely to spoil
it; decadence and the downfall of the Republic were foreseen. Yet
in spite of these sorrowful exhortations, accompanied as they were
by the threat of dreadful penalties, the sumptuary laws remained a
dead letter. The devoted *confidenti* continued to report offences,
but no one was ever punished or received more than a mild rebuke.
It is difficult to believe that the dreaded Ten, however feeble they
appeared, were unable to enforce austerity; what baffled them seems
to have been the fact that austerity went clean against the fashion,
and their own wives were the leading lawbreakers. What was more,
because of the dearth of suitable hotels in Venice, the chief families
were expected to entertain distinguished guests – an arrangement
which gave a lot of latitude. In these circumstances the noble houses
did their dazzling best by way of hospitality and a display of luxury
was quite in order. Similarly, many of the laws relating to gaming-
rooms, receptions, shops and cafés were generally relaxed. Rigorous
application would have dulled the fair fame of Venice as a pleasure-
city and kept the flow of visitors away.

It is less easy to see why the Inquisitors were as indulgent as they
were towards the *philosophes* of contemporary France, whose works
were all condemned to public burning and all enjoyed a large, and
more or less public, sale, The secret agents merely reported them
as they came out, and this they could certainly do without delay:
the informer Manuzzi managed to get hold of the Italian translation
of *Candide* with the glue still tacky on the covers.[34] He had no trouble
buying it, the bookseller having also offered him the original
French version and the news that he was expecting 'something
else good in the religious line' at any moment. Casanova is another

who eagerly forwards a list of banned books available in the shops. Voltaire, Rousseau, Marmontel and Helvétius figure prominently, as do Lucretius, Lucian, Aretino and Machiavelli. He gives the names and addresses of some who buy as well as sell the forbidden literature, ending only for lack of space to complete the catalogue, and yet the Ten took no action against anyone so indicated. Also damned were lubricious books, 'written to excite unhealthy passions by means of indecent tales in ribald style'. but there was on all sides a roaring trade in them. Such works were usually in French, though customers were more interested in the pictures than the text. They were 'highly obscene and scandalous items', and Casanova's explanation for the vast demand was calculated to discourage any censor. 'A book,' he sensibly says when compiling the above-mentioned catalogue in December 1781, 'is never so popular as when authority bans it. Being banned makes many a licentious author rich.'

These, then, were things about which the Inquisitors, perhaps considering them non-political, were tolerant enough, but dire retribution awaited the Venetian who failed to obey the sacred commands to other departments. Or so it was believed, and that, in the eyes of the government, was what chiefly mattered. Fear, in their opinion, produced more good behaviour than did anything else, and the tales of horror went carefully uncontradicted. No special tribunal is ever much beloved, but none was ever painted quite so black as the Consiglio dei Dieci. Libraries have been written to denounce its parodies of justice, its secret hearings, the confessions extracted under torture and its terrible curbing power. So deeply did our grandfathers shudder over these accounts that it sounds improbable even now to dismiss them all as fables of mystery and imagination, designed to appeal to people who liked that sort of thing, and far divorced from truth. The only tortures were probably those Casanova tells of – the being kept in ignorance, as were prisoners in the Piombi, of the reason and duration of a sentence, and the impossibility of getting news out or visitors in. One would be undermined by boredom and inaction and the purgatory be just this waiting for something definite, this not knowing whether to hope for or to dread it.

The secret executions are a legend that arose from natural deaths, three examples of which may be found in the year 1755 alone.

There was outcry at the death of a twenty-one-year-old prisoner in November and rumours that he been left 'to perish of consumption', though he was in fact a hairdresser with lungs affected by the powder used in setting wigs. Then it was said that Francesco Rossi and Michiel Zanetto had been suffocated in prison, when they asphyxiated themselves by lighting a fire on a cold night 'with coal, *acquavite* and other materials'.

The famous Inquisitors' Poison, too, though used in the dim and distant past, was no more than an unpleasant memory. They still kept some in the store-cupboard but, as their secretary reported in 1717, 'there are only a few boxes left, that Serpicelli is said to have prepared, but the instructions have disappeared and it may have lost its strength'. Obviously they would be foolish to rely on it for secret executions now.

Much is also heard about the death sentences pronounced by the Ten against persons who had fled to countries far away and whom they wished to deal with at a distance. And yet these covert murder-mandates seldom came to anything, it seems. The French-born Count de Bonneval, for instance, though condemned to death in Venice, rose to the rank of three-tailed bashaw in the service of the Turk. The *Dominante* ordered its ambassador to dispatch him in 1729, but eight years afterwards he was still cutting a dash at the Ottoman court.[35]

What is the inevitable conclusion? Surely that the dreaded tribunal was more dreaded for its sheer, self-sought impenetrability than for anything it actually did. All the documents suggest that the Inquisitors made their justice feared by hideous intimidation, which was quite enough to overawe the people and engender a wary deference for their supreme authority. If they mentioned the Ten, we are told, the Venetians did so with lowered glances and a precautionary finger pointed at the sky. But it is true to say that no clanking of chains disturbed their usual levity. There was no smothering reign of terror, nothing sinister about Venice. It was simply – and this was the whole object – that the thought of the prison-cell and the executioner kept the generality from meddling in affairs of state.

Indeed, it would have been strange had a body created 'to preserve freedom and prevent the abuse of personal authority' proved to be itself a tyrant; and stranger still, as René Guerdan pointed out, if Venice, with all her safeguards against despotism, had tolerated any such thing from her most powerful council. At a time when the *lettre de cachet* was still employed elsewhere, she was careful of individual rights. Here no one might issue a search warrant himself; there must always be a collaboration of authority, and not even the Inquisitors could set this rule aside. They had to pass a unanimous vote before a man could be imprisoned, were it only for the purpose of giving necessary evidence. Venice, it should be remembered, was the first state in Europe to abolish torture and limit the time for which anyone might be held without trial. In its anxiety to avoid judicial error the government never seized a wrongdoer until it had collected all the evidence against him, with the result that arbitrary arrest was impossible and the criminal frequently had time to get away. The legend of savage repression is contradicted again and again as soon as fact replaces fantasy. The truth about the state prisons, vastly different from the myth, will be examined later, and the gaols where the Ten were said to keep so many alleged innocents in secret durance were almost empty. When the French flung wide the doors to let the 'victims of despotism' out, they found a solitary inmate up in the Leads – *sotto piombi* – and four persons in the Camerotti underground. To compensate for the disappointing haul the sons of liberty paraded one of these victims round the town, but unfortunately their hero, after twenty-two years away from the world, had grown very fond of his cell and never ceased imploring them to take him back. Then the poor man gorged on chocolate, wine and sweet cakes and died of a surfeit four days later, and so resolved an undeniably awkward situation.

But as new ideas spread, the Council of Ten, though never as bad as it was said to be, aroused such aversion that the Senate decided on reform in 1761. Yet the process was neither swift nor thoroughgoing, for six years of enquiry and committee meetings produced only an apology for reform, with the mandate of the Ten curtailed in some specialised and minor fields while their responsibility for the safety of the state remained untouched. They could still intervene in all that went on and their power, despite appearances, was still intact.

Their mistrustful supervision bore as heavily upon the nobles as on the common people and it is a fact that, simply by not re-electing them at the prescribed intervals, the dominant patrician caste could have abolished that board of tyrants easily, with no revolution and no violence. Yet they never used their right to do so and one may fairly assume that this was because every aristocrat cherised hopes of being an Inquisitor himself some day. There was, too, the reverential respect for a time-honoured institution, to alter which in any way would be tantamount to attacking the Glory of Venice.

However, in 1779 there were found two members of the impoverished nobility ready to lay such scruples aside and bring to the Great Council a plan for reforming not only the Ten but every other part of the Venetian polity. One of these men, Carlo Contarini, made an impassioned speech on the distress of the people and the luxury and immorality of those who ruled them. And for once the people, normally unconscious of the sad state they were in, appeared to pay attention: such a ferment broke out that the first uprising in Venetian history seemed about to take place. It did nothing of the kind, of course, and the imprisonment of ringleaders and suspects caused so little protest that alarm had clearly been ridiculous. Any attempt at reform was henceforth doomed. The oligarchy would resist it in the council chamber and there would be no worthwhile support outside. In the end it was Bonaparte who drew the executioner's sword to do away with all the established machinery that had worked, smooth and uneruptive, for the best part of ten centuries. Without it the Serenissima could not survive, and he killed the longest-lived republic the world has ever known.

Laws affecting relations between individuals, and between the individual and the state, were, like the public institutions of Venice, seldom altered save on points of detail. The codification of 1678 had merely classified the law by subject and heading and upheld the principle that 'written law is to be interpreted in the light of custom, which may also modify and even override it'. We must therefore look beyond the written word for anything approaching a complete picture of the Venetian legal system. This was further developed than any other then in force in Europe, coherent and flexible at the same time, and some of its provisions, notably those to do with commerce and arbitration, anticipate our most advanced legal thinking. It was administered, moreover, by men of integrity, immune from bribery, intrigue and pressure.

The chief courts were known as *Quarantie*, from their original forty constituent members, each being the highest tribunal in its own sphere. The *Quarantia Criminale*, or *Serenissimo Consiglio*, ranked first; it had originated as the Doge's council and the magistrates who belonged to it still spoke in the Senate. Civil cases were heard, according to their subject and degree of importance, by one or other of the remaining *Quarantie* and conducted by barristers who, though they belonged to a respected calling, sound to us like ham actors. They had perfected a style of the calm, flat opening that grew louder and more heated as they went on, throwing themselves about like lunatics, thumping with clenched fists until the desks before them shook and rocked. Contemporary accounts are full of howling and histrionics and rending of garments; a barrister would frequently stand forth naked to the navel, then scramble into a spare shirt at the far end of the hall.

The whole atmosphere of the law courts seemed singularly well adapted for these performances. Goethe affirms that the civil hearing he attended was the best entertainment he got to all the time he was in Venice. 'One of the lawyers would have been first-class as a *buffo*, padding out his rôle on the stage,' he says. And this was on a relatively dull day, with none of the fireworks that could delight the connoisseur on a good one, so that the great man's main diversion was to see the by-play with the court hourglass. There was an ancient and peculiar custom of Venetian law by which clerks and secretaries could speak or read extracts for as long as they liked, but an advocate was strictly limited to an hour in any one session, however long that session might go on. A clerk therefore kept the hourglass on its side for the reading of documents or specialised evidence, but as soon as counsel opened his mouth it was set upright and the sand began to trickle through. The second he finished, it went back on its side again. The great knack, for the lawyer, was to insert some lightning remark, some sally or witticism to make the ever-appreciative public laugh and keep the clerk constantly tipping the glass up and down for time in and time out, until he got in a terrible muddle.

Criminal courts were seemlier by far, owing to the presence there of the *avogadori*, whose function resembled that of an attorney-general. Elected by the Great Council, they were, however, much more than public prosecutors. The Golden Book was in their keeping and the promulgation of laws could be postponed on their authority. They received arraignments and accusations but could not act against a criminal directly. They might only bring a case before the Ten, often to see it taken out of their hands and judged in the secret, unopposable manner of the Ten.

In the ordinary courts an accused person had all the safeguards of a good judicial system. There was always a lawyer to help him: prisoners' aid was known in Venice many hundreds of years before it came to this country. Methods of examination were legally laid down, with no trick questions or traps for the weak or ignorant. Evidence was not taken in open court but before a group of magistrates, and reported later, so that nothing that happened in court, no threat or pressure, could affect a witness upon whose accuracy might hang a man's life or reputation. For Venice was terrified of judicial mistakes and had her own peculiar formula of appeal. When a death sentence was pronounced on what seemed insufficient evidence an usher from the *avogadori* appeared without delay and spoke to the judges. All he said was *Ricordeve del povero fornareto!* on which four simple words the sentence was immediately quashed. They referred to the tragic time when a poor baker's lad went to the gallows for a crime he never committed and of which the real author had been discovered later. The judges of that case were then executed in their turn and their confiscated property paid for the two small red lights kept burning night and day before a mosaic of the Madonna on the façade of St Mark's, twin reminders for all those charged with administering the law.

What happened to the prisoner after condemnation depended on his social class, on what he had done and on which court had condemned him. Minor delinquents served their usually short sentences in the various houses of detention scattered about the city. There was one of these *cofanetti* in each district, used by the Ten for such of their prisoners as were not to be detained in secret for an unspecified period. These unfortunates would go to the dark and solitary cells known as *le Quattro* where they were, however, allowed an oil-lamp and could call the gaoler if they needed him. From here they went, for varying terms, to fortresses away from Venice such as that at Cattaro, which had an evil reputation, a graveyard of dangerous persons who were to be got rid of speedily without the public clamour of a trial. As Casanova says, the air of Cattaro was fatal. This was putting it mildly, with the ways and means the government had of increasing the fatal effect. Carlo Contarini, the lawyer who attained too much influence in the Great Council, was a strong man, but when the Ten wanted him out of the way all they had to do was send him to Cattaro and he was dead within the year.

Beneath the ducal palace were the nineteen underground dungeons known as the Pozzi. They were another kind of hell, exactly like tombs, faintly lit through narrow gratings that let in two feet of standing water from the lagoon outside. In each of these 'wells' was trestle bed and mattress, more or less clear of the flood, where the wretched occupant could crouch or lie. Soup and a pitcher of drinking water came every morning, and a ration of bread which he had to eat at once, for the nightmare place was alive with rats trying to snatch it from him. To the *Pozzi* went those whose death sentences for crimes under common law had been commuted to life imprisonment – an ironic mercy, considering the martyrdom it meant. For the unhappy creatures did not die quickly, despite the ghastly conditions. Casanova, though it is unwise to take his unsupported word, claims to have known one who had been there thirty-seven years. At the fall of the Republic most of these sewers had stood empty for a long time and only five men were found there. The less sinister *Camarotti* that were used instead had been built in the sixteenth century along the Rio del Palazzo, where the sea was visible from the windows. They also looked straight on to the pavement, so that prisoners could talk with passers-by. The penniless might beg their bread through the bars, and those in funds order meals from such inns as were within shouting distance for, by some quirk of the organisation, official hospitality stopped short of feeding the inmates of these particular cells. Meanwhile, the terrifying threat of the almost deserted *Pozzi* was kept alive, part of the government's settled plan of scaring everybody out of their wits.

By one of history's many absurdities, and despite the dire reputation of the other prisons, it was the mild *Piombi*, the Leads, of which the Venetians were really frightened. They had all heard of the *Piombi*, and all agreed they were unbearable. Up in the attics of the Doge's palace, under a lead-covered roof, the fearful thing about them was the exposure to heat and cold, although in fact a layer of wood three inches thick was carefully laid between the ceilings and the roof. They were reserved for political prisoners and the regime seems not to have been too awful. Casanova was there in 1755 and in this case his description is generally accepted as an accurate one. Arriving with his head full of inauspicious tales, he was amazed to learn that he might furnish his room as he pleased and use his money to buy very passable food. He could even have his fellow prisoners to dinner and regale them with excellent dishes of maccaroni cheese. Far from being a sordid den, the room was about thirteen feet square and the warder swept it daily. Nor, of course, was he so closely guarded that he could not prepare and carry out the great escape which, but for the cleverer-than-thou tone in which he told the tale, would have been recognised as the boldest of the century.

The story was written, with the object of reingratiating its author with the government, in 1788, so there was some ulterior motive in its kind words about the *Piombi* and the emphasis on how well the detainees were treated there. One critic, annoyed past bearing by Casanova's conceit of himself, suggested that he should take 'a little Venetian lead with his dinner every day, as Agathocles the potter's son went on eating from clay dishes when he was a king'. But though errors and embellishments have undoubtedly crept in, we may believe the narrative on the whole and infer, as from many other sources, that the *Piombi* by no means lived up to the alarming reputation they enjoyed at home and abroad.[36]

Alone among Italian states the Serenissima had no official police, for the number of down-at-heels *sbirri* she maintained – three in 1718 and only one in 1764 – could hardly be glorified into a force. But for the assistance of the *fanti*, who were underlings of the Ten, Venice would have been about as well equipped for the prevention of crime as a village with a rural policeman. And the *fanti*, though neither gentle nor pleasant-tempered in their ways, had only limited powers and were not officers of the law in any real sense.

This, to us, surprising state of affairs arose from the basic, underlying principles that governed the Republic. In order to ensure their probity and disinterestedness, the boards of magistrates must always be shielded from the risks of too much power. All those beautifully balanced councils and complicated elections, that frequent, punctilious scrutiny of every office, all the laws and traditions, had for object the preservation of civil liberty. No one, however highly placed, not even the Doge himself, could make the smallest decision without the agreement of other counsellors or *savii*, so stringent were the precautions against despotism. And despotism, it was felt, was what a police-force could lead to very easily. It was not the sort of thing a board could run with much success, yet anyone in undivided command could fall into temptation: they might all wake up one morning and find the police had been handed over to some political faction.

Rather than call in professionals, therefore, Venice chose to rely upon well-disposed persons for the keeping of public order. In case of serious trouble (which never arose), there were always the *cala-fati*, the caulkers from the Arsenal, swinging along in every procession, full of martial vigour to overawe the population. When it came to catching, or actually punishing, criminals on the run, an appeal went out to the bandits who prowled at large on the mainland and these unconventional allies were rewarded with bounties, and pardon for their own offences. It was a cynical method, but effective. There was also the network of informers, ubiquitous and Argus-eyed, sending in denunciations so that the courts could clamp down unerringly on any misbehaviour.

The lack of public disturbance was also largely due to the fact that nobody thought of creating it. Venetians were renowned for their docility. They appeared to the Grand Duke Paul of Russia as one big, happy family, models of loyalty and obedience. No police were needed to control them, even when they got excited. They never brawled in the theatres, where no one had to keep order. If the commons went to see a ducal banquet they made way or left the palace at an usher's sign. Any crowd that did gather was dispersed with surprising ease. The Princes of the North, as the Grand Duke and his wife were known on their travels in 1784, saw the onlookers rush into the arena at the bullfight given in their honour; and they saw exactly three guards get them all back behind the barriers again. A Frenchman who was present observed that in his country there would have been guns and sabres out, but here 'one *fante* single-handed can cope with anything'. Whatever was happening, Missier Grande, chief of that meagre band of constables, had only to show his red robe and quiet was restored.

Foreign powers, as we have seen, disregarded Venice and snubbed her ambassadors, for she was undefended and no one need respect her. The army was indeed non-existent to all intents and purposes – seven or eight thousand men, and only three thousand of them actually soldiering. The rest were an unruly civil militia, unarmed and unremunerated. The old fortresses that had been the bulwark of the Serenissima were more than half dismantled and many of the cannon useless. The troops had no notion of how to drill or even keep ranks. Their officers, innocent of all military accomplishment, were recruited from the petty mainland nobles: a patrician of Venice was naturally deflected from the army whenever possible, in case he went up in the world by holding a commission. Not that a comission would have meant very much, as it happened, for the army was no part of the body politic and an officer's uniform was only the mark of his job, bestowing no dignity, accorded no special respect.

The fleet, too, that had been the glory of the Republic in the days of her greatness, had declined to nothing. When commerce flourished, Venice could command experienced crews; men, it was said, who fought with all the fury of property owners defending their possessions. But now the sailors had no hopes of gain and she had to raise them from among adventurers with neither experience nor spirit, and make outrageous concessions to retain their services. Sailors, in fact, were well-paid thieves – far better paid than the soldiers, who often deserted to the galleys instead – and free to do their stealing unrebuked. The general idea seemed to be that 'you had to overlook it' and theft was treated as the lightest of naval crimes. Casanova tells of a boatswain who replied to a citizen complaining of the depredations of one of his crew, 'Watch out for him, then, and if you catch him, beat him. But don't put him out of action – he's worth five hundred ducats to me, and you'll have to pay.' The law itself offered as much compensation if a *galeotto* were hanged, and in 1778 an inspector of the forces summed up the various malpractices as leading to insolence, penury and indiscipline.

It was not for lack of high-sounding senior officers that the navy came to grief. In time of peace, command was held by a Provveditore Generale da Mar, who yielded place to the Capitano Generale da Mar in time of war. There was an admiral of the oared ships, another for the sailing vessels and a third for the galleasses, or great galleys. There was a Capitano del Golfo, a Superintendent of the Galleys, an Admiral and *Patrono* of the ships, all exercising their authority, in a conflict of tangled function, over a disintegrating fleet. And how entirely and characteristically Venetian the resonant titles are, combining as they do an allure of age-old history with something of the impresario's craft. They are pointers to the fact that 'the art of using symbols to disguise reality and smooth out of sight anything that did not quite fit in'[37] had by now become the policy of the state.

Such, then, were the dispositions of Venice in the eighteenth century. For hundreds of years they had seemed to add up to a masterpiece, and now they were sadly out of date. Yet the Venetians had every faith in their republic and no desire for change. They were happy, and believed themselves free. And they had been free, ever since politics first became a closed preserve where they did not intrude; freer than any nation in Italy, or indeed in Europe. An anonymous writer defined the extent and nature of this liberty:

'You must never in the least meddle with Affairs of State: You must commit no enormous Crimes punishable by Justice, which, by their notoriety, may oblige the Government to call you to account; and in all other respects you may do what you please, without so much as fearing to be censur'd. This is the sum of Venetian liberty.'

But the interests of the people were all the better served for their having no voice in the direction of affairs. Their work was protected, their wages were fixed at reasonable rates. Taxes never impinged on them, exempt as they were from the levies paid by property owners from the Doge downwards, from forced loans and dues on landed revenue or earned income. Customs duty affected only luxury goods. Essential foodstuffs were all tax free and the poor could buy provisions at less than cost price from the state monopolies. But all this determined effort to lighten the burden of the lower classes was very poor economics. It forced the government to cut expenses and let fleet and army go to rack and ruin; it put urban improvement out of the question, though fortunately much had been done during the previous century. The great financial expedient was accordingly to get the individual to pay, whenever possible, instead of the state. Prisoners paid the warders' wages as well as their own keep. Prostitutes, faced with sumptuary laws and drastic regulations, bought exemption by means of taxes. Ambassadors personally defrayed expenses abroad[38] and the shipping companies had to take them there for nothing. Public and private entertainment of important visitors was the contribution of the nobles. Every incoming Doge overhauled the ducal palace, where most of the staff and doorkeepers were paid by foreign ambassadors. Hospitals were run by the guilds or by charitable organisations. The famous hospital of the Incurabili (i.e. for venereal diseases) was founded by two patrician ladies, horrified at the plight of syphilitics, and twelve patrician girls were the first nurses there. All sorts of good works provided public relief and unemployment pay, while the state merely urged priest and lawyer to remind the faithful, and anyone coming to make his will, about charity being a sure road to heaven. Nor were these exhortations in vain. Hospitals and dispensaries, old folks' homes and rest homes, were built and run on gifts and legacies. Any association started for the benefit of others could count on money and support.

Obviously, the place was unique. In most countries of Europe the revenue was squandered by the rich. Here, where Aldus Manutius had chosen to set up his printing-press, the rich were using their revenues to subsidise the government. A curious state of things indeed, and one that made Venice in that libertine age 'the world turned upside down'.

CHAPTER TWO

SOCIETY

I THE NOBILITY

In the special kind of patrician democracy that was the Most Serene Republic the nobles retained all governing power and jealously controlled its workings. This dominant place they had reached by means of great deeds and epic service in the golden centuries; the might of Venice was built upon their courage and tenacity. Now, when there was no more sailing away to glory, they still considered their privileges well earned by the dedication of their time and loyalty, and of their fortunes if need be, to the state, but peace and quiet grew ever more attractive to them and they wished for no disturbance. Tradition, ingrained habit and strong prejudice all held them back from any notion of reform or change, and it was largely this narrow viewpoint of the ruling class, this happy settling into unadventurous ease, that brought disaster in the end.

They were a closed caste, as we have seen, and the simple citizen could no longer climb by merit to their ranks. He might have quite exceptional gifts, acquire great fame and prove a paragon; praises would shower freely down, but no honours that meant anything would come his way. The most he could aspire to was *nobiltà da terra ferma*, which gave him no political rights and was held in contempt by the aristocracy proper; and even this was rare and singular good fortune. In 1770, in time of urgent financial need, forty of these *terra ferma* nobles, provided they were very rich and paid a levy in proportion, were allowed to join the patriciate, latecomers to whom the nobles of Venice extended a chilly welcome and refused to accord any importance at all.

Commoners who had bought themselves in, sometimes centuries before, met with similar disdain. The old aristocratic families were tenaciously attached to their rights and their long pedigrees, and

4 The Grand Canal, by Canaletto

5 Colonnade of the Procuratie Nuove, by Canaletto

6 The Piazzetta

never compromised. It was a point of honour with them. They were especially high-handed with the great merchants, foreigners for the most part, who had been entered in the Golden Book a hundred years before to encourage their donations towards the war in the Morea. And yet these despised parvenus lived in luxury that would have done credit to all the despisers put together. Their palaces were like something from an Eastern fairy-tale, their banqueting-tables were set with gold plate for a hundred guests at a time, and those who saw them say their wives were hung with jewels like so many queens. But not all this opulence served to obscure their lowly origins. The Fonsecas had sold sugar before they went in for banking; the Widmanns had been street porters, the Castelli drapers; and nobody forgot it. Their acceptance into the real patriciate was nothing but a fiction.

This, then, was where the theory first broke down that nobles all had equal rights and privileges. Nobles were equal before the law, but far from being so in the sight of man. Within their class were clear cut divisions, set by usage and tradition. The cream of the cream were those descended from the twelve tribunes – always compared to the twelve Apostles – who first elected a Doge in 697. Next were four families going back to the ninth century, and these, of course, were the four Evangelists. Another eight, emerging a hundred years later and bereft of scriptural significance, joined forces with Apostles and Evangelists to form the leading category of patricians, the *lunghi*. Behind this undisputed elite came the *corti*, led by twelve families raised to the patriciate during the Genoese wars of the thirteenth century, and by the 'ducal houses' which had at one time or another provided a Doge for the Republic. The Nuove Famiglie, who were last, ranked according to the dates of their ennoblement, with the newest, who had paid for the honour, at the bottom of the scale. By tradition the oldest families claimed all important offices of state from more recent arrivals, though the latter were in a majority on the council boards. When it came to voting, however, the prestige of a great name would often swing the balance and help them over the difficulty.

Parallel to this hierarchy of lineage was another, that of money. Some of those great magistracies were beyond the reach of any noble, however exalted, unless he had means to sustain them. Not only were they unsalaried, but the Republic in its usual thrifty-minded way required the official to meet the whole expense of

c

office. You had to be able to afford some very grand housekeeping to be an ambassador, and to become a Procurator of St Mark was a more costly business still. That was the farthest anyone could go, apart from being Doge, and although the dignity carried no political influence the holder was greater than a Roman prince: the nephew of the Venetian-born Pope Clement XIII chose to be known as a Procurator rather than as Prince Rezzonico. The year 1765 saw the advancement of eleven Procuratori and huge sums disappeared to pay for celebrations. In 1713 one of the Pisani family spend 36,000 ducats, and Pietro Mocenigo in 1779 poured out 40,000 on 'wine, food and showers of coin' alone – something in the region of £200,000.

Nor could a poor man aspire to the Senate, for which he did not even qualify unless he came of a long line of senators. The distinguished members of the Quarantie, on the other hand, who formed the legal aristocracy, were not necessarily very rich. Here the requirements were a really good education and complete independence, though an adequate fortune was naturally one of the things that made such independence possible.

But it was far from true to say that every aristocrat was a man of wealth. Old family fortunes had been diminished or entirely swallowed up in the chances and changes of life, to say nothing of the effects of personal extravagance, and there existed a whole definite class of ruined noblemen. Being so poor, they were not expected to seek office, though they still shared with their luckier brethren the political supremacy that was theirs by right of birth. They were a resentful lot, sour and envious, open to bribery and therefore much mistrusted, for their frame of mind was thought to constitute a risk to law and order. Their main colony was in the district of San Barnabà, near the Rezzonico palace, and the Barnabotti, without a shadow of worldly consequence, eked out their lives on tiny allowances provided by the Senate. They rubbed shoulders with the richest grandees in Venice under the golden ceilings of the Sala del Maggior Consiglio, then returned to their dingy rooms for a slice of watermelon and a plate of polenta. Living as they did from hand to mouth, they tried to make extra money gambling, Some went in for confidence tricks – not too successfully, though, being seldom able to inspire the requisite confidence – and many sold their votes. 'In them,' says Pompeo Molmenti, 'were seen all the faults and opinions that spring from the combination of poverty and conceit.'[39] Corrupt and corrupting, restless, seditious, they preyed on the need of one, the ambition of another, and on any vulnerability they could find.

When disturbing new ideas from France reached Venice the Barnabotti were the first to embrace them. As much out of spite against the old aristocracy as from the hope of fishing in troubled waters, they became wholehearted supporters of the Revolution. By this time, the last quarter of the century, their numbers had grown as Venetian prosperity declined; they were many, they were subversive, and on both counts were dangerous. The Great Council accordingly thought it wise to make their most forward agitator, Giorgio Pisani, a Procurator of St Mark, in an effort to channel off their inconvenient enthusiasm. It was to regret its diversionary tactic soon enough, for Pisani, once installed, revealed his simple doctrine: get rid of the Doge and share out the property of all the rich patricians among the Barnabotti. This was too much. On May 29, 1780, when the new and unconventional Procurator gave an entertainment to celebrate his election, the guests were inundated with little notices full of rhymed menace – *Ancuo ingresso e doman processo* ran one couplet – roughly, 'He's in today, but the trial's under way'. Even this was too kindly a forecast, for it never came to a trial. Pisani was arrested two days later and immured, first at Verona then at Ferrara where he died, all reputation gone. After this the leading patricians felt justified in their exclusive attitude and never weakened again as far as the Barnabotti were concerned.

The three hundred or so families of the noble class – 3,577 presons in 1766 – made up a very small part of the population, perhaps two and a half per cent. A great family was known as such by its great name, and titles, though they existed, were relatively unimportant. There were plenty of *marchesi* about, but they were all of foreign extraction and had been *marchesi* somewhere else before they were citizens of Venice. Some nobles went so far as to adopt the style of Count and claim they got it from their ancestors, and since the phantom honour gave them neither rights nor precedence nobody challenged this form of self-promotion. The particle is often used in works of history, and can be found in contemporary memoirs, but only as a concession to French usage; a patrician rarely added *da* and a territorial name to his own. The distinguishing *Ser* was enough for him, and when he belonged to the Gran Consiglio his only right was to the style *Nobil Homine*, while his wife

67

had that of *Nobil Donna*, abbreviated respectively to N.H. and N.D.
Originally no one was an Excellency unless he held one of the chief
offices of state, but by the end of the century every patrician was so
addressed.

The young nobles entered the Great Council at the age of
twenty-five.[40] There were no especial moral, educational or cultural
requirements and usually none would be necessary, for all were
sure to have had good moral direction and excellent schooling.
Most went to the university at Padua and some studied farther
afield, out of Venetian territory, returning home at twenty-two to
begin their careers and apply themselves to the art of government.
If they were relations, friends, or even aquaintances of ambassadors
or *provveditori* they might go abroad as attachés; others would serve
as honorary assistants to senators or magistrates. All of them were
early put to learn something of how the administration worked and
the conduct of official life, and the Signory set great store by these
beginnings. The straw-covered basket of medlars carved on the
Scala dei Giganti symbolised the youthful patricians and the
subordinate tasks that ripened and prepared them for the responsi-
bilities of government later on.

Thus careful of the training of her élite, Venice was no less so in
protecting them from the invasion of doubtful or irregular intruders.
A name entered in the Golden Book gave full right to membership
of the Great Council, but every year that noble directory was most
attentively revised. Should a patrician marry into the middle class
the name of his son was deleted unless a special court, enquiring
into the mother's family, descent and circumstances, decided otherwise. But the case was rare, since the marriage of an aristocrat had
to be approved by the Great Council in the first place and it was
seldom indeed that they blessed a union with a woman of lower
rank. An exception could be made if the lady's father were a
terra ferma noble or belonged to one of the privileged professions of
medicine, spice merchanting or glass manufacturing. But she had
to be very rich, all the same, and in the best families such misalliances
did not occur. A peer in England was none the worse for giving his
hand to a peasant girl, but in the Most Serene Republic the patrician
who married beneath him was depriving his children of noble rank
and any prospect of ever being Doge. If the lady of his choice were
a servant, or in any other 'base or lowly station', then it was goodbye
to his own nobility too and he became an ordinary citizen.

The outcome of these iron rules was to make a closed circle of the patriciate and to sacrifice that blending together of bourgeois and grandee that had such happy results elsewhere. (It was doing wonders for the British aristocracy at this very time.) On the other hand, and with the exceptions noted, all a patrician's sons were noble, not the eldest only, as in some other European countries; and though brothers had no automatically equal claim on an estate when their father died, yet they were equal before the law.

These young men, making their bow on the Broglio, admitted to the Great Council, had before them lifetimes passed in the pursuit of public office. They had over 800 employments to choose from, some far more important than others and all of very short duration. This transience was, in fact, the chief of many arrangements calculated to make the middle class feel that aspirations to power were simply not worth while – the more promise any given charge might seem to hold out to the embryo dictator, the briefer was his tenure. Senators and the Council of Ten were elected for twelve months, the Doge's counsellors for eight. The *savii* served no longer than six. Elections followed one another in a continual general post, with enormous scope for intrigue among the swarm of applicants for every job. The applicant's part was to make himself as pleasant as possible to the largest possible number of voters, and with this practical object in view the rich nobles would be as agreeable to their poverty-stricken fellows as though everybody were as good as everybody else. The intricacies of compliment and courtesy seemed indeed to establish a kind of egalitarianism, a friendly democracy among aristocrats. The candidate who thought he could dispense with the sometimes obsequious brotherly love that was in order at election times was known as *duro di schiena*, a ramrod, and risked having a long wait for a plum post, however well qualified he might be.

And yet it cost no pains for these patricians to display their charm, so naturally was charm at their command. Courtesy, amiability, politeness, were not only the tradition of their kind, but its main characteristic. Goethe appreciated the look they had of 'men effortlessly wise, untroubled, sitting lightly to life, and every one of them animated by a sort of gaiety'. Apart from their beguiling of voters, they showed the most scrupulous delicacy in their behaviour to others at all times. Baretti[41] quotes the example of a highly-placed Venetian who scolded his son for asking a stranger whether his country could boast any square as fine as the Piazza. Especially were they magnanimous to inferiors, with an intimate kindness that Carlo Gozzi tells us was almost universal. His memoirs recount how his uncle, Almoro Tiepolo, tripped one evening in his flowing patrician robe as he stepped from his gondola. His gondolier, reaching to save him from falling into the water, dropped the oar, which knocked against his master's arm and broke it. He did not realise what he had done and Tiepolo never murmured until he got to his own room. Then all he said to his valet was, 'Be careful, my arm is broken in two.'

This was the consideration of pure good breeding, with no slovenly democracy about it, or low familiarity. Friendly as they were, the nobles knew their place and behaved in all circumstances in such a way that no one else forgot it either. Small details of bearing, speech and gesture told the tale. 'You could recognise an aristocrat in the depths of his gondola,' said a visitor, 'just by watching him raise or lower a window.' Let the parvenu imitate with all the care he might, he could never be mistaken for a man of birth in the plainest coat. And this superiority of look and manner rubbed off on the servants, too. George Sand was to observe that no public boatman ever rowed with anything like the majesty and elegance of a palace gondolier – proof that the good old traditions were still alive at the time of her famous visit.

Characteristic of the patricians was their close-knit family life. Aristocracy mistrusted the breakaway. When parents died the family possessions were not divided up; the children lived on in the palazzo, and, since none had an individual share, they rarely quarrelled. At the first sign of discord, arbitrators were called in to nip it in the bud. This smooth domestic atmosphere, one must admit, owed something to the fact that all daughters would have been firmly disposed of, to husbands or to convents. The prime object was naturally, to marry them to rich men, but in any case to men with plenty of relations, for this was important when voting time came round. A suitable dowry was paid and the girl relinquished any further claim on the family funds. Daughters who did not marry, and marry early, entered convents, each with the statutory endowment and an allowance for pocket money, and they, too, gave up all right to anything more from home. We shall speak later of the life of non-vocational nuns.

Their brothers, left behind in an ancestral mansion invariably large enough to shelter a great many people, led a communal existence. A steward, usually a priest, was employed to manage their income and give each a monthly sum to pay his personal servants and cover private spending. A brother ran up debts – they were met from the general fund and docked from his *mensata*, or allowance; another was elected to expensive office (and all office was expensive) – the general fund financed him. It was a scheme that went very well with the prime object of increasing the family's political importance; and even more it helped the patrician in his chief moral duty, accepted counterpart and justification of his enormous political privileges, that of serving the state not only in person, but with all his worldly goods.

As a rule only one of the sons would marry, sometimes delegated by his brothers to carry on the line, and he then received the largest share of income. The Président de Brosses believed the tale that the one-for-all-and-all-for-one principle extended beyond the family fortune to the family wife, arguing with his accustomed cynicism that the arrangement, though immoral, obviated *l'embarras de la précaution*. Besides, everybody was at least sure that his sons came of his own blood. Saint-Didier, too, tells of a go-between who briskly diverted the designs of a foreigner upon a married lady with the information, 'Nothing doing; *già quattro cognati in casa*' – four brothers-in-law at home already. In fairness it must be said, however, that neither Saint-Didier nor the Président is really trustworthy on questions of this kind.[42]

But this practice of one marriage per family, even if morally unimpeachable, may well have had some bearing on the decline of the patrician class as a whole. The bachelor brothers, with no domestic ties or possessions of their own and no means of making careers for themselves, were apt to drift into the aimless life that beckoned in Venice to gentlemen of leisure. Many, on the other hand, set aside personal ambition and devoted themselves to the interests of the married brother who was now head of the family. If all the opportunities for high office went to one man, there was compensation in the fact that capital did not dwindle away in divided inheritances. Impoverished nobles were, with reason, regarded as a menace, and the Venetians approved of anything that led to fewer of them.

Government was also careful to prevent the rise among the

aristocracy of any group which might aim at political domination. So important was it to have all the nobles on one level that they were even required to look the same. Their costume, while differing from that of commoners, was allowed no touch of individuality, and so they were all regimented into the *veste patrizia*, a sort of Roman toga or full, gathered gown which was supposed to satisfy the vital but contradictory conditions. The wider the sleeve the more important the wearer, and since a nobleman was correctly greeted by a kiss on the edge of his sleeve, those hailing the truly great had to bow very low indeed. The cloth of this gown was lined with squirrel-fur in winter, with silk or ermine in summer[43] and varied in colour for the different ranks and offices, purple-red for senators and Procurators of St Mark, scarlet for the ducal counsellors, violet for the chiefs of the Quarantie Criminale. The leading magistrates wore wide belts with plaques and dangling ornaments of silver. Other nobles had plain, one-coloured robes, usually of black, and all wore a matching stole over the left shoulder.

This severe uniform was heavy, cumbersome, inconvenient, and all the more annoying because the clothes it hid were romantic and elegant to a degree. Fashion came from France: knee-breeches of cotton or woollen cloth, white silk stockings, tricorne hat, lace at the wrists and throat, and coat so heavily embroidered with gold or silver thread that the material was invisible underneath. The skirts of this French coat were modified by the end of the century into little more than a sort of ruffle round the waist. It was worn open to show the long waistcoat, or *camiciola*, of silver or gold brocade or flowered silk, and what with painted procelain buttons and braids of pastel-coloured ribbon, the ensemble had such a feminine turn that Gasparo Galerno was moved to wonder 'whether the stronger sex were not changing into the weaker before our very eyes'. And indeed, although the noblemen of Venice by no means set themselves up as models of elegance, yet their finery was quite as lavish as that of their wives.

How understandable, then, that they should hate concealing all this fanciful raiment with clumsy gowns that made them look like elephants. Chafing under the regulations, they are to be observed throughout the *Settecento* trying to discard the *veste patrizia* for the freedom of the graceful *tabarro*. This was of light material and generally in some bright colour, and did not get in the way or prevent one from walking properly: a kind of overall, kept on even in the hottest weather and favoured by men of the middle class and everyone above the rank of artisan. The women wore it with a *mantellina* over the shoulders and bosom. The poor patrician males, left stifling in their noble robes, resolved at last to adopt the *tabarro*. At first they used it on their private walks when they did their best to avoid recognition, and muffled their faces if anyone accosted them. But they grew bolder as time went on and more brave souls came forward every day to flout the purposes of the Ten. That supreme tribunal, in an effort to stem the tide of revolt, abandoned its wonted solemn reminders about the rules for wearing the unalterable *veste patrizia* by law established and introduced severe penalties – five years in a dark dungeon aud a thousand ducats' fine. But not even such stern threats had much effect for long. The unseemly practice still went on, the nobles increasingly disregarded their official wear. The *tabarro* was seen on the Piazza and in places of public resort; it was seen on the Broglio itself. The *Provveditore alle Pompe*, whose business it was to enforce the sumptuary laws, repeated his warnings and set his spies in vain. No one was taking any more notice.

Nor, of course, did anyone suffer serious consequences. The uncompliant nobleman, we learn from a document printed by Giovanni Commisso, was called before the Inquisitors' secretary and the following admonition was read out:

'We are astonished to hear that you have had the audacity to appear in the streets in a *tabarro*. This scandalous conduct, made worse, as it is, by your station in life, leaves us little choice but to inflict upon you penalties in accordance with that station. For this occasion, however, being satisfied that you must be already ashamed of an action so imprudent and obnoxious, we shall administer only a well-merited rebuke; together with the warning that it is to be inscribed in the records of this court and known to those who will succeed us here. If therefore you at any other time commit a similar offence you will be liable to such severe and exemplary punishment as befits the dignity of this court, which must require of all, and of patricians above all, strict heed and absolute obedience.'

Thus warned, the guilty party went home, changed, and returned to his pleasant pursuits in a comfortable *tabarro*. If again noticed or accused he received a second, identical lecture, but however often this happened no punishment materialised. One can quite see why the decrees of the Ten remained inoperative. On pain of death, café owners, barbers, keepers of *casini*, theatre doormen and the like were all forbidden to allow on their premises any noble wearing the *tabarro*; all did so, and all got clean away with it. The *tabarro* went from strength to strength throughout the century until at last togas were met with only in the Doge's palace, where they were kept in a cloakroom like gowns at a lawcourt, and where so great a personnage as Ser Vicenzo Zen appeared in a *tabarro* in the Senate itself.

Authority had no better luck with periwigs, the fashion for which was brought from the French capital by the patrician Scipione Collalto in 1668 and at once energetically forbidden by the Ten.[44] They might have saved their breath. Gilded youth and bald old age combined against them and the Venetians, docile as they were over politics, were far too used to making a mockery of dress regulations. The periwig had such a huge success that the Senate decided to sanction it on payment of a double tax. Tax or no tax, it became the national headgear and the fashion spread from the noble to the middle class. Soon, if you did not conform, you risked being taken for an uncouth creature, or wilfully behind the times or, what was worse, one of the common herd. There were periwigs of many kinds to choose from. The *groppi* was a design with curls all knotted together; the hair of the *cortesana* fell forward over the left shoulder and behind the right; the *parrucca alla delfina* was high in front, with a little silk bag for the hair at the back of the neck. Different styles came and went and a multitude of barbers (every one an 'artiste') lived by making and looking after wigs. When Lorenzo Correr died in 1757 the newspapers drew attention to the fact that he had been 'the last of the patricians to wear his own hair'.[45]

The nobles lost their source of income when Venice lost her possessions in the Levant. The Barbary pirates had no mercy on Venetian trading-craft, and to carry a handful of armed men on board did nothing but add to transport costs. Things might have been different could the Serenissima have outfaced the corsairs at sea, but her ships, as we know, were painfully few. The small defence fleet she suddenly decided to construct in 1759 was fitted out for show alone, costly and little used.

Sleeping partners in these stay-at-home days, the nobles entrusted their money to maritime business houses who took all the hazard and paid interest at 6 per cent, which was more than it would have made in ordinary business. Thus, though they could no longer increase their capital by the kind of venture on which it had been built up in the past, they could still draw a good income from it. The obvious remedy would have been to develop the mainland, or *terra ferma*, but the patricians of Venice retained the mercantile spirit of their ancestors and were simply not farmers. Any farms they owned they visited at grape-picking and harvest time, not otherwise. There were many who merely walked about in dusty shoes, making believe they had been to the country property, without actually setting foot there.

Not a few of the patricians, apart from the miserable Barnabotti, led lives whose reality scarcely matched their outward and apparent circumstances. These were the nobles who received their friends in the smallest apartments of their vast, forlorn palaces, there to offer them nothing but a slice of watermelon; who sent the solitary manservant out for a dish of polenta and ate it surrounded by the inherited picture gallery in the dining-room; and who from time to time spent a year's income on one evening's entertainment that 'put the splendours on display and brought the old opulence back to life'.[46] Others could no longer keep up pretence of any kind. Casanova, visiting the highly-esteemed Senator Zaccaria Vallaresso in 1743, and thinking to find a dream of luxury, was amazed to see that the entire furnishings of the big salon consisted of four worm-eaten chairs and a battered, filthy table. Nobles whom their peers thought deserving of and able to afford office had to refuse it on the score of expense, and some could not even pay the set fine, doubled on a second refusal, of a thousand ducats which was imposed on top of a year's banishment. The fact that the priesthood was an escape-road from these penalties brought some gifted and distinguished men into the Church.

And yet a poor noble was the exception still. The patriciate as a body might be poor, but the day of great wealth was not gone, and many a family had ten gondolas tied up at the watergate, eighty indoor servants and an income counted in tens of millions of florins. They lived in tremendous luxury, with a lack of heed that sometimes verged on the indecent: Caterina Querini smiled when the pearls from her necklace scattered to the floor as she danced with the King of Denmark, and went on dancing over them.

These more-than-oriental grandees could be petty and parsimonious, however. With one hand they lavished a fortune on the mounting of some spectacular pageant, and with the other refused anything more than twelve lire a page to the best poets in Venice. The owner of a sumptuous villa on the Brenta cuts his gardener's wages by four lire as he spends thousands of ducats on a hothouse for exotic plants. The Dogaressa Mocenigo, agreeing to stand godmother to the son of the steward of her fief of Cordignano, hastens to indicate that she cannot possibly make the usual presents; and then at her husband's death pays for 16,000 lb. of wax candles and funeral black for the eighty servants of her household. Aristocratic ladies blazing with jewels passed the long evenings over embroidery frames in the homeliest corners of majestic palaces.

And those Venetian palaces were an indication of how many rich nobles there were still, with the end of the story already in sight. Many of the buildings were old – Commines in the fifteenth century had called the Grand Canal the most beautiful highway, with the handsomest houses, in the world, and from then on Venice was unmatched for great and splendid mansions – but additions made in Casanova's lifetime could hold their own with anything of earlier date.

Old or new, however – Gothic with Romanesque detail or Saracenic trimming, specimens of the high baroque or forerunners of the neo-Classical return to the antique – the palaces were as much museums as private homes; more so, perhaps. They nearly all retain the atmosphere of magnificence and it is now possible to visit some of them and appreciate the setting in which the lords of Venice lived. What strikes one immediately is that cosiness was not the object. The huge porticoes with their exotic lanterns, the colonnaded courtyards where marble statues stand among the low green shrubs, proclaim the fact at once. A Venetian palace is the showplace for a patrician family and as such it is designed. The vast salons of the *piano nobile*, used only for receptions, are floored with marbles patterned in mosaic and strewn with rich carpets. Ceilings are great spans of gold, or painted masterpieces. The walls are gorgeously hung with damask or gilded leather, or panelled in precious marble. This style of decoration never appealed to the French and the marquis de Montaigu had 'all that sort of thing' hidden under superb hangings of his own at his embassy, while the Président de Brosses, who disapproved of coloured stucco rioting on doors and window-frames, spoke of 'tasteless prodigality'.

As for the elaborate furniture, few royal residences could have equalled it. Everything, large or small, was beautiful and rare. Venice had continually contrived new types of chairs and cupboards, tables and desks. She had imported little ornamental jasper columns, vases and goldsmiths' work and the baroque had added its profusion of looking-glasses, Murano chandeliers, painted furniture and allegorical figures carved in ebony. There could be little informality among such crowds of *objects d'art*, but they gave an air of richness that went well with the princely palace-façades.

The family would usually live on the floor above, where rooms were smaller, lower and more convenient, though every bit as full. The main salons were deserted save for the receptions which though dazzling, were infrequent, for the nobility did not share the widespread Italian taste for such diversions. Even the *conversazioni*, then the main attraction of society in Rome, were not over-popular in Venice and foreigners found them deadly. For one thing, it was difficult to join in the gambling that absorbed their fellow guests; Venetian suits had different names and they could not recognise the pictures on the cards. For another, contrary to the Roman usage, no sorbets were served. All you got in the wealthier houses was a slice of watermelon and a small cup of coffee round about eleven, and at midnight, says Brosses, you went off with your stomach rumbling and had a proper supper at home. The mental nourishment would have been as sparse, he adds, for those cold and formal gatherings did not exactly facilitate the exchange of ideas. Even light chatter was hard going. 'Venice,' concluded René Gourdan, 'had no conversation.'

For conversation could so easily have led to politics. Cipher though she was among the nations, the Republic still jealously preserved all the forms and customs that had served as valuable weapons in the past, first and foremost the absolute secrecy masking all she might decide to do and all she had decided on. It was supremely important that the nobles, every one of them more or less involved in state affairs, be protected from the perils of indiscretion and careless talk. What better way than to curtail their opportunities for private conference? For this reason entertainments in Venice were always the same: full-dress gala occasions with never any

77

chance to withdraw for a serious *tête-à-tête* in any quiet corner.
Gasparo Gozzi sketched these show-piece gatherings:

'I have been at parties where no one could bear to stop talking
for a second, where you could hear neither question nor answer
but only a great combined voice. All throats merged into a single
throat and made a noise like water cascading from an overflow;
joy and good cheer burst forth on every side.'

It was unlikely that state secrets would or could be divulged, or
private opinions confided, above a din that drowned an orchestra.
(And several orchestras would be playing, too, in the various rooms.)

As far as possible, strangers were kept away from these receptions
and might attend only if the Inquisitors approved. Even in everyday
life no one trusted them: it was not really wise to speak to a foreigner
in public view. There was more than a hint in Venice of the Iron
Curtain mentality.

This unfriendly arm's-length meant social excommunication for
ambassadors. The Serenissima had no outside interests and nothing
to conceal any more, but the old, undeviating rule still held about
hiding everything from foreign eyes. The arrival of an ambassador
was greeted, it is true, with all official honours, but these were
regarded by the nobles as so much glorification for themselves and
by the commons as yet another spectacular titbit. A brilliant
procession wound along the decorated route, the palaces were lit
up after dark, great stands of torches shone in the streets and
fountains ran with wine. Government and populace joined in the
festivity, with bands playing loudly in the background. The embassy
itself stood open all night through to anyone who turned up for a
drink or liked to help himself to a memento in silver or porcelain.
(Such unconsidered trifles disappeared at all Venetian junketings
and no one was supposed to notice or object.) There are instructive
details in a manuscript describing the entry of the marquis de
Montaigu:

'The amount of food and drink consumed was much increased
by reason of a crowd of Jews and other low people who got in in
disguise and went off with all they could lay hands on. Over
seven hundred glass and crystal vases were stolen during the
night and more than five hundred pieces of porcelain and
faience.'

Next day the ambassador would be admitted to solemn audience in the ducal palace, where he presented his letters of credence to the Doge in the presence of the Senate. The speech he made was by tradition full of highly flattering references to the well-known and never-failing wisdom of the Republic and the unique virtues of her political system. This was the sole direct interview he ever had with either Doge or government. All business was thereafter done by letter, and the devious and complicated procedures left no loophole for contact or discussion, even of the most formal kind. The only way an ambassador could gain information was by using bribery and corruption.[47]

These unreliable methods were further impeded by the firm rule that forbade any noble, under pain of death, to have dealings with the foreign envoys or their staffs. No patrician might entertain or visit them and must avoid a greeting should they happen to meet. It was treason to say a word to them, a hanging matter to linger a moment in their company. A senator of the great Tron family who ran into the French ambassador when visiting a priest turned tail 'as if the plague were in the house'. Another nobleman fell into conversation with a young masker and made his apologies to the Ten without delay on realising the man was Jean-Jacques Rousseau, a secretary of M. de Montaigu – temporary employee though he was, and not well thought of by his master.[48] Patricians had been known to pay with their lives for faults and failings in this dangerous direction: Leonardo Loredan was executed for commerce with the Spanish ambassador when all he had done was to steal that gentleman's mistress. There was an outright miscarriage of justice over Antonio Foscarini in 1622 and his was a grimmer affair than the Président de Brosses believed. He heard that Foscarini, without speaking to a soul, walked through one of the embassies on his way to a lovers' rendezvous; he was in fact executed for treason, accused by the Ten of having entered the Spanish embassy for the purpose of meeting foreign diplomats. The spy who denounced him on this baseless charge was convicted of false witness soon afterwards and put to death in his turn, but though the government admitted error its apologies were half-hearted and its attitude on the subject unrelenting and unchanged.

A despatch from the French ambassador of August 25, 1764, mentions a case in which it did not even bother to apologise. This time it was the parish priest of San Mattia who was prosecuted by

79

the Ten for alleged correspondance with Montaigu and spared the death sentence in the hope that he might eventually name his accomplices. Condemned for life, the old man had rotted in prison for years when the accusation, quite by chance, was proved to have been false. He was declared innocent and set free, but 'the balm of his own good conscience was all the compensation he got'.

The Inquisitors attempted to pass their harshness off as concern for the diplomat in their midst who, so they said, deserved protection against spongers and imposters. Towards the hungry nobles, perpetually on the lookout for extra cash and none too scrupulous as to how it might be earned, they were pitiless. It was not the fact that these men were in the market-place that made them anxious – the real worry was lest the Barnabotti, tired of being shut out from government, should sell themselves to a foreign power for the sake of improving their lot. And above all they dreaded the risk from nobles in great office, who were kept under most careful supervision and against whom the Ten would proceed in full severity.

Ambassadors, thus outcast from society, had to rely upon each other's company, or that of their own nationals. They were not left quite isolated from all the gaiety of Venice, however, for they could always illuminate the lighter side of life by consorting with beautiful women. Sad to say, the French embassy set some rather poor examples. The Count de Froulay abducted a nun. With M. de Montaigu all was 'bacchanalia, courtesans, games of chance, etc.'. As for M. de Bernis, although he was busily building up the character of perfect ambassador he was to exhibit when representing king and country later on in Rome, the striking stories Casanova tells of him are damaging, to say the least, although we may be reluctant to believe them entirely;[49] while it was difficult, if not stupid, to ignore the beautiful women, in Venice of all places. Nor should we hasten to condemn the French alone. Other ambassadors were just as bad, albeit pursuing a course of conduct well established among diplomatic missions to the Serenissima. Some might be said to have pursued it too zealously by far; there was an English envoy who died as a result of sexual excess with a harlot from the theatre.[50]

The nobility meanwhile had to forego all the pleasant additions which the polished and stylish corps of ambassadors and attachés contributed to the intellectual and social scene in other capitals. They remained a class narrowly circumscribed, and since they claimed no divine right to their position nor any sort of natural superiority, their only justification lay in public work and their only privilege was to serve the state. Riches were no advantage under the civil law, while criminal law doubled its rigour for the patrician whose victim was a commoner. A French aristocrat could have Voltaire thrashed and fear no repercussions, but Venice was the one place in Europe where no master could do the same by his own servant. In Italy, indeed, it was always best to rely on a well-placed boot by way of castigation.

The ruling classes exercised all their unchallenged power in the interests of the lower. The people lived under their protection, side by side with the protectors. All mingled freely together at the public festivals, one paying no mark of deference to the other. Aristocrat, plebian and courtesan might have their quarters under the same roof. The greatest lady might make a personal friend of her maid, and it was quite usual for the patrician to give his son a godfather of lowly birth. The nobility of Venice were obviously very different from the European nobility as a whole, to whom, indeed, they appeared as so many deluded egalitarians, madly courting revolution.

II THE MIDDLE CLASS

Between the aristocracy and the large labouring class there came the men of middle station, people with considerable influence in and on the life of the city. Their work was done in government offices, in the shops of the Merceria or counting-houses at Rialto, even in the dens where news-sheets were put together. They were relatively few in number, about a fifth of the population, growing fewer still as the century advanced and the rich bourgeois tended to live more and more like the patricians, while the poorer members sank into the class below.

They were a very mixed lot and those at their head, the mass of officials in charge of the complicated routines of government, were themselves a finely graduated band. High among them came the secretaries, busy in the Doge's chancellery compounding dossiers, drawing up reports, drafting laws and diplomatic instructions – documents which, according to Antonio Lamberti,[51] they were much given to embellishing with *non comuni viste politiche*, unorthodox political comment of their own. They included what he calls 'a squad or two of imbeciles' but their ability was for the most part undisputed, their good sense acknowledged and their integrity

81

beyond question. We have already seen with what respect they were surrounded, how they walked with the nobility on state occasions, how their wives were bidden to parties by the Doge. The *segretari* were known as the *gentiluomini del populo* and were indispensible to the nobles, with whose interests their own were bound up. They strove, not always very convincingly, to imitate the noble attitude and way of life. Wanting tradition, they did not get the thing quite right, however, and displayed a disagreeable hauteur towards the lower orders and even to the *terra ferma* patricians. They lacked the grace of openhandedness and their wives were said to be too fond of thrift, a middle-class virtue. Their respectability was also most unusual in Venice, and the theory that meanness was behind it all made it seem less praiseworthy.

Below this rank of superior registrars, so proud of themselves and prouder still because their position was perhaps a trifle shaky, proliferated the whole little world of lesser clerks, petty bureaucrats and holders of such modest employments as might give a man some small authority and standing. These, too, were favoured beings, for though their earnings were low their place was fairly with the middle class and they clung to all its manners and ideas.

The liberal professions were lucrative, at least for those who were good at them. The 240 licensed barristers included some ten or a dozen stars and about twenty who commanded very high fees.[52] Incomes for the rest varied with their talents and their way of using them. Even the least gifted could scrape a living through the touts who chased up briefs on commission. Goldoni as a briefless barrister filled the time by working out what he would earn if a case or two came his way; 40,000 livres at least, he thought, 'a lot, really, for a country where things cost half what they do in Paris'. Everything was done to swell a client's bill by getting him involved in legal extras chargeable on top of the niggardly three sequins that were the approved rate for a court appearance. And since an appearance was limited to three-quarters of an hour, one way to solvency was to make as many as possible: the most straightforward affair could easily be spun out to fifteen or twenty separate sessions.

Medical practice was carefully regulated, and nowhere was free-lance doctoring frowned on more severely. It was an offence to hand out a cup of herb tea, bathe wounds in an emergency or recommend an ointment to the woman next door. This being so, the doctors generally put a stiff price on their prescriptions and on the potions they prepared themselves, often from plants they grew in their garden-plots. The one loophole in the system was the latitude enjoyed by barbers, who might treat simple cases with triaca, or Venetian treacle. This concoction of gum, frankincense, opium and Cretan wine was an original Venetian recipe, a supposed panacea for many ills. Similarly, the apothocaries did best by selling sedatives, based on opium, to the numerous sufferers from food poisoning or people whose drinks had been tampered with. They also saw to the making up of the 'sovereign remedies' ordered by the medical men. This was an exactly-controlled process and three supervising witnesses had to be present before the druggists could begin.

By far the biggest group among the middle class consisted of manufacturers and merchants. The detailed figures for 1766 show 5,500 of them, in varying degrees of prosperity. They were honest, industrious folk who followed the law in blind obedience, ridiculously heedful of the hundreds of frequently idiotic regulations that hindered their activities. The bourgeoisie included also painters, musicians, copyists of music, clock-makers, draughtsmen and, generally speaking, all whose calling raised them above plebian level.

But despite these interior gradations, all were members of a separate world with a moral code, a conception of honour, and customs of its own, a world whose structure and spirit were to be profoundly affected by the widespread social changes of the eighteenth century. Before about 1720 little is heard of it. Its houses were closely shuttered, its outlook narrow and its life retired. There might be song and gaiety in Venice but the middle classes did not want to know. Whether from humility or native caution, they retreated from the times, indifferent alike to scandal and the intrigue of politics. The only news they liked to hear was strictly practical. A ship was in – what was she carrying? What were the current prices for whatever it was that they produced or traded in? The rates of exchange? The latest bankruptcies?

These, of course, were male preoccupations. None but faint echoes ever reached the womenfolk, recluses in their modest homes, with crossed kerchiefs and high head-dresses, their monotonous hours filled with housekeeping and saying the rosary and chatting occasionally to the neighbours in lisping Venetian. There are descriptions of their little universe in the *Memorie per servire all'istoria dell'inclita città di Venezia* by Girolamo Zanetti,[53] and of those

83

unexciting, invariable conversations, punctuated with sighs and proverbs. They talked about insolent, lazy servants, self-willed children and giddy-minded females; how people took too much coffee and chocolate and similar drugs that only upset their stomachs; how the price of food went up. The subject-matter was scanty and what there was they dwelt upon interminably. If peas were scarce and going to be dear, or the lagoon fishermen knocked off for a day with one of their recurring grievances, the topic was picked over and exclaimed about for weeks.

Masculine discussion was on the same sort of level and it is clear from their comments on how to behave, how to bring up the young, and on everything else in general, that the gentlemen were somewhat out of touch. A famous scene in Act II of Goldoni's *I Rusteghi*, (*The Boors*, plainly illustrates their rearguard frame of mind:

'Oh, you're quite right, you never see young men nowadays as they were in our time. Remember? You did what your father said you could, and no more and no less.'

'My two married sisters, I don't suppose I set eyes on them ten times in all my life.'

'I hardly used to open my mouth, even to my mother.'

'To this very day, I've never seen a play or an opera.'

'They hauled me off to an opera once, but I slept right through it.'

'When I was small my father said, "Do you want to see a peep-show, or would you rather have two pennies?" And I took the pennies.'

'I was the same. Always saved my tips. I added all the farthings up until I had a hundred ducats. Then I invested them at four per cent, and that meant four more ducats every year; and now, when I draw them, I'm so thrilled I could count them for ever. It's not avarice, it's just the thought that I *got* them, when I was still a boy.'

'And where would you find anyone doing that now? They throw their money away, ruin themselves.'

'This liberty, that's what's behind it.'

'True, true. As soon as they know how to dress themselves, they're off.'

'Yes, and you know who puts them up to it – their own mothers.'

'Don't tell me! I hear things, I hear things. . . .'

And unhappily Goldoni's old men put their principles exactly into practice. One of them insists on his son's taking a wretched footmen with him wherever he goes, although the boy is of an age to be married and the fine flower of the patricians were just then making a great point of going about with no attendants at all. Another will not let his wife have visits, even from her own near relations. A third is planning to marry his daughter off without telling her to whom. All she hears is, 'In the presence of these gentlemen and their wives, and of my wife, who is like a mother to you [i.e. the girl's stepmother], I am telling you you are engaged.' The man? She will know who he is later, which is always soon enough. Girls went to Mass with their eyes fixed on the ground, vigilantly chaperoned by some elderly kinswoman. Once married, they were huddled into dark clothes with no ornament or touch of prettiness. Fathers were stern sentinels of virtue and young men not unnaturally hesitated. The welcome that might be waiting for them can be imagined from a speech in another of Goldoni's plays, *L'Uomo Prudente*, in which the bourgeois householder addresses an intruder who, for purposes of his own, has contrived to cross the threshold:

'I'm warning you, don't you look at my wife or my daughter, either little or long, and don't you set foot in my house again . . . I may as well tell you, just between you and me, there's a trapdoor under one of the stairs, and I'm the only one who knows how to work it. It turns right over and drops you in a pit full of nails and razors.'

All these honest merchants, undeviating husbands and guardian brothers were occupied exclusively with the preservation of goods and family honour and never dreamed of interfering in matters of public interest. Not for them a sojourn under the leads. They neither heard nor desired to know about such things. They went to church, took off their hats when the Angelus rang and would no more turn into freethinkers than become religious fanatics. The established order had in them its surest prop, and they regarded as emissaries of Satan all who wished to change it. Faithful bondsmen to the past, they were quick to condemn any new departure.

Yet they were not morose and sour all the time; they would not have been Venetians had cheerfulness not kept breaking in. This it did quite often, and they regaled themselves in simple, seemly ways. Buffoonery amused them and they appreciated good cooking.

They enjoyed cards, and a little dance at home and family picnics in the country, and were altogether more sprightly than their frowning faces would lead one to suppose. The two married couples in *I Rusteghi* present an illuminating picture of what they were really like and go far to explain why austerity could not last. These people, too, were swept with the rest into the whirl of pleasure they had so recently and piously denounced as fatal to salvation, and so swift was progress that it happened before a quarter of the century was gone. That is to say, in no time at all the daughter of the *Uomo Prudente* would be playing the *zentildonna*, receiving love-letters and making assignations; she too, when married, had her *cicisbeo* or *cavaliere servente*, like a lady. Fathers of families meanwhile would no longer disapprove it all as needless luxury but go the ruinous road themselves, giving masquerades and vying with the nobles in the costly delights of summer in the country. 'To be like other people' – the standard excuse – they too would sit in the cafés of the Piazza, haunt the gaming-rooms and frolic their way through Carnival as readily as the next. Sure sign of emancipation, their women took to wearing jewellery, and less was heard about dead capital in this connection. They began to keep somewhat better state. Those who could afford it lived in luxury, as did many who could not. Circumstances altered morals, so that the old-fashioned bourgeois would hardly have recognised himself in this new guise. Says a character in a play of Gasparo Gozzi:

'I remember how, when I was young, we had just one servant-girl – an old woman, rather; she went through the rooms at night with a small oil-lamp in her hand. If she heard anyone knocking she went to the window and raised the lamp and called, "Who's there?" Someone would reply from below, "Let down the basket." And she let down the basket and appeared a moment later in the family salon with a letter addressed *alle mani del signore osservadissimo* so-and-so; news of some vessel unloading, or loading, maybe, and what the profits on the cargo were. If anyone knocks at the door these days three or four valets go dashing to answer it. You are *illustrissimo* now on the letters they bring in, and there's a basket of pears or eggs from the tenant-farmer too – only we have to call him an agent, of course. . . . And which do you think means more in the end? The little old woman with her lamp, or a mob of footmen waving torches round?'

It is not fair to generalise, but clearly Gozzi was thinking of the small section of the middle class who had made money and set out to live like many of their betters, with no apparent aim save pleasure. In spite of their broader outlook and tolerance of new ways, however, the majority would continue serious-minded. They enjoyed life, for this was Venice, where life was to be enjoyed, but most of their time was devoted to business and to domesticity, which had grown less tedious nowadays. It is they who inhabit the stage of Goldoni, straightforward, uncomplicated people, uncontaminated by prevailing laxity. Good-living, good-tempered husbands; sons a little dissipated, but nothing really wrong with them; gay, witty women. And if these ladies were not in fact the pure gold their dramatist-portrayer says they were, yet they were certainly far less profligate than most of their fellow Venetians.

But if the bourgeois and his wife were going out and about to an increasing degree, their class was by no means dead nor were its principles forgotten. Its basic attitudes had not changed with taste and manners. It remained in the second half of the century a true bourgeoisie, more than ever attached to its old traditions and proud rather than ashamed of what it was. It had a great sense of solidarity, and stood by its own with boundless generosity in time of need. Molmenti relates how, when an official mislaid 5,974 ducats and was condemned to death, the neighbours came to the rescue and collected far more for him than the sum required.

The middle class was in fact rather smugly proud of itself and of its honourable citizens, making bold to think them superior to the aristocrats who believed a title justified a life of idleness. Yet there was no wish to encroach on the nobility. The bourgeois may have developed what we should call social awareness, but that failed to turn him into an agitator, and no wish for reform emerged. Things were different in other countries in those years, but here he made no attempt to break the political monopoly of the patriciate.

It was otherwise in the realm of the intellect, where the nobles had also gone unchallenged: the Doge Foscarini once said the same families have always directed the Republic with wise counsel and glorified her in the arts'. Henceforth, however, it was not only the scarlet-robed law-givers who figured as humanists and learned men. From Francesco Algarotti the grocer's son to Rosalba Carriera and Tiepolo, the middle class was to produce most of the artistic and literary talent. Goldoni himself was so completely bourgeois in character and background that he could never create anyone from high life on the stage, and the elegant women in Pietro Longhi's pictures remain always mild, home-keeping bodies, playing at great ladies.

With honest money in the bank, with less bigoted opinions and an increased response to art and letters, the folk of middle condition came to fulfil in Venetian life a rôle they would have scorned before. In the comic theatre the tale unrolls in the development of the plain and simple merchant Pantaleone. When the century opens he is the destined dupe of lover, valet and serving-girl, but we see him translated as the years go by. He still appears slow on the uptake and cherishes some narrow-minded notions, but he is no longer the butt. He is now the one who talks sense and inspires confidence and gives advice that people listen to. It is he who points the moral and sustains the plot.

And the Venetian third estate was rather like Pantaleone. No violence attended its birth and none was in its nature; also, it came too late into the world to snatch political power, as did its counterparts elsewhere in Europe. Its members, all shrewdly watching their own advantage and traditionalists to a man, never bothered with such things as ideology or claiming their rights to this, that and the other. They were far too busy managing their own affairs.

III THE LOWER CLASSES

Manservant, lady's-maid, layabout; caulker at the Arsenal, gondolier, Murano glassblower; the fisherman, and the man who hawked the catch; silk-weaver, lacemaker, the girl stringing pearl necklaces and the woman opening shellfish – these were the commoners of Venice, crowding the wharf and the workshop, at every counter and in every street. They formed a huge class and they went for nothing in the scheme of things. Law after law, their political prerogatives were whittled away while they stood by and applauded the spoiling process, steadily convinced that, nullities though it made them, they were absolutely free, no doubt about it, the freest people in the universe. Many were the songs that hailed their Venice as 'liberty's eternal home'. Every time they went out or gathered in a theatre they sang them lustily – how could they suppose such stirring invocations were deceptive, or untrue?

And when all was said and done the working people had, as Misson observed, the joys they really wanted. No one had the slightest intention of taking away their sessions in the wineshops, their card-games, or the lovely look of Venice, or anything else that made their lives worth living; and they certainly never complained.

There had been nothing difficult about their relegation. The labouring class were pursuers of pleasure in any case. All that was needed was 'to put pleasure within their reach and at their own level'.[54] The nobles provided the simple gratifications that appealed to this frivolous proletariat – fêtes and balls, and water-jousting on the Grand Canal, six months of Carnival in the year, heedlessness and hilarity. And enormously the proletariat relished it all, with no hesitance or question. What was the point of losing faith in those who made the days so happy for them? From time immemorial everybody knew that patricians were naturally right and infallible; why suddenly change one's mind and get involved in telling them what to do?

Veneration for the Republic throve in this climate of good government. The people called it their 'beloved mother' and had nothing but gratitude and respect for the oligarchy at its head. Montesquieu would have us believe that working men were so deeply respectful that they did not even protest at noble bills unpaid. It is strange to find a normally intelligent observer relaying such nonsense, but someone had been telling him fairy-stories: 'If they go three times to a creditor and he says he will have them beaten if they come again, they do not come again.' Apart from the fact that it was a serious crime to have an inferior beaten, all the evidence shows that dealings between noble and commoner, even in money matters, were marked by trust and friendliness, with very real relationships developing in other spheres than those of business. When nobles had godchildren of the working class the bonds of affection and near-kinship were cultivated on both sides with almost religious devotion, Not, of course, that worldly advantage was left out of reckoning – the child with a good selection of god-parents was correspondingly well protected on the road.

These gentle commoners of Venice, strangers alike to intense hatred and long grievance, did not in the least desire emancipation. Life's inequalities aroused no envy in them. Class warfare was limited to unexplosive quarrelling, resolved in smiles and hand-shakes. At the elections of parish priests and beadles, for example, where all parishioners might vote, it often happened that one candidate was supported by the noble, another by non-noble, householders. The parish would split into twin camps with no holds barred, and each party daubed praises of its own man and crude remarks about his opponent all over the walls. But as soon as the result was known, the winners set to with trumpets, fire-crackers and celebratory rockets and the losers joined them with no shadow of resentment.

Lively, gay and loyal, loathing the police and loving their city with such passion, the Venetians were remarkably tractable. They never shoved or hustled in the street. If they had disputes, they never came to brawling, and any passer-by could soothe them down at once. They were indeed what Montesquieu called them, the best people in the world; a little tempted to mockery perhaps, for they were natural wits, but they were also courteous and not uncivil in their irony. They cared nothing for the affairs of others, and so never thought of interfering in them. They did not stare. They did not dream of criticising anyone's clothes or appearance and were quick to offer help if he got lost. Heedless to a degree, the Venetian lived from day to day, oblivious of accident or illness, the possibility of losing his job, or of any other misfortune the morrow might produce. Nor had he the least notion of saving money for a rainy day, and a traveller notes how the people 'spend what they earn with the enthusiasm of a miser cramming it into a strong-box'.

Above all, they were a nation of artists. They loved beauty and created it as easily as they breathed. The gift is evident in the miracles that came flowing from the lace-makers' bobbins, the delicate shapes that grew from the glass-blower's tube, the gold-threaded materials woven at the looms. Everything the Venetian labourer did had the rhythm of poetry, whether he rowed a gondola or cast a fishing-net. The most ordinary groups composed themselves into pictures or poems, such as that scene, like a harvest festival, that so enchanted William Beckford in 1780:

'It was not five o'clock before I was aroused by a loud din of voices and splashing of water under my balcony. Looking out, I beheld the grand canal so entirely covered with fruits and vegetables, on rafts and in barges, that I could scarcely distinguish a wave. Loads of grapes, peaches and melons arrived, and disappeared

in an instant, for every vessel was in motion; and the crowds of pur-
chasers hurrying from boat to boat, formed a very lively picture.'[55]

Venetians seemed to make graceful scenes and charming prospects
such as this by instinct, presumably because they lived surrounded
by works of art and got their eye in – they possessed what Gasparo
Gozzi called *una certura misura*. The faculty extended to impalpable
things as well, and toil and pleasure were touched with lyricism. It
irradiated their dialect with captivating diminutives and melting
love-words. The people appreciated this language of theirs and
were the best of audiences for story-tellers and purveyors of tales.
They bred fine *improvvisatori* and more than one genuine poet, for
they had a passion for poetry and could reel off whole cantos of
Tasso by heart. As for singing, that was part and parcel of their
daily work, their rest and recreation. Every hour of the twenty-four
was filled with wondrous serenades, with lingering recitatives and
lilting, fleeting ballad-snatches. The treasury of their music was
inexhaustible, rich in the kind of tunes that set the feet tapping –
tunes the women sang to tambourines at the street-corners, when the
oldest among them would quickly find herself singing alone while
all the others danced, and the crawling hours were suddenly,
momentarily lightened by the gay refrains.

Limited though their existence may have been, these carefree
people always had a good standard of living, certainly much higher
than that in other parts of Italy; and this was true until the end
of the century, when economic decline flung so many workmen on
to the streets, poverty-stricken and unemployed. Until that time,
and surprising as it may seem if we rely on the bare official statistics,
real poverty, out-and-out destitution, was almost unknown. The
figures show 18,000 persons dependent on public or private charity
in Venice in 1760, but we should remember that anyone *senza entrata
e senza mestiere* was included: anyone, that is, without visible income
or who was unregistered with a trade guild.

And by no means everyone coming within this category would
be a beggar or a pauper living on charity. In a land where the
great aim was to do as little as possible, many people contrived to
find their basic needs without actually performing any task at all.
This was no mere idleness, but a course deliberately chosen in
preference to any of the comforts they might have earned by labour.
The bright ones managed to subsist on someone else, some patron

to whom they would compose dreadful poems as occasion offered. The patron's part of the bargain was to dole out money and – his main function – to feed them in return for flattering table-talk. Such were the *cavalieri dei denti*, colourful characters found time and again in the plays of Goldoni. Others pursued a lean career of shifts and expedients as card-sharpers, petty criminals, sellers of fake relics, general-purpose interveners in any shady transaction and, it goes without saying, panders. Anyone who felt himself insufficiently gifted for these or similar undertakings could try to turn a penny by handing ladies out of gondolas or doing odd jobs – delivering a parcel or a letter, putting people on the right road at night, helpfully standing aside to give a better view when a procession passed. Such services were always worth a tip in this city of the *buona mancia*.

True-blue beggars confined themselves to displaying their deformities and sores and rattling their wooden bowls under the noses of the passers-by. By the century's end there were so many of them that they became a real social evil, though up to that time they were more numerous and better tolerated in other Italian towns than here in Venice. In Rome their activities were looked on as an invitation to the practice of one of the cardinal virtues and encouraged under police protection as having Gospel warrant, but the Venetian attitude was altogether different. So long as work was available the beggar was considered a criminal who ought to find employment and earn his daily bread.

By one of the curiosities of Venetian life, however, this much-scorned mendicant did very well indeed. The foreign visitor, here to enjoy himself and ready to appease his conscience by generous almsgiving, naturally bore a part in this prosperity. It was reported to the Council of Ten that the son of Count Bonafede had become a beggar and was 'paying for his vices' with the proceeds. The adventurer and versifier Lorenzo da Ponte tells in his memoirs of being invited home by a beggar to whom he often gave money, and how home turned out to be excellently furnished and well supplied with books. This particular beggar had a very beautiful daughter too, who was offered to the guest in marriage, with a thousand ducats of dowry.

The working classes were relatively well off, as their clean and comfortable houses showed. Obviously these were worlds apart from the great palaces but, though simple, they were well-found, agreeable dwellings. Venetians, we repeat, did not inhabit hovels.

Their diet was frugal, its sole luxury being excellent coffee. (The art of Turkish coffee-making was a heritage from Constantinople.) The ordinary wines were nothing to speak of, insipid if sweet and, if dry, harsh and rough. The people usually drank *garbo*, a mixture of water and marc hardly calculated to produce a strong, full-bodied brew. Artisan families celebrated on feast-days with Greek wine or the red wines of Verona, which were said to be delicious, though wine-making then was a somewhat drastic process and the result perhaps not over-palatable.[56]

Nor was the bread they ate exactly fit for kings. Even when fresh it could be so dry and solid that you had to take a hammer to it, as you might to army biscuit. It looked inviting enough, but then looks were deceptive. Meat was plentiful, for 500 cattle, 250 calves and any amount of fowls and goats were slaughtered every week. A great deal of fish was eaten, naturally enough in a sea-city, and if supplies failed – as they often did, the fishermen being annoyingly addicted to concerted strikes for trivial and at times completely foolish reasons – a serious situation arose. What made it worse was the government's way of doing nothing to get the strikers back to work, although the protests of the public were sure to reach the ears of the Ten. During one such emergency, in August 1737, voices at King Louis' embassy, in horror at the official unconcern, were heard proclaiming that they ordered these things better in France: 'most of the confounded fishermen would have been hanged by now, instead of calling the tune and dictating to the Doge himself'. Criticism was no kinder at the Papal Nuncio's, and reported by the same spy; the town without fish, Monsignor's household with nothing to eat – an outrage. If the strike fell, as in this instance, on a Saturday when meat was forbidden, there was perforce a general fast, since not everybody wanted eggs and milk. People had to console themselves with the reflection that 'it wasn't for the first time, after all'.

The native abstemiousness of the Venetians was a great aid in reconciling them to these occasional gaps in the supplies, but theirs was a virtue tinged with laziness. With so many stalls selling fried fish and fritters, the women took small trouble in the kitchen. The usual excuse was that the smell of cooking-oil would annoy the neighbours, but they are damned by the fact that they also bought their pasta pre-cooked; no Italian housewife can get lazier than that.

93

Nor did they cook vegetables at home, but let their baskets down from the windows to an itinerant greengrocer and hauled up helpings ready boiled, with salt, pepper and seasoning all complete. Even the national dish was brought round ready for eating by those who specialised in its preparation – *pidocchi* soup made from the sea-louse, a kind of mussel found in the lagoon, and as popular as was bouillabaisse at Marseilles.

Whatever one may think of Venetian indolence, this habit of buying cooked, and therefore more expensive, food, argues a degree of prosperity, and wages were certainly higher here than elsewhere at the same period. The minimal annual pay for a young hand newly out of his apprenticeship and with no family to keep was sixty silver ducats; while the recognised workman earned not less than a hundred if married, and a hundred and twenty if he had children. Wages, in fact, were adjusted to match domestic expenses in splendid anticipation of modern family allowances. The rate of exchange varied during the century, but the silver ducat of eight Venetian lire was, generally speaking, worth five *livres* of French money.[57] The *livre tournois* and the 'germinal' franc, which was to remain more or less stable up to 1914, were of equal value, so we may reckon that the Venetian labourer earned on average 600 French francs at pre-1914 levels, Taking into account the rising cost of living in France since that date, this average labourer comes out with 200 new francs a month, or about £180 a year.

But this was probably not the pittance it sounds. Methods of production have altered, people's needs increased. A true comparison with modern times is almost impossible and those 200 francs were in fact an adequate monthly wage. A good craftsman in contemporary Rome could look for no more than twenty *baiocchi* a day, which was only three-quarters as much, and he was by no means on the breadline. It was less than half what a French workman earned, admittedly, but life was very different in the two countries. Venice, say those who knew both, was three times cheaper than Paris, and Arthur Young, a trustworthy witness, found that things cost five times as much in London.[58]

The question of price-comparison is further complicated by the all but insoluble muddle of Venetian weights and measures. A pound of sugar, coffee or chocolate was not, for instance, the same as a pound of candles, butter or meat. A different standard obtained for heavy merchandise, another for the silk and drug trades. The division of the several pounds into ounces, carats and grain-weights also went by diverse rules, while other goods, such as cereals, were not reckoned in pounds at all but by the *moggio* or by the sack. There have been many problems and arguments, and it does not really help to know that the *moggio* was something like five bushels, the sack rather less. Measures were as protean as weights. The foot-unit of length was not what a Frenchman would have called a foot. Six feet made one perch, and a square perch was a *tarola*. Eight hundred and forty *tarole* were one *campa* and five feet made a *passa*. Liquid measures altered with the liquid, the unit for wine being the *bigoncio*, which comprised fourteen *staie* of ten *ingiustare* each.

To make confusion worse confounded, money itself could not invariably be taken at face value. *Zecchini*, or sequins, were usually put on a scale and accepted only at their actual weight's-worth: Casanova had a very troublesome interlude with the State Inquisitors over a sequin that was two grains light.[59] If it all seems too baffling, we may take comfort in the fact that it often baffled the Venetians too, and look round for useful points of comparison, such as the prices charged in hotels or private lodging-houses. Here three or four lire a day ensured an excellent room and good food, two bottles of wine and generous meals. This was rather less than a pound sterling nowadays and far below what one paid in other parts of the continent. It is easy to see both why so many foreigners lingered in Venice, where they could make a much better show than ever they could at home, and how the wage-earner enjoyed a decent standard of living on what sounds at first to have been scanty pay.

These good conditions for the working class, although they declined progressively and were poor enough by the century's end, were due to the remarkable way in which labour was organised by the *scuole*, or guilds. Venice had always given the guilds protection and encouragement, unlike other European countries, where they were despised or even persecuted, and they were venerable institutions with an important part in public life. Not only were they allowed to run their own affairs and order those of their members as they saw fit, but questions of industry or commerce were always laid before them and no decision made until their opinion was considered.

They took honourable place at public ceremonies and great official occasions, and at Corpus Christi the guilds went in procession, their banners proudly borne aloft, beside the leading magistrates of Venice. The beginning of every reign saw them at the palace, music playing, flags flying, to pay the newly-elected Doge their complimentary visit, and he returned the courtesy in state. The patricians presumably regarded the guilds as an outlet for popular feeling, and treated them accordingly.

Each of the eighteen brotherhoods was itself a small-scale republic with its own electors, constitution, its *banca*, which formed a kind of senate, and its *gastaldo* who was more or less a doge. Within this miniature state masters and men decided together, in democratic fashion, what was best for their profession and the welfare of those who practised it. Excluded though he was from public affairs, the workman could thus say his say and count for something in his own sphere, and even got a relish of the plotting and intrigue he loved so much.

All trade problems were settled by the guilds and guild decision was supreme. It never challenged the general precepts of authority, but authority would never interfere with what it did. The brotherhood fixed wages, dealt with disputes, allotted raw materials, laid down types and patterns, checked the methods and standards of all members. So detailed were its attentions that anyone who actually made anything did so under a mass of restrictive regulations which, tight as they were, undoubtedly preserved the quality of workmanship. The Venetian trademark was beyond price, especially on textiles, for which the dyeing, colour-blending and designs were tested and controlled in every detail; and through this age-old care were produced the marvellous fabrics that were by long tradition the glory of Venice.

Apart from all technical preoccupations, a guild was responsible for the running of its workshops, the promotion of its best craftsmen and, most important of all, for a relief-system which in many ways looked ahead to the social security of modern times; one, moreover, administered by those primarily concerned.

There was not only moral authority behind the guilds as they carried out their many tasks, there was the power of money too. Each member paid a subscription in proportion to the profits he made, and those who had done well often left a large part of their goods to the brotherhood at death. To do so was a recognised obligation, shirked by none, and the guilds as a result grew very rich. Some were able to lend money to the state in difficult times, and all kept up and decorated the churches of their patron saints.

7   The Stone of Proclamation

8   The Prison

Their headquarters were splendid buildings that rivalled the cele-brated *maisons des métiers* in the Grande Place of Brussels.

Each guild maintained its hospital and school, and without such schools there would have been yet more illiterates in Venice than was in fact the case, for the government took few pains to educate the children of lower condition. The commissioners *ad pias causas* ran some primary and secondary schools[60] but the road to further learning was closed to the workman's son unless some priest, struck by his intelligence, taught him enough to get him into a seminary. This did not necessarily mean that he became a priest himself; he might be a lawyer or a doctor, or enter the civil service as a secretary.

The guild schools were less ambitious. Their curriculum, combin-ing the general with the technical, aimed only at producing *garzoni*, or apprentices. Boys must come from well-conducted, steady homes and there were searching investigations. Certificates had to be forthcoming, securities advanced. When schooling and apprenticeship were over the boy, if he had studied hard and behaved properly, became a workman. After a year or so he got through the professional examination that qualified him as a master and could then have a business of his own. With luck and talent he might prosper very well, and many a master craftsman ended up with a palazzo as magnificent as anything the nobility could show.

They were good, solid institutions, these brotherhoods, fostering the simple virtues of loyalty to a profession and devotion to one's work, of charity and mutual aid. In this latter department, as in provision for the future, their own arrangements were notably efficient. A member was cared for and given money if he were ill and helped in his old age, while trouble was taken to see that he should never starve yet never feel humiliated. Less demanding tasks were put in his way as his strength failed and no grant came in the guise of charity. He need not worry about his family as death approached, for widow and children were sure of income and friendly support. Clearly, the *scuole* were model organisations. When the French in 1798 suppressed them in the name of liberty the people lost their corporate security, and with it, lacking as they did any natural urge to save, lost all they had. In these straits they turned to government charity and the workers of Venice became, for the first time in their history, a proletariat.

D

It is impossible here to review each individual guild, but we may perhaps glance at a few of those that counted as most important or appear especially picturesque. First place belonged to the glass-blowers, who styled themselves gentlemen on the grounds that they had been ennobled by Henri III when he visited them on his way back to France from Poland. The mysteries of their art came first from Syria, and glassmaking flourished in Venice from the eleventh century onwards. There were so many furnaces by the end of the thirteenth that the Great Council, for fear of fire in certain districts, particularly in Rialto, removed them by decree to Murano, an ancient city on a group of five islets about a mile off the northernmost point of Venice. After 1292 Murano was the centre of the industry and reached its greatest importance in the sixteenth century: its 30,000 inhabitants, though still an integral part of the Serenissima, had political autonomy, a Great Council and a Golden Book of their own. *Cristallo di Venezia* was unrivalled then in Europe, though later on many other glassworks, notably in France and England, competed with those of the lagoon. Things improved with the invention of looking-glass to replace the old steel mirrors in the great mansions, but the secret soon leaked out and by Casanova's time the Murano industry was obviously on the wane. Glass-blowing was weary work and the guild, the best organised and the richest in Venice, ensured comfort in their declining years to men whose strength was exhausted in the heat of furnaces kept going night and day. Absolute loyalty was expected in return for the high wages and other benefits and discipline was rigid. The glass-blower who left Murano to work abroad was condemned as a traitor and his flight constituted an attempt against the security of the Republic.

Then there was the Arsenal that had been the glory of Venice when she was fighting her victorious wars and spreading her power at sea. This was the master-instrument of all her conquests, the bulwark of the western world against the Turks. It lay at the city's edge, within high, crenellated walls crowned with fifteen massive towers, an enormous enclosure built over the Zemelle islets, the most formidable armoury and the mightiest naval dockyard in the whole of Europe. It was entirely self-sufficient, turning out its cannon, weapons and ships of every type independently of any other establishment or industry. There was continuous, jealously-guarded progress in its methods. It had a hand-picked labour force and an incredible rate of production: when need arose, a galley a day came off the slips with all her armament and rigging.

Though less active, the Arsenal was still employing two and a half thousand men in the eighteenth century. In its upper rooms was ranged a wonderful collection of firearms, swords and body-armour that drew visitors from far and near to marvel at the evidence of bygone greatness. Sixty thousand guns were shown and six thousand pieces of ordnance, some of them, said Lalande, with muzzles so large that you often saw three or four children crouched together inside. If your tastes ran to art rather than ballistics, then this remarkable museum also included sculpture and old masters, and the famous lions of Piraeus united war and virtù at the very gates.

This last relic of departed worth was something the Republic delighted to show distinguished guests. In 1764 the Duke of York, brother of George III, was received here in state, although it was, alas, no longer possible to manage for him the surprise that had entertained Henri III in 1574 and build an entire galley in the course of the afternoon.[61] This time they had to be content with doubling the number of women sailmakers, to whom new clothes were issued, and with bringing in more ships, so the vast dockyard would look a little livelier for the one-day gala. Eighteen years later, on January 22, 1782, the Grand Duke Paul spent seven solid hours admiring the armoury.

The men who worked here were cosseted with good pay, a generous relief system and worthwhile privileges. They could buy certain provisions, notably wine, free of tax, which meant virtually at half-price. They marched round the red standard of Venice in official processions and theirs was the honour of providing the standard-bearer. Large groups of *arsenalotti* came by turn to the Doge's Ascension Day banquet, sat at his magnificent tables and ate from silver dishes with important fellow guests. This was not only a compliment, it was profitable too, each man being allowed to take away the four flagons of muscatel wine, the box of preserves and bag of spices set before him, together with a silver medal to commemorate his presence at the feast. The company would also make bold to carry off the plates and silver drinking-cups they used and authority, by custom, overlooked their pilfering. The Doge, as we know, was carried into the palace by sturdy Arsenal men on the day of his coronation and these lucky porters became the heroes of the districts where they lived. Lastly, it was from among the *arsenalotti* that the Grand Admiral was chosen, with a minor responsibility hardly up to that resounding style and title. His task was to pilot the *Bucintoro*, and it was but once a year that the *Bucintoro* left the port, weather permitting, for the ancient ceremony at which the Doge solemnly threw his ring into the waves and married the sea. The costume of the Grand Admiral was, however, absolutely splendid and the humblest caulker might hope to wear it for the brief allotted span. A golden prospect, open to all.

There was usually a very practical ulterior motive for any action of the Republic, and these favours lavished at the Arsenal were meant to ensure the dockers' proverbial loyalty, which it was essential to confirm. In the absence of an organised police force the Signory counted on them to combat signs of unrest. These fortunately were rare enough, but the men had specific orders just the same to occupy strategic points in case of any alarm. All they actually did by way of protecting the government was to find a guard, fifty strong, who stood, impressive but uncalled for, outside the ducal palace when the Grand Council was in session, ready to intervene. But the defence of Venetian law and order was the merest sinecure and their aid was invoked only when fire broke out.

In the water-streets of Venice, they said, the gondola replaced the horse. The Président de Brosses affirmed that 60,000 people rowed for a living, but that would have been nearly half the population and he was exaggerating wildly. The census of 1766 showed the more reasonable figure – sixteen times more reasonable in fact – of 3,776 *barcaioli* in the city and the lagoon.

Casanova would recognise the familiar Venetian gondola unchanged. The slender length, the notched prow rearing from the water, give it the look of a fish swimming tail-first; a bizarre creature with something Egyptian about it, Henri de Régnier thought, and, perched on its back, the little wooden cabin like a carriage with the wheels cut off—the *felze*, a small private boudoir with occupants never seen and assumed always to be lovers. In a *felze*, observes a visitor, you were in a room of your own, free to read or write, make love or talk to a friend. The seat on the left was the place of honour, for from the other you could not see well enough to give directions to the gondolier. Elders, betters and women were put on the left, and there the private gondolas carried the owner's arms or monogram on a shield of polished copper, while those for hire had images of the Virgin, of St Mark or some saint of the boatman's special devotion.

The sumptuary laws in the eighteenth century decreed that all gondolas should be alike, for the prevention of rivalry seemed the one way to safeguard public order. Black was the only colour permitted and black paint or pitch had to be applied to every visible part of the boat. The cabin, with its black upholstery, was cushioned in black leather. Details not expressly covered by the laws, such as boat-hooks and lanterns or the wrought-brass holder where a light was put after dark and a flower during the day, were as ornate as possible, but the general effect was sable over-all. Gondolas were sombre craft and going into a *felze* was rather like entering a catafalque. 'A kind of black-hung tomb where you bury yourself five or six hours a day,' was the Chinese Spy's sarcastic way of of putting it. But Chinese or French, or whatever he was, his viewpoint is foreign, for the idea of black as funereal, or even sad, would not occur to a native. Venetian coffins were draped in red and the hearses floating over to the cemetery island of San Michele were the same colour, which was also worn by undertakers' men.

Certain gilded and gorgeously carved boats, such as the state gondolas for important persons on official business, were exceptions to this rule. Ambassadors might have any colour they chose, and embassy gondolas were much bigger than ordinary ones and fitted up like the most luxurious travelling carriages. Also of different colours and embellished in various ways were the *peotte*, big covered boats for twelve passengers, used only on the Grand Canal with a cargo of ladies on regatta days, or for following the *Bucintoro* on its triumphal progress towards the Lido when the Doge went out to wed the Adriatic. Nor was black compulsory for the great *burchielli* that plied between Venice and the islands and towns nearby, and one of which brought the Président de Brosses from Padua. He was extremely pleased and wrote to his Burgundian friend Bernard de Blancey:

'I cannot remember whether I told you how we left Padua on December 28th last. We embarked on the Brenta canal with the wind against us, as usual, but with two good tow-horses on the bank we *ingannare'd* the devil and our attendant bad luck.[62] Our boat was named the *Bucintoro*, a very small off-spring of the real

Bucintoro, as you may imagine, but charming all the same, quite as handsome as the long-distance boats in France and far better kept. There was a small cabin for the servants, then a saloon hung with Venetian brocade, with a table and two long, leather-covered benches. It had eight proper windows and two glass doors. We found our quarters very comfortable and for once were in no hurry for journey's end.'

Goldoni has left us another glimpse of the Padua *burchiello*, 'a fine boat with looking-glasses, carving and pictures, that goes a mile in twenty minutes and where you can relax, sit down or doze in absolute security'.

With so few bridges and quays and no public transport, journeys of any length had to be by water and a large fleet of gondolas was needed. Those crowding gondolas, many more of them than nowadays, were the characteristic, essential feature of the city. Everywhere you saw them, waiting at the tall painted posts outside somebody's house, riding like a flock of sea-beasts at the landing-stages, breathing in rhythm on the water as they rose and fell; like shadows, supple, proud and noiseless, slipping over the bright canals. Most of the gondoliers plied for hire in their plain shirts, wide sashes and small caps, and those in private service wore livery, though only those employed by foreign princes or the Doge's family might have gold or silver trimmings. The state gondoliers seen at official fêtes and regattas standing on the prows of the gilded gondolas in gold-laced red velvet jackets and carrying enormous hats, were only part of the pageant. They could not possibly row in this array and were being towed by the smaller craft that carried musicians and trumpeters.

But such privileged creatures were rare; the ordinary gondolier worked away with his single oar. He stood on the forepart, facing away from his master, who was thus left in privacy, though a few boats might have a second man at the stern. The method of rowing, with the whole weight tipped forward and leaning on the paddle, was not a very safe one, but all the *barcaioli* used it. Long practice gave them poise and balance and they never fell in, manoeuvring with miraculous precision. This mastery, however, came only after a protracted apprenticeship, punctuated by many duckings; the 'Venetian stroke', that hardly ruffled the surface with its gentle plash, was exceedingly difficult. Nevertheless, in the days when it was smart to row your own gondola, there were athletic young noblemen who put on the appropriate jacket, cap and sash, went off for lessons from some experienced gondolier, and managed to get the hang of it.

At the junctions of the narrow canals the boatmen would break the magical quiet with the 'wailing noise in incomprehensible jargon' that was their warning cry. There were gondola-blocks, as there are traffic-blocks today, and though the *barcaioli* were deft at getting out of them, occasional crashes would occur. A move in the wrong direction, a shout misunderstood, and two black canoes might run together and tangle their tall-necked beaks with the six iron teeth. It looked like a battle of ill-tempered swans with great necks lunging, and made raging furies of the normally placid Venetians. Quarrels erupted, as they do between headlong drivers on dry land. The epithets of a more heroic age rose readily to their lips, undesirable comparisons drawn from the animal kingdom, accusations of villainy and murder. Heaven was involved as they flung insults at one another's saints – 'Your saint's a washout, your Madonna's a whore.' The air was thick with fulmination, oaths and blasphemy. Hands itched to get round throats and oars were brandished as though to fell the foe. Peace did not automatically follow the extrication of the gondolas and long after they had floated away the echoing revilements came back down the canal, growing ever more fearful as distance made the exchange of blows progressively less likely. But the battle was always with words, never hard knocks, and a moment later the clear, true voices rose in the sweet songs that were the normal accompaniment of gondoliering.

For the boatmen could not live without singing. At night, we are told, a solitary voice would sound over the water, audible far away, and always someone would hear it and reply with the next line of the song. The cadences crossing and re-crossing echoed in the dark and made the melody vibrating and alive.

But the gondoliers were also acknowledged experts in abuse, and when actors had a rough time the strongest language was always supposed to come from *barcaioli* in the audience. Their verdict decided the fate of many a play; Goldoni even arranged seats specially for them. They were indeed a goodly company, proud of a profession whose secrets and traditions were passed from father to son, and heroes of the famous water-jousts. Portraits of honoured and victorious forebears hung on the walls of their houses with trophies, flags and pennons won in the regattas.

They did more, however, than row the gondolas. The gondolier was a jack-of-all-trades and in the relaxed, amoral climate had blossomed as an accomplished go-between, an occupation he described as *fare l'ambasciata*. He knew all the good addresses and the unsuspected little stairs. He was in the confidence of lady's-maids.[63] Often he had a tactful and delicate touch, as witness this very Venetian anecdote of Goldoni's about an acress-love of his in the 1730s, for whom he used the pseudonymn Passalacqua:

'The Signora Passalacqua prevented my leaving, assumed a gay tone, looked at the sky, said the weather was wonderful and invited me to take the air with her in a gondola she had waiting. I said no. She laughed at me, insisted, took my arm and pulled me towards the quay. What could I do? We got in, and a gondola is as snug as the prettiest boudoir. We went out into the wide lagoon that surrounds the city and there our practised gondolier closed the small back curtain, steered with his paddle and let the boat go with the tide. We chatted away. All was lighthearted and agreeable. Soon, night was coming on, we had no notion where we were and it was too dark to see my watch. I opened the curtain and asked the man what time it was. "I don't know, Sir – just about right, I should imagine." "Then get on," I cried, "back to the Signora's house at once." He began to row towards the town, singing as we went the twenty-third strophe of the sixteenth canto of the *Gerusalemme Liberata* [which is all about kissing and parting].'

CHAPTER THREE

LIFE, MANNERS AND CUSTOMS

I THE CAREER OF PLEASURE

What had long been second nature to the city of Venice – addiction to the delectable side of life – had taken over entirely by the eighteenth century and she was an enchanted place of serenading, masquerade and pleasure. Every citizen, as Stendhal was to find, had 'the sort of character that makes for happiness' and she became the modern Sybaris, where enjoyment was the main consideration. She let others dwell on guilt and misery and gave herself up, amid noise and frenzy, to perpetual saturnalia. From this existence, so delightful and so useless, nothing could attract her, nothing deflect her for a moment from her own voluptous version of life. Until they actually broke above her, she ignored the fatal storm-clouds piling up all over Europe. Her reaction to the clashes and quarrels of her neighbours was to keep out of them and thus avoid being badgered for an opinion. The world strained towards the future as happy-go-lucky, fatalistic Venice closed her eyes to the whole thing, smiled and had a good time. She chose to be happy. She would devote her remaining energy to happiness, and there was something heroic, a touch of real gallantry, in the way her people went about the pursuit of pleasure.

The Venetians in their opera-house setting might have been denizens of fairyland. Money-grubbing, ambition, material preoccupation of any kind, seemed no concern of theirs while the fête went on non-stop around them, its centre the Piazza, the Piazzetta and the banks of the Grand Canal, its echoes reverberating in the furthest *calli*. Darkness made no difference, for there was no real night in this town of contradictions. 'Here,' says Goudar, they are getting dressed when the rest of the world is going to bed,' and Ballerini, agent to the Venetian ambassador in Paris, considered that a *conversazione* should ideally begin two hours after midnight.

Some very picturesque elements came crowding with the rest

to the metropolis of pleasure. Poets, newsmongers, parasites and moneylenders; peddlers of obscene literature; virtuosi bereft of their instruments and actresses and dancers disengaged; quacks and soap-box preachers, astrologers, fortune-tellers and story-tellers; croupiers, pandars and prostitutes – all and anyone who made a living out of pastime and could offer a spice of sin. Mingling with them were financiers on the run and improbable Highnesses, swindlers, harlots trying to look like ladies, and similar people, countless and questionable. If the devil could take the roofs off Venice, Beckford thought, what a variety of lurking-places he would uncover, and what innumerable adventurers lurking in them! Adventures and love affairs were going forward everywhere, comic, casual and passionate; the baffling city had so many steps that led round hidden corners, so many unobtrusive doorways to unpublicised apartments, such a complication of water-lanes. From the press of minor figures intriguing over love and money a few stand out in memoirs of the time: John Law of Lauriston, living now by what he won at cards, and failing to persuade Montesquieu of the virtues of his notorious banking system; the Count de Bonneval, future three-tailed bashaw of the Turk; Cagliostro with his elixir of youth and his recipe for manufacturing gold; Ange Goudar, thief, wit and spy; and Casanova, their grand prototype, whose fame was to eclipse them all.

Such dubious individuals were lost, however, in the throng of honest pleasure seekers, blessed in their search with inexhaustible good humour, holiday spirit and lightness of heart. They had a candid, happy attitude that disposed them, like children, to laugh and joke at anything. The least absurdity was greeted with a pertinent rhyme and gravity was a solecism, out of the question save at political ceremonies. Life was based on merriment as speech on pleasantry. Everyone appeared cheerful, everyone, from Doge to gondolier, was full of mirth and banter. The Président from Burgundy thought the whole Venetian way of life uproarious, and it was here, according to the tale, that Aretino laughed himself to death in the sixteenth century.[64] Everyone was laughing at everything and nothing and at everyone else. Nobody minded being laughed at, and being called ridiculous gave no offence in Venice. It was a great asset to be able to amuse people and Casanova wrote, among other things, a 'plan to dispel the spleen'. Puns and word-play were much cultivated, though wit is hard to discern in many of the practical jokes designed to raise a smile. Some, such as the laxa-tive-pills-for-ladies joke, were downright crude, and Casanova recommends pills to cause 'unretainable wind' as part of the plan. The harmless bourgeois was presumably not entertained at finding his spectacles in his soup or a cheese or a dead rat in his bed, though naturally it was the onlooker who was supposed to laugh, not he. But comedy permeated the air, outdoors and indoors and even in the lawcourts with their burlesque oratory. Laughter and singing were heard by the canals; traders carolled away as they proffered their wares in the meanest alleys, and nights of love went by to the sound of the boatmen's ditties.

And love itself – a subject to which we shall return – was not a passion but a game, one of life's charming customs. 'The soul,' says Sainte-Beuve, discussing Casanova's *Memoirs* in an article of July 1833, 'came into the picture only as something extra, an amenity or relaxation for the senses.' The fleeting embrace, the little rage, the transitory variance, made up the Venetian love affair. It was all buoyancy, ease and tenderness. Love was life and fulfilment, but love soon followed love and was quickly out of mind.

'Here are no old people in this country, neither in Dress or Gallantry,' wrote Lady Mary Wortley Montagu to her daughter on September 5, 1758, and for all that one could see, it was quite true. How should age indeed, gain any ground here where nothing was oppressive or more than skin-deep, everything so pleasant, and existence, gliding like a gondola over the lagoon, consisted of billing and cooing? It was enough to be blissfully alive and unperceiving, for all the world as though the French proverb were true and one's temporary circumstances were settled and permanent. Lady Mary also said, 'no body grows old till they are bed rid', and she was right again – people took to their beds to die and not before. Some managed to end with a witticism, like her beloved Francesco Algarotti[65] who, when given a dainty velvet nightcap during his last illness, exclaimed, 'Good God, you're trying to make a very handsome corpse of me!' But death was not an acceptable subject for conversation. The thought of it might have been entirely absent, so seldom was it mentioned. No one recognised it; why, therefore, prepare for it? To do so would have been too much like giving it a welcome. When it did arrive it was dispatched hastily to its island home on San Michele. Venice was no place for the dead, any more than for regrets. Venetians were less upset by bereavement than were other people, and even dead children, regarded as having gone straight to heaven to plead for their parents at the throne of grace, were referred to as 'family advocates'.

Life, from adolescence to its last earthly hour, was all springtime for these unprofound beings. They never knew misfortune and hardly anything was sent to try them, since pleasure and entertainment effectively smoothed all annoyance from their path. They would not have recognised what the term 'world-weary' meant. You only had to listen to them, with their single expression for 'wickedness' and 'sorrow' and their *Ah! che consolazione!* for a stroke of good fortune. They never had a moment's boredom, which was just as well, for they could not have endured it. The Venetian who declared, 'Being bored is the worst thing in the world, I'd rather be miserable,' was not a jaded libertine but a highly respectable and exemplary patrician lady named Giustina Renier, niece of the last Doge but one. If ever her fellow citizens of the Settecento were ruffled at all it was over paltry inflictions; someone delayed them on the way to a rendezvous, or an unseasonable shower had spoilt the set of a wig. 'It goes to my heart to tell you,' wrote Algarotti to a friend, 'I am clean out of Spanish snuff.'

Detached from serious and possibly thought-provoking problems ('thought' and 'trouble' were the same word in Italian), these people with their exquisite good temper and delightful unconcern became passionately involved in the most trivial of current events. Their news-sheets are full of what they talked about, to beguile their elegant idleness, under the arcades of the Piazza di San Marco. Should a one-eyed tenor be allowed to sing the part of Bajazet at the Teatro San Crisostomo? What about the preacher at San Lorenzo who compared Esther to the Virgin Mary? Did the Russian Grand Duchess actually kiss Conterina Barbarigo? Was the prior of Sant'Aponal suppressing his indignation at an impertinent female and is that why he has now dropped dead? The Pregadi have decided to widen the Fuosa channel, but is this the moment to do so? And that barber who shaves you with extract of balm! And that cat, producing dog-headed kittens! And the details of dreams that were exchanged, and the snippets of personal information: some patrician's gambling losses, the merits of foreign noblemen staying in the city and the attractions of their noble wives. No wonder that no one grew seriously heated about such little scraps and oddments of conversation.[66]

More exciting topics were pursued, less publicly, behind the coffee-houses in dim parlours known, from their theoretical purpose, as chess-rooms. 'Gossip-rooms' would have done as well, for these were the great scandal centres of the town. Here everything was mulled over that gave cause for amusement or a raised eyebrow, and spiced in whispers with Decamaron-like detail. The frantic tittle-tattle that went on tended to spoil the accepted picture of Venetian tolerance, for this retreating to the back premises, there to thrash out every bit of information on somebody's love affair, did not exactly fit in with the friendly ease and freedom that obtained beyond the door. Outside on the pavement you might sit down by a woman and woo her openly for all the world to see. You could escort her home and cause no comment. The strict condition of this tolerance was, however, that all the world *should* see. As soon as an aura of mystery was detected, forbearance gave way to curiosity and spying began. The scandalmonger's standard excuse was that serious interests were forbidden and he had nothing else to talk about, but no great harm was done, for the most piquant morsel was abandoned for ever after a week or two and the loungers fell on the next new thing with equal zest.

There were so many of these loungers that one could well believe the saying that Venetians worked only when leisure permitted, in any spare time they had between diversions. New arrivals might pardonably assume that the inhabitants were all persons of independent means who had settled down to enjoy life. They sang songs about the delights of labour, but this was obviously a pleasure they were prepared to do without, and they had hundreds of proverbs about the slavery of work to contradict the rousing choruses. (One, that equates the studious man with the poor lover, pithily disposes of intellectual toil as well.)

Many were the Venetians who followed the bad advice enshrined in the national proverbs, some because they could afford to and others because it suited them. Pierre Jean Grosley[67] outlines the typical day of the rich and leisured bourgeois:

'Up at the fourth hour (which was not too early, if we remember the idosyncratic division of time.) and off by boat for a dip in the sea, coming back through the Piazza; sit in a dressing-gown and have a cup of chocolate, and take a stroll until one. Next, a good dinner, two or three hours' sleep and start again around seven, paying visits on foot or by water until midnight, consuming in the process vast quantities of lemonade, coffee, chocolate, ices and so on; then a separate supper. Such is life in Venice.'[68]

Such, at least, was daily life, for this programme omits all mention of the night and its less innocent recreations. The complete Idler's Credo is found in Casanova: 'I went out to pursue my business, by which I mean my pleasures.' Even those who actually did some work managed to fit in long rest periods; even Goldoni, writing sixteen plays in one year, never forwent his social enjoyments. 'We saw the family,' he recalls in his memoirs, 'we dined with friends and went to the theatre.' Or, again, 'Good food, cards, concerts, balls and banquets in plenty.' The well-to-do middle class devoted very little time to business and their programme was matter for yet another proverbial rhyme:

> Alla mattina una messetta,
> Al dopo dinar una bassetta,
> Alla sera una donnetta.

Nothing could better express the prevailing sensuality, addiction to gambling, and lip-service to religion:

> A little trip to morning Mass,
> A little hand at cards, to pass
> After-luncheon hours, until
> A little woman, later still.

Side by side with the lucky possessors of private incomes, and equal sharers with them in the carnival life of Venice, was the near-criminal swarm whose problematical activities we have already mentioned. These were the people who could organise a quintet or an evening out, or find you a furnished apartment; who hovered so tenderly over the visitors. Whoever wanted to go shopping, or spend his money on music or women or good things could be sure of willing helpers. And the visitors might number as many as 60,000 – which is a lot among 130,000 natives – every one of them seduced by the magic of the place, attracted and held by what was the real Venetian poison, the mere delight of freedom and leisure in 'the most beautiful, the most charming and the happiest city on earth'.

Many of them, having known the sky-and-water spell and the rest of the lavish enchantment, succumbed entirely and came back for more. From the world of letters, from the underworld and from the most polished society, all pre-Revolutionary Europe flocked to the feast. Most of these people were rich, they were often amusing and they adored diversion. They were guests whose very presence made the banquet gayer. Their hours were pure pastime, the careless exhilaration seemed like plain good sense, the festival went on; and Venice never knew, was incapable of realising, that it was so nearly over.

II FÊTES AND ENTERTAINMENTS

The *Fête Venitienne* so poetically distilled in Watteau's famous picture[69] was no brief recreation to lighten the monotony from time to time, but a permanent state of affairs. Venice had been the richest city in the world; as a poor one she kept the tastes acquired in happier days, the love of luxury, of balls and glowing processions and every kind of splendour. Her daily life was highly agreeable in any case and a never-ending succession of special occasions made it even more enjoyable. There was never a day in the perpetual *Fête Venitienne* that did not celebrate some saint or hero or anniversary, when some king, prince or ambassador was not welcomed with impressive pomp. The fanfares sounded jubilee and everyone joined in.

The churches were thronged to the doors for the great religious festivals, especially San Marco, the largest of all, when the Doge went there in person, attended by the various Councils. Then eyes and ears alike were overwhelmed by golden hangings and scarlet silk, by lights and music and glittering mosaic, and the celebrations were echoed by secular holiday-making and a rain of fireworks after dark. On various feast-days the Doge would visit each parish church in turn and sit on his throne beside the altar, having come with a brilliant entourage by way of streets decked with flowers and greenery. The humblest districts strove with the rest to do him honour and some of these picturesque local festas drew huge crowds. On Christmas Eve the whole government went by gondola to venerate the martyr's relics on the island of San Giorgio, where they landed by the light of thousands of torches and were followed by hundreds of illuminated boats. On the third Sunday in July the Doge passed over a bridge of boats to the church of the Redentore on Giudecca, for this was the anniversary of the ending of the plague of 1577 which had claimed Titian among its 50,000 victims.

On May 1st the ruler and all his dignitaries went to the Vergini convent at Castello and returned bearing armfuls of flowers.

The great dates of Venetian history, the taking of Scutari, the victory of Lepanto, the arrival of the bones of St Mark, the capture of Constantinople or the execution of Marino Falier, were magnificently remembered. So were many less important anniversaries, some of events so trivial or so far removed as to have lost all impact, so that several were struck off the list and others grouped together to share a day between them.

But whatever the show was about, the chief, immutable attraction was always the ducal procession. The Doge in his mantle of gold, the children supporting the ends of the long trumpets that were carried before him, the corporations, the *arsenalotti* and guild-members marching in order, all were there, unchanged for centuries. Everyone, without distinction of class, hastened with unvarying enthusiasm to the great parades, which were provided as often as possible. A parade kept authority in touch with the people, and it kept the people suitably dazzled. This was sound policy, for what public ever tires of fairy-tale spectaculars? Moreover, simply by being present and cheering, they were themselves actors as well as audience, for some of the dazzlement was designed for the visitor too, and a contented citizenry was part of the show.

Fond as they were of these sumptuous and stately pageants, the Venetians were also mad about less formal celebrations, such as their *sagre*, or parochial feast-days, which seemed to affect them with a kind of mania. Every parish had a saint of its own and the process of honouring him must leave the saints of all the neighbouring parishes far behind. And honoured he was, when his day came round, in a wondrously decorated church, with loud, convivial conversation accompanying the sacred offices and nuns passing to and fro with nice cool drinks.

But if the church-going part of the festival was gayer than usual, thanks to these ameliorations, other aspects of the *sagra* were more animated still, with the whole district humming and buzzing like a fair. Streets were strewn with flowers and spanned with triumphal arches, houses were decked with garlands, flags and tapestry. Hawkers rigged up their booths under bright, streamer-hung awnings and drove a mixed trade, selling holy images and frying fritters (essential to any popular treat) in pans of oil. At the corners there were clowns on makeshift stages and champions from nearby parishes in furious competition over sports and games. The girls in their brilliant dresses danced all night – sleeveless bodices of scarlet, silken skirts, Persian-patterned aprons, breast-knots of ribbon and white slippers. Every engaged girl wore a rose in her hair to discourage troublesome suitors, and the men rivalled the women in nimbleness and grace.

They loved to dance the *monferrina* and their favourite *furlana*, a sort of *tarantella* with the same rhythm and abandon. The *furlana* tune – there was only one – was used in French ballets of the period to evoke Venetian atmosphere and the dance itself was popular everywhere. Everywhere, that is, but in society gatherings, where the *zentildonne* went through the boring steps and lifeless evolutions of quadrille and minuet. What they liked, of course, was to go slumming to a *sagra* ball where they could wheel and whirl in the *furlana* and amply compensate for the sedate conventionalities at home.

A *sagra* could easily burst out of its own parish and fill the whole town with excitement. This was certainly true of the Giudecca festival, where people went in flower-laden boats and stayed, with the lamps burning, until sunrise. The gardens of the island could not contain the gaiety, and rafts with make-believe gardens were moored on the water by way of extensions. Instead of the usual fritters, fried sole would be served to the coffee drinkers while orchestras played softly and violin tunes were endlessly repeated. It was a joyful occasion that dissolved all barriers. Noble and commoner, great lady and courtesan were all happy together, and even prelates were seen to join the merrymaking.

Government employees were badly paid, and soldiers were never paid at all, but the state forwent none of the grand official spectacles. Poverty-stricken but determined to disguise the fact, it still gave its ostentatious welcome to important visitors, still tried to match the splendid effort made for Ferdinand II, Grand Duke of Tuscany, which cost it 50,000 ducats in 1628. As much was spent in 1767 for the Prince of Wurtemberg and later for Joseph II, both recipients being deeply impressed, not to say thunderstruck; it was even hinted that the display had made them rather jealous. At one of these fétes benches for the public rose against the columns of the Procuratie as high as the capitals, with a tribunal for officials in the form of an archway facing the basilica. First a series of allegories celebrated the Triumph of Peace, who was duly crowned with the fruits of Plenty while Mars and Bellona, in a charming spirit of forgiveness, offered their services. Four pairs of white oxen drew the divinities on and off in carts, to music, song and dance. No sooner was Peace securely triumphant than there was some bull-baiting, with able-bodied young men yelling *Viva San Marco!* and the enthusiastic audience seeming about to invade the ring until a glimpse of Missier Grande in his red robe made them think again.

In 1784 a spectacle was laid on for the visit of King Gustav III of Sweden, but the high point had been reached two years previously for the 'Princes of the North', Paul of Russia and his wife, a visit that was perhaps the prime example of what the Republic could do when her diplomatic interests were at stake. Concerts, masked balls, regattas, processions and gorgeous banquets, the San Benedetto draped in blue silk for gala nights – nothing was forgotten, with, for culmination, the Piazza transformed into an amphitheatre for the usual grand evening entertainment.

Since there was nothing now but pageantry to furbish up the banners of St Mark and to maintain their ancient glory, everything possible was done to outshine the pageantry of former days. Naturally, however, the state avoided shouldering all the expense and the only celebrations it paid for entirely were those of a ducal election, when it did the thing in style. Millions of official ducats went on the coronation of Alvise IV Mocenigo in 1763; as he entered the palace with the Dogaressa in her cloak of gold, to the roar of cannon, Venice might have been the *Dominanti* still. But otherwise, when a show of splendour was required, the signory saw to it that the leading families bore a share of the cost, leaving them often enough to organise the whole spectacle and pay for it themselves.

And it was unheard of for the leading families to decline. They considered themselves honoured in using their fortunes for the good of the state and did so generously when the flattering opportunity arose, to show their own importance. The Pisani offering for the Prince of Wurttemberg cost them 18,700 ducats for a single evening, for which they turned the whole Bacino into a magic garden, with copses full of nymphs and music among the trees and on the water. Ca' Rezzonico was completely redecorated when the family had their superb ball for Joseph II. The sumptuary laws were suspended and the Venetian ladies took full advantage of the fact – a witness says they 'dripped with precious stones'.

Apart from such red-letter entertainments, the rich nobles gave plenty of their own accord. The veritable triumphs that hailed elections to the great offices of state – often far more gloriously than the occasion warranted – were financed by the newly-chosen magistrates themselves. When Lorenzo Tiepolo became a Procurator in 1713 his procession dazzled all beholders. One of the Pisani, on assuming a position of no particular importance, spent 30,000 ducats merely on archways with inscriptions congratulating himself. The shops of the Merceria, too, always contributed pennants and colourful hangings, and portraits of the hero of the hour, set off with learned emblems and poetical eulogies.

The sumptuary laws without doubt served to dim the splendour of family events among the aristocracy. Wedding processions no longer swept down the Grand Canal in a line of decorated gondolas. Christenings were diminished now that infants were not swathed in priceless lace and carried to church on enormous platters of gold. Nevertheless, there was still considerable scope, for the *provveditori alle pompe* could never get witnesses to prove infringement of the code.[70] Funerals alone remained as stately as ever, perhaps because the government set the example with its ostentatious rites for a dead Doge. There were no restrictions save on the number of candles used.

The private host, so long as his hospitality could be seen to uphold the prestige of the Serenissima, could safely break the regulations, and it was not usually difficult to find a distinguished man to entertain, or an ambassador to welcome. Then the state-rooms shone with candle-flame, and tables loaded with flowers and fruit and crystal suggested the Palace of Spring to one observer, while another speaks of the combined appeal to eye and imagination of 'delicate wines, beautiful statuary and magnificent centrepieces'.

Greatest show of all was the fête of the Sensa, when the Doge carried out his unique and poetic right to marry the sea on Ascension Day, celebrating at the same time the victory over Frederic Barbarossa, when Venice fought for Pope Alexander III, to whom the Emperor did homage before St Mark's in 1177. Alexander had given the Doge a ring in gratitude and told him, 'Let posterity remember that the sea is yours by right of conquest, subject to you as a wife to her husband.' The marriage had been solemnised yearly ever since. The Doge in the name of the Republic went forth in dignity and wedded the Adriatic, 'widowed so often,' as Casanova said, 'and still as fresh as when she was created'. That was the day they towed the *Bucintoro* from her berth at the Arsenal, a huge vessel a hundred feet long and twenty wide, with a ceremonial upper deck and a rowing-deck below. She was the last and latest of several editions, admiringly described by the Président de Brosses:

> 'I consider the *Bucintoro* one of the most beautiful and interesting objects in the world. It is a big galleass, or very large galley, covered outside with the finest carving and gilding. The interior is an enormous parqueted saloon, with sofas round the walls and a throne for the Doge. Down the middle a row of gilded statues supports the roof, or bulkhead, which is carved and gilt all over. So are the window-recesses, the stern balconies, the rowing benches and the helm, while the whole is tented over with flame-coloured velvet, embroidered in gold.'[71]

He might have added that a very mixed company of allegorical persons, pagan gods, saints and demons were on display upon the ceremonial deck, and that the ducal throne, its canopy held by two *amorini*, stood on the poop, facing the window from which the sanctified ring was thrown into the water. Goethe thought it inaccurate to say the *Bucintoro* was overloaded with ornament, for it was an ornament in itself. He compared it to a monstrance, and found it the perfect image 'of what the Venetians had been, and believed themselves to be'. In 1798 the French burned that floating monument to the pride of the Republic, the more easily to strip the gilding applied seventy years before at the staggering cost of 60,000 gold *zecchini*. They had thought of taking her all the way round to Rouen and down the river to Paris, but she was considered unfit to stand the journey.

For the *Bucintoro*, despite her splendour, was no sailer. Every other consideration had been sacrified to décor and she was a mere showboat, flat-bottomed and helpless in the slightest sea. It was always on the cards that the Doge and all his retinue would be plunged to a watery grave by a gust of wind, and so fulfil the prophecy of the Turkish Sultan who used to say that the far-famed marriage might well be consummated one of these days.[72] As we have seen, the vital decision rested with the Grand Admiral elected at the Arsenal, and since his life was forfeit if the vessel were lost or damaged everyone could rely with the utmost confidence upon his prudent view of the weather forecast.

On that morning all Venice was astir. Gondoliers put carpets and hangings in their boats, banners and tapestries were draped from windows, and warships and merchantmen, flags unfurled, took station from San Marco to the Lido. Messengers ran about the *calli* delivering parcels and posies, for it was customary to send presents to ladies on Ascension Day.

The time came, the bells rang and the Doge emerged from the palace in his state litter, preceded by fifes and trumpets. First went the *capo della polizia*, and a brilliant train of ambassadors, grandees and senators walked behind the Doge. He went on board at the Piazzetta and the *Bucintoro* sailed for San Nicolò del Lido over flower-strewn waters, saluted by all the forts and all the ships at anchor in the basin. Behind her came the chief magistrates in big, gilded boats, then the embassy gondolas and those of the Nuncio and Patriarch. Military contingents sailed, with piercing fanfares, in a second group of twelve and a third comprised the heads of the *scuole* with their banners and standards flying. Next were the *peotte* of the noble families, likewise beflagged and garlanded, with gilded oars and gondoliers in rose or sky-blue uniforms; and then the citizens in crowded craft which, though less splendid, were also hung with flowers and bright festoons. The triumphal progress ended by the lighthouse on the Lido island, where the Doge threw his ring into the waves with the time-honoured formula, 'We wed thee, oh sea, in sign of true and perpetual dominion.' At this, the climax of the day, the bells pealed, the massed trumpets rang out and the huge crowd shouted itself hoarse.

More casual was the order of return, when the procession broke ranks and the sight was, if anything, finer. The gondolas went dancing over the lagoon with their loads of gorgeously-arrayed men and of women flirting fans; lengths of velvet and silk trailed among the blossoms that floated like a carpet round them. The Doge then gave a lavish feast at which the French ambassador, by old-established diplomatic privilege, presided as co-host, and the people came as usual to watch it all. Afterwards, everyone repaired in gala dress to the Piazza for the opening of the Feria, a marvellous exhibition of commerce and art, where the best that Venice could produce was ranged on the double row of stalls. There were the glowing fabrics, the wonderful glass, the masterpieces of goldsmiths' work, and pictures by the greatest painters of the time. For two weeks, exclaiming, laughing, joking, the solid, cheerful crowds would pass before them, doing the rounds. The square was transformed into a fairyland of glittering crystal lamps, and the cafés from end to end of the arades proffered their chocolate, their Cyprus or Samian wine and delicate, delicious water-ices for a special treat. Outsiders poured in by the thousand to this paragon of fêtes, for they knew, as one historian writes, 'that the world had nothing else so rich and colourful to show, nor such a setting, nor so voluptuous an atmosphere'.

Naturally, when it came to settings, none could better the lagoon and the Grand Canal for water-borne games, and full use was made of them. Regatta followed regatta all summer through, with the added sporting interest of races for professional gondoliers. These would take their trophies home to be the family's pride for generations to come, but when amateurs were competing a regatta was for social amusement only.

The Fresco regattas of Holy Week, though little more than occasions for jaunting about in gondolas, were always the most popular. They began just before sunset and went on until it was dark. As many as three or four hundred contestants would row from the church of San Geremia at the far end of the Grand Canal to the Ponte della Croce, and though in early days there was real racing, with victory to the first across the finishing-line, a Fresco regatta was never a life-and-death affair. For behind it came a small, tapestry-hung fleet, gay with martial trophies, marine deities and characters out of plays, and the field was mainly occupied in exchanging fond glances with the ladies who sat among these exotic emblems.

Every Saturday in summertime there was a procession of *peotte*, wreathed in flowers and bearing mythological tableaux. These were handsomely mounted, and all sorts of characters appeared. In May 1740, Lady Mary Wortley Montagu saw the boat of the Pisani family with twenty-four statues for the twenty-four hours of the day, and the moon rising among stars. That of the Contarini displayed Mount Parnassus with Apollo, Pegasus, the Nine Muses and Fame. 'Signor Soranzo represented the Kingdom of Poland', complete with provinces and rivers, and had a band in Polish costume. The Querini 'had the chariot of Venus drawn by Doves, so well done they seem'd realy to fly upon the water'. The Doria family chose Diana hunting in a forest; trees, hounds, stags, nymphs and peasants were 'all done naturally'. The Triumphs of Peace and

Valour were not forgotten; there was a group of Neptune and Cybele and another of Flora, 'adorn'd with all sorts of Flowers', in a chariot 'guided by Cupids'.

The Venetian beauties in their luxurious gondolas attended these shows among the less distinguished audience jammed into hired boats. And indeed the processions were by no means the chief attraction, for the music played and the gondoliers sang and there were smiles and sidelong glances and dresses cut generously low to add excitement to the scene.

Sport – the real thing – had declined from its old standing with the general softening-up of manners in the eighteenth century. You got farther nowadays by talking pretty nonsense to a girl than by killing a bull in her honour or getting your head cracked open in the annual fist-fights on the Ponte dei Pugni.[74] Nobody went to the riding-school at the Mendicanti, hardly anyone practised target-shooting on the Lido. Even *calcio*, that tough and distant ancestor of football, which seems to have surpassed its American descendant in violence, was abandoned:[75] the patricians had once been passionately addicted to this game, but now preferred indoor sports or the card-table. Fencing, however, retained a degree of favour, for many private quarrels were still settled by duelling. A century before, the young bloods had duelled on the slightest pretext and the lawyers and *segretarii* had been yet more enthusiastic, but their keenness faded when banishment, and even death, became the punishment for the first man to draw. The other was then held to be acting in self-defence and had nothing to worry about, so the duel took on a novel aspect, as each antagonist tried every trick he knew to get the opposition to launch the attack. If neither party would actually make a start after a long string of aggressive and insulting remarks, the affair might end up as a set-to with bare fists. Alternatively, the witnesses might be asked to find some gentlemanly and Christian compromise, and there was always someone somewhere ready and able to concoct a formula of apology that could safely be tendered without loss of honour.

III CARNIVAL

There were six months of Carnival in the Venetian year, the longest lasting and most famous of the fêtes. The opening bout was from the first Sunday in October until Christmas, and it began again when the bell rang for vespers on the feast of the Epiphany, when it lasted until Lent, with a further fortnight at Ascensiontide. Public festivities and the chief governmental elections were also marked by days of Carnival, so that for a good half of the time the town was given over to licence and excess. These were seasons that bore out the contention of the Chinese Spy that the voluptuous air of Venice was in itself a threat to good conduct – 'pageants, pleasures and amusement everywhere'. He was quite right. Traditional usage and convention ceased to matter and all restraint was cast aside and the protections of mask and disguise conferred free speech on everyone.

The mask or *bautta* was not, as elsewhere, a simple affair covering mouth and eyes. In Venice it was a sort of enfolding cape or mantle with a black hood over the head and shoulders, the whole surmounted by a little tricorne hat. The actual mask part is described as being 'closely modelled on the white mask of classical times, its beaked outline altering the face into that of some strange bird cut in chalk'.

Perfect for its purpose, the *bautta* became almost a uniform for Carnival. From Doge to kitchenmaid, everybody wore it, man, woman and child of every age and station. Servant-girls went masked to market, mothers carried babies in masks in their arms, the lawyer wore a mask to plead in court.

The long domino-cloak or *tabarro* so widely used in Venice was generally adopted at Carnival time. In the *tabarro*, unless a skirt should happen to show beneath the hem, it was impossible to tell the sexes apart, and so the women took care to lengthen their dominoes until they swept the ground. In the whole packed Piazza di San Marco no one could be known or recognised again, unless perhaps it were Casanova and those who, like him, affected the display of a gold-braided velvet coat under the half-open *tabarro*.

But he and his friends were eccentrics and all the rest were agreed and determined on concealment. If a woman knew whose chatter she was listening to, whether he were a senator or her own shoemaker, it would ill become her to give any sign of recognition. A man would never hint that he recognised a woman; she would have broken off the encounter at once. It was just not done to indicate that you had pierced a disguise, and when someone spotted the Papal Nuncio in *bautta* and *tabarro* and besought immediate blessing everybody, as Montesquieu recalls, was dreadfully shocked.

Watertight anonymity was in fact the great lure of the Carnival, the relish that made it what it was. Goldoni calls the mask 'the most advantageous thing in the world', and there was nothing a masker dared not do. Before him difficulties melted away. Whoever he might be, he could join any company, go into any salon, sit down to cards, take part in the conversation, pay the women extravagant compliments. Women, for their part, could walk about as they fancied, enter the cafés or the lowest haunts there were, and have unmentionable adventures. Maskers could even get into the convents whenever they wanted to. Who was to forbid them, when nobody could possibly tell whether they were male, female, rogues and vagabonds or authority personified? All the barriers were down. There were neither rich nor poor, police nor *facchini*. There was only *Sior Maschera*, and who was to set limits for that faceless personage? Noble and commoner were confounded, as Casanova says, 'prince with subject, the ordinary with the remarkable man, lovely and hideous together. There were no longer valid laws, nor lawmakers.' Difference was obliterated, the social structure cancelled out. Dissembling was suddenly good behaviour and deviousness a merit, as the élite of the underworld rubbed shoulders with the worthier multitude.

With rules and regulations thus abolished, even the inquisitorial spies were no more heard. Doubtless they were far happier being free and easy like everybody else, while all around them, safely masked, the innocent raillery and less innocent intrigues went on. Speech and action were bolder, mischief was brewed as securely as though behind locked doors. Alibis were child's play. The whole tangled skein was obviously a great moral danger. 'At Carnival time,' wrote a contemporary, 'you see all kinds and classes of women, married, unmarried and widows, masked and mingling with the courtesans in every square and meeting-place, ready to do anything, publicly, with anyone who asks them, old or young.' With all this lust and risk and stimulation hovering in the air, how pre-eminently was Giacomo Casanova the right man in the right place, the very epitome of Venetian Carnival.

Many people adopted disguise as well as the mask, and sought from that *valet de l'imprévu* yet further protection for their vagaries. Invisible in any case, they sought also a new identity. Young men, and others not so young, abandoned the *tabarro* and plunged among the throng in fine fantastic costume as heroes of legend or history, or the lovers and grotesques of the *Commedia dell'arte* – Mattaccino attired in white with a plumed hat, the Magnifico in his long coat, black-robed Doctor Graziano or chequered Arlecchino. Choice was unlimited, the street was full of Moors and satyrs, of turbaned dervishes and feathered Indians, English blue-jackets, tartars, typical syphilitics and typical murderers.

Every wearer entered into his part, and it was this that made the masquerade successful; only a good actor would attempt to carry off a disguise. If you saw a harlequin, he was capering round and murmuring compliments to all the women; Brighella cracked jokes like those of Brighella on the stage; the Capitano bragged of high, imaginary deeds and Pierrot – only they called him Pedrolino here – mooned about in a world of his own. All Frenchmen were flighty, all Spaniards arrogant, judges prosy and medical men pedantic. Mock disputes broke out, with the crowd taking sides, speeches were declaimed and ridiculous conversations held. Wit was agile and spontaneous. An English traveller said that everyone was funny during Carnival, when one day afforded more wit than you otherwise heard in a week.

Inevitably, some people overdid things. Odd muddles ensued when the women dressed as men, or men dressed as women and imitated womens' voices. At one time there appeared a special brand of beggars known as the *pitocchi*, in clothes of brocade and velvet carefully slashed to shreds, with bright patches over the rents. It was Casanova who first thought of this idea, but unfortunately the pretended beggars soon turned into real ones, for though they said their begging was a joke and that they took money only 'under protest', the government heard that they sometimes badgered in good earnest and this particular costume was henceforth forbidden. Another thing that had to be stopped in 1775 was the blasphemous spectacle of men and women in ecclesiastical dress, wearing mitres and swinging holy water around. Everybody, too, disapproved of the *bernardoni* who added artificial sores to their beggars' disguise, and of the *teatini* who represented large, half-witted children.

Often the maskers joined in groups on allegorical floats hung with tapestry, green branches and flowers. They might stage a battle between Negroes and beplumed Indians, or a donkey-cavalcade of peasants from Calabria; a squadron of German mercenaries shook their lances or the Papal soldiery marched by, each man with his umbrella.

Trouble intruded from time to time, of course, among the make-believe. Gangs of revellers would invade the coffee-houses with whistles and catcalls, rolling drums and ringing bells at unexpected moments until the uproar, as the Inquisitors were informed, 'drove men deaf and blind and stupid'. But the Inquisitors were interested only in speeches against the government and could do nothing, in any case, because they could never catch the culprits. No witness had ever seen or heard a thing, or knew a single person involved. The wretched *fanti* were lucky to escape with nothing worse than rude words, such as those reported by Angiolo Tamiazzo on January 30, 1788, when he urged moderation upon an ebullient masker: 'Then sod you,' came the positive rejoinder, 'bloody you and all the other bloody spies.' It is little incidents like this – and there were many of them – that show the extraordinary effect of Carnival, for normally no one would risk saying any such thing even to a suspected law-man. Tamiazzo, excellent fellow, kept calm and placidly wound up his account, 'Nothing further occurred and disturbance on these premises continued to the usual hour.'

But with all its excesses, the great fête was something more than an uninhibited carouse. The lovely masking was a marvellous sight and its figures from other lands and times were creatures of the poetic and lively imagination that was the essential delight of Carnival – endlessly inventive, frivolous, brimful of gaiety and happy for ever in the passing moment. It is easy to understand why the whole world was bewitched.

The Piazza and the Piazzetta were the focus of it all. There the maskers gathered at the café tables or surged to and fro in a deafening, dizzying parade. Drawn now by tootling and tattoos from a distance, now by a gaudy riot of pictures, flags and notice-boards under their noses, they moved from one trestle-stage to another, from contortionists to wrestlers, from stuntmen to animal-showmen. From the bird-trainer with the calculating canaries they could turn to a gold-bespangled dentist pulling teeth to the accompaniment of loudly-beaten drums; or stroll across from the apes and bears to see an Irish giant. Amazing feats of strength were performed, the most popular being the *forze d'Ercole* or human pyramid of twelve, eight, four and two men, with one more at a terrifying height supporting a child above him in the air. Or a man on a rope slid to the ground from the top of the Campanile, face down and holding on with his feet; this was the *volo*, or *saltamartino*. The acrobats always

123

crossed themselves before they began and at the Angelus fell to their knees, with the rest of the bare-headed spectators, and crossed themselves again. Several minutes' reverential hush would then ensue, before the hullaballoo broke out again, louder than ever before.

If tricks and strong-man acts did not appeal, there remained, in this age of Cagliostro, all the soothsayers and cabbalists, all the hucksters with the elixir of life for sale. The fortune-teller sat among a collection of spheres, retorts and globes, breathing prophetic words into a tin speaking-tube. The customer held this tube to his ear so no one else could hear, and if he looked pleased the sage would ring a bell to announce that by the virtue of his art he had, as Misson says, 'dived into a very secret Affair', and the astonished bystanders, without fail, took off their hats as religiously as though they were listening to the *Salve Regina* chanted at an execution. In quiet corners, or in such quiet corners as there were, the ballad-singers retold, with many embellishments, the exploits of the paladins of Charlemagne or tales from the *Gerusalemme Liberata*, throwing in dragons and sirens and hippogriffs, with extra love scenes to liven up the doings of the Christian champions.

The mob could be dragged away from the Piazza only when some better spectacle happened to turn up in real life – a hanging, perhaps, on the Piazzetta, a thief in the pillory, a body found in the Grand Canal. And having looked at it, they turned back to their diversions. In the whole century we hear of exactly two things distracting them for any length of time. One was the rhinoceros exhibited at Rialto in 1751 and the other was Count Zambeccari's air-balloon, whose flight in 1784 was recorded by Francesco Guardi.[76]

Far beyond this main centre, of course, the stir of Carnival overflowed. Into the Merceria, where the shops outdid one another in elegant and arresting window-display and where even the druggists gave rein to fancy, claiming attention in 1729 with 'a few jars of leeches and a wreath or two of live vipers'; into the streets, where there was merrymaking of all sorts and they danced the *furlana* to the strains of spinet and violin; and outside the palaces where the commons stood to see their scarlet-gowned senators and their nobles in ball-dress, and to collect the *zecchini* scattered by generous-minded signori on the balconies above.

But the Piazza was always the true centre of activity and always black with people. Or rather, so full of a motley, rainbow-hued

concourse of devoted pleasure-seekers that it would be hard to guess
just how many it held when the revels were at their height. Could
there have been a hundred thousand, as a visitor believed? Certainly there was never an inch of space to spare and every human
creature was ruled by frenzy and delirium. The clock and the
rules of conduct went overboard together. All the eating-houses
were open in the middle of the night; everybody seemed to have
gone mad in the pursuit and cultivation of pleasure and dissolute
behaviour. No one entered a shop save for food or drink, toys or
trinkets. Books, even obscene books, were a drug on the market,
the dealers lamented; reading seemed a lost art. Differences of rank
dissolved. Venice danced and sang, applauded the mountebanks
and arranged its love affairs, given over to gratification and delight,
for six whole months of every livelong year.

IV SUMMERS IN THE COUNTRY

When the hot weather came the rich quitted the town and went
off to their country houses. This was an established habit of the
nobility and not to follow it was social death. Those whom poverty
anchored to the spot shut themselves up for the summer in their
dilapidated palaces, not to be seen on the Piazza until autumn came.
If for any reason they had to emerge they wore masks, and it was
for their sake that masking was allowed out of Carnival time.[77]

In the eighteenth century the middle classes, too, had taken to
spending summer in the country, and there the rich merchant
lived side by side with the aristocrat. Once away from Venice he,
who might neither rival nor emulate his betters at home, was free
to wear a curly wig, and rings on his fingers, and to strut about with
a sword. His wife might change her dress a dozen times a day, go
out and gamble and wind up the evening at a ball: many a bourgeois income was mortgaged for years to come after a season of even
small-scale patrician life. Often, however, there was very little
choice about such summer holidays. A merchant could easily
lose his credit by passing those revealing months at home. His
business would suffer and his family go down in the world; he
might find it more of a problem to get his daughters settled. He
went to the country, therefore, and frequently his sacrifice to
the gods of public opinion plunged him into the very difficulties
he had been hoping to avoid.

The attitude of the nobles, even those who could well afford the *villegiatura*, made their visits, too, more of a social convention than a genuine rural enjoyment. No one who really liked the country would have tried so hard to change it all. The parks they made were entirely artificial, with formal pools and fountains where-ever a pool or fountain could be introduced, huge trees tailored into arbitrary shapes, avenues laid out with a ruler and covered with clean sand. White marble statues were planted on all sides. Any touch of nature would have spelled vulgarity; cows in a field, a donkey at grass or dogs romping been dreadfully out of place.

There were great numbers of stately patrician villas on the main-land[78] and hundreds on the Terraglio, the highway to Treviso. So many stood along the Brenta that Brosses was quite discouraged and never went near, pleading that the sightseeing involved would have taken several years. Molmenti rightly considered that many were fitter for kings than private owners: great, luxurious palaces with fifty rooms and more, salons opening one beyond another, wide galleries and statued porticoes. The state apartments were frescoed by the most renowned painters with the sensual pleasures of life. Here is the 'blond, rosy flesh, bare and available'; here 'the smiles and parted lips, the trysting and plighting and swooning away'. The very kitchens glimmered and glowed with colour.

Existence in these enchanted palaces was just what the décor seemed to indicate, with every day one long, delightful programme, well described as 'Carnival without the mask, folly undisguised'. The Inquisitors were far away, the sumptuary laws were set aside and serious things forgotten. In Venice the patricians seldom enter-tained at home, but here in the country they proved enthusiastic hosts. Friends passing through, and even friends of friends, were pressed to abundant and delicious meals, to glittering evening par-ties and visits that went on and on. So free and easy were they that dozens of people no one had ever met tended to turn up for the sake of the good cheer, or just to swell the company. Antonio Longo[79] recalls how he once took fifty-three guests for a sail and how they all decided to stop at the villa of the Senator Giambattista, there to be warmly welcomed to a ball to which they had not been in-vited and to remain ten days. Lady Mary Wortley Montagu records another such carefree intrusion:

'I had a visit in the beginning of these Holidays of 30 Horse of Ladys and Gentlemen with their servants (by the way, the Ladies ride like the late Ds of Cleaveland). They came with the kind intent of staying with me at least a fortnight, tho I had never seen any of them before; but they were all Neighbours within ten mile around.'[80]

Lady Mary, being English, was only moderately taken with this way of doing things, but the native-born adored it and behaved so generously with open-house and table that not a few spongers managed to infiltrate with the rest. But nobody turned such people out again, for they contributed their fair share of amusement. There was indeed a whole category of hangers-on who spent their time and earned their dinner by making the party go. From Goldoni we learn of their dancing a burlesque version of the *furlana*, regardless of whether music accompanied them or not; playing the violin without knowing the first thing about it; singing stridently and churning out ridiculous, far-fetched rhymes. They were impolite to everybody and unruffled by the snubs and occasional slaps they got in return as long as they raised a laugh. Thimble-rigging, doing complicated tricks with ribbon and a pair of scissors, producing a bird out of a pack of cards or eating macaroni with their hands tied behind their backs, it was all one to them. They were professional buffoons, like the court jesters of the Renaissance and the guests seconded them happily with practical jokes of their own. (Casanova recounts a horrid one that nearly killed a man with shock.) The great thing was never to be upset, and to keep laughing. If you couldn't take a joke you only looked stupid; you were there to enjoy yourself, after all.

The rustic timetable left little opportunity to follow your own devices. It would have been rather difficult to evade the collective activities, and no one thought of doing so in any case. The first meeting, for chocolate, took place late in the morning, for early rising was no part of the routine. This moment, wrote Goldoni's Jesuit acquaintance, the versifier Giambattista Roberti, with its 'spicy sips and spicier conversation', was 'the most delightful that friendship could contrive or afford'. The stimulating chatter continued in long walks round the gardens, ideal settings for elegant, leisurely flirtation under the indulgent gaze of marble nymph and satyr. Next, an unhurried, ample luncheon with a great display of fine cookery, though the fineness lay mostly in exotic sauces and fancy presentation. Meals were served in a succession of rooms, one each for meat and game and a third for the puddings and ices. This probably helped you to guess what was actually on your plate, but the vast array of food entailed made the simple life appallingly expensive, which was sad for the bourgeois doing his best to keep up with patrician splendours.

Sometimes, as a break from heavy, formal eating, an outdoor expedition was arranged. Guests would gather laden with maize-flour or bottles or knives and forks and crockery, and the more stalwart were put in charge of a large copper cauldron. Then, in some open glade, they would all cook polenta and have a cheerful picnic on the grass, with fine lace tablecloths.

Afternoons were sacred to the *trottata*, a ritual airing in small carriages, on horseback or, most often, by water. Everyone boarded the roomy *burchielli*, some of which took eighty passengers and whose cabins, unlike the black *felzi* of the gondolas, had looking-glass and pictures and hangings of light-coloured silk. In these charming boats they sailed to visit the villas of friends or to attend the fêtes that each host gave in turn and competition. Floral arches welcomed them, bands were hidden among the trees and allegorical scenes were played on garden terraces.

Evening was always a full-dress occasion, with admirable music. Orphan girls of the Ospedaletto were sometimes brought from Venice to sing serenades and opera, and there were theatricals and dancing. The card-tables were set, and lackeys carried fruit and ices round. People vanished into the gardens two by two, to the small, convenient arbours of boxwood and oleander. This was the time for 'truth and probity, a meeting of hearts and hands, when darkness made it easy to tell all'; or so said an essayist in the *Nuova Veneta Gazzetta*. Dawn broke, the sun was up, and everybody went to bed.

The long, full day had been one of unremitting entertainment. The Venetians had gone through nine months of continual jollity before retreating to the country, but far from having a rest they were twice as eager, for they never wearied of amusing themselves. One inevitable result of this was that many nobles spent so much on luxury that nothing was left for bare necessities. The bourgeois after his costly summer season had recourse to moneylenders, but a patrician could borrow at low interest from the convents, which

10   Gala Night at S. Benedetto Theatre, by Francesco Guardi

hardly ever wanted their money back. This very convenient system was to be brutally abolished when Napoleon suppressed the convents and took over their property. The nobles were then faced with foreclosure and had to sell up, so that half Venice was on the market at a time when the political situation meant that nobody wanted to buy and a palace fetched little or nothing. Many of the patrician familes were ruined overnight. But they had led the dance and they met the hour, when it came, without complaint.

Meanwhile other and more prudent citizens were content with summer trips to the islands in the lagoon, and nobles with neither country houses nor friends to send them invitations spent the months at Padua, where there was always plenty to do. Padua had beautiful gardens, good plays and an agreeable society in which young people could more or less please themselves. The visit began, moreover, with the enchanting journey down the Brenta canal.

Was there ever a pleasure cruise like that of Goldoni and his gifted companions on the Brenta, ten of them in that lovely boat, furnished with books to read and instruments to play? They travelled slowly through the day and stayed at carefully chosen places at night, music their main pastime. Goldoni being the only non-musician and, as he says, 'no good at anything', occupied himself with making a verse chronicle of the voyage to recite to the others after coffee. They had a concert on deck every evening and people on both banks crowded to applaud them, waving their hats and handkerchiefs. Cremona gave them a rapturous welcome and a very good dinner, after which they continued their performance. The local music-lovers joined in and there was dancing until dawn. Every night it was the same, and Goldoni's account of the whole delicious interlude prompted Taine to say he could imagine no more spontaneous, all-round, intelligent way of enjoying oneself; which was a perfect comment, and perfectly true. Venice, however, had yet more lures in prospect for the man of pleasure.

V GAMBLING

To say that Venetians were gamblers is to be guilty of understatement. Play was more than relaxation, it was a serious occupation, a consuming passion with them. For more than a thousand years, without the aid of cards or dice, the nobles had gambled in their sea-going affairs. It was a gambler's game to charter a ship, lade her with goods, then sit at home and reckon up the profits, awaiting her return. There were always galleys that never saw the Bacino again, cargo and crew gone down in a storm or captured by corsairs, and then the only thing to do was double the stake. And so it went on, double or quits, with even the largest fortunes perpetually at hazard.

The patricians, used as they were to this constant fluctuation between wealth and bankruptcy, were lost when the great maritime trade of Venice practically disappeared. It was then that they turned to cards for the excitement they had come to need and gave themselves up to the gambling passion with an intensity that infected and damaged the whole fabric of society and deeply alarmed the government. All over the city people took to gambling, day and night. They used the well-heads, they sat on steps among the passersby, and everywhere they cheated. This was so even in the private salons, some of which were crooked to a degree: a nobleman could teach his young daughter 'to rig a faro game so that she could not lose'. The split between the theory and practice of what was right and wrong was obviously deep and wide – the polished phrase, the poise and elegance on the one hand, and on the other an effrontery and a line of conduct borrowed from the criminal classes. Marked cards and loaded dice were among the mildest methods used to part an innocent from his money and the Great Council finally passed a stringent law that virtually prohibited gaming. But, as over-emphatic legislation often does, this failed in its missionary intent. Secret sessions were not very difficult to arrange and soon the law might as well never have been passed at all.

Taking the lesson to heart, the state decided to license play under proper control and for its own benefit. The Ridotto was opened as an official establishment in 1628 and stayed in business until 1774 with ever-increasing popularity, so that its luxurious rooms in a palace near San Moisé had to be extended more than once. Anybody in a mask was admitted, entry without one being a privilege reserved to patricians and their wives, and it was hard to move at more than a snail's pace through the dense crowd in the six communicating salons. A profoundly silent crowd, be it said, where decorum demanded a restrained bearing and impassive expression at all times.

The favourite games were *biribisso* and *faro*. The first, a sort of roulette, was introduced in France with terrific success by the Venetian ambassador Giustiniani, and the second resembled baccarat. At each table a bewigged and gowned patrician held the bank, generally on behalf of a syndicate. The punters sat quietly round in orderly fashion, with never a hint of argument as the ducats and sequins passed between them. Nightly huge sums were won and lost and only the state, taking a percentage of the stake money, remained solvent and added considerably to its revenue. Bankruptcy followed bankruptcy as private fortunes melted away at the Ridotto like the snow in summer. What the commoners lost nobody knew, but disaster in the higher reaches of society was more or less public. It was noticed when senators were selling furniture, pictures and *objets d'art*; their palaces, too, very often, Or they were seen at the money-lender's begging the wherewithal to live or to get back to the tables once again.

The Signory chose to ignore this deplorable exhibition for a long time, but the scandal grew worse and worse and in 1774 it took the fearful decision to cut off its gambling revenue. It asked the Great Council to 'suppress the vice at its chief centre' and, almost by mistake, the requisite law went through. Many of the counsellors, on the assumption that there would be a large majority against, had felt safe in supporting it, for the sake of appearing on the side of the angels, and we read in Casanova how when the votes were counted the Maggior Consiglio found to its consternation 'that it had made a law it disagreed with, and the legislators gazed at one another stupified'. But the Ridotto was not to be saved by stupefaction, and its closing down was an unparalleled calamity for the whole of Venice. Life came to a standstill. 'All the Venetians,' wrote Goudar, 'are a prey to hypochondria; the Jews go round with faces as sour as lemons, shops are deserted, the mask-makers starving, and gentlemen who have been used to dealing cards ten hours a day find that their hands are withering away. Evidently, no state can keep going without the aid of vice.'

But the paralysis was soon over. On all sides, clandestinely, the card-games started again, in the back-rooms of barbers' shops, in the salons, the *casini* and cafés, and even in the *pestrini* which had hitherto confined themselves to selling whipped cream and wafer biscuits. The fever was stronger than ever before. In most theatres there was now a gaming-room as an alternative to play or opera. The whole world gambled, the poor as eagerly as the rich, wagering their watches, rings and trinkets to join in. People staked the clothes they stood up in; a well-born *abate* named Nicolò Grioni once had to dash home without a stitch on. Real addicts were even known to bet their womenfolk.

And now the *casini* began to serve a new purpose. Every noble, from senator to young man about town, had a *casino* as, had he been French, he might have had his *petite maison* in Paris, but here, instead of being a separate building, it was a small, discreet set of rooms, part of a house let off in similar sets. These were little hidden *casini* for the noble ladies too, and Madame du Boccage, Goldoni's Parisian friend, speaks with envy of their privacy and prettiness.

'A middle-class sort of house; a dim lantern to see you up the stair; the key in your pocket, and in you go. You can rest, see friends or have a *tête-à-tête*, just as you like, with no risk of gossip. I have seen more than one of these charming oases and they offer far more freedom than women here are blessed with.'

The *casini* were mostly in the warren of alleys near San Marco, beautifully furnished and decorated, ideal for informal chats as well as lovers' rendezvous. Casanova calls some of them 'temples of luxury and love'. Here the patricians, who so seldom visited one another's palaces, would drop in without ceremony. Sometimes several people shared the expenses of a *casino* and met and talked and read the papers there. The habit was adopted by the bourgeoisie, with *casino*-clubs for the various professions, and even the manservants had *casini* of their own.

These, then, were the little sanctuaries which, when the Ridotto closed its doors, turned into gaming-rooms. Larger ones were opened which were to all intents and purposes public resorts, since any gondolier could get you in if you fancied a game of *bassetto*. Some were questionable lairs where a squalid rabble of rogues and harlots mingled with the best blood in Venice; places that admitted anyone in a mask, and a simple eye-mask, a false nose or beard seemed to be quite enough disguise. Morals were nowhere. Ballarini, agent of the Procurator Andrea Tron, reports that women who ran out of money 'gave themselves to anyone so they could stay and gamble'. The *confidenti* sent in some harrowing accounts of the unholy atmosphere, the awful goings-on and the uproar that sounded as though murder might be done at any minute.

Authority had tolerated the *casini* as decent meeting-places, but now decided that enough was enough. Had their laws been fully operative not a *casino* would have survived, but needless to say they were not, and spies reported the scandal and the shocking incidents in vain. The Signory knew itself powerless and had to let things go. Illegal gambling hells multiplied from year to year, as did new, fashionable ways of losing money. One of these was *spigolo*, a fore-runner of poker, of which an agent named Camillo Passini, with characteristic and commendable devotion to duty, successfully worried out the rules, in October 1776.

'I beg to submit that this game is played with a pack of fifty-two cards which count at face-value from ace up to king, all court-cards counting ten. They are dealt three at a time to two players. A winning hand must include either a pair – any pair, sixes, fours, eights; or three of the same suit, that is a *flusso*, of clubs, spades, etc.; or three running values – seven, eight, nine, for instance, or ace, two, three – which constitute a *sequenza*. The *gilé* or pair beats everything and a *flusso* beats a straight, which scores least unless it is a straight flush, in which case it beats even a *gilé* and is beaten only by a *gilone*, i.e. threes. When both players have a flush or a straight the game is decided by counting up the points. Bets are made after dealing and before the cards are seen. When the hand is finished there is another round of betting, for more or less than the amount lost, either for a sum equal to all the money on the table, or with an agreed ante of, say, one sequin. Losses may, therefore, be large. This is how they play *spigolo* at the Moro coffee-house, at the sign of the Guardian Angel under the Nuove Procuratie. The Noble Gentlemen Francesco Balbi and Angelo Foscarini play there night and day, as do the Noble Gentlemen Alvise Renier, Nicoletto Pisamano and others. Some arrive, morning and evening, in scarlet *tabarri*, and borrow masks before going into the cafe or inner room. The Noble Gentlemen Carlo Constantin Querini, Fortunato Balbi and Silvestro Dandolo have been seen to do this. The host keeps a supply of masks to lend out, which are returned to him on leaving.'

People also made opportunities for gambling by playing childrens' games like *cala carte* for grown-up stakes. In this version of beggar-my-neighbour chits were given to those who collected the most cards or points, and considerable sums changed hands when the value of the chits was high. This went on in full view, on the public boats or the benches of the Piazzetta.

It was in Venice that playing-cards were first thought of, in the 1400s, when they began as an album of fifty items which, the designer thought, 'might be nice to amuse the children'. A contemporary next evolved a game with them as 'an attractive pastime for those of riper years'. By the eighteenth century 'pastime' was hardly the right word; card-playing appeared to be the only thing Venetians ever did. Seasoned enthusiasts simply never stopped save when the coffee-houses and *casini* closed early in the morning. They then went to the Erberia, where the jostling boatloads of vegetables, fruit and flowers would be discharging on the quay. There the victims of recklessness or ill-fortune, as Casanova shows them, enjoyed a soothing stroll, in company with everyone else who needed to recover from a night's career or perhaps drew a defiant breath of morning air.

The government venture of the Ridotto had not really catered for the working class, who could rarely afford to go. But the gambling itch was every bit as strong in them as in their betters and they too required an outlet. For them, therefore, the Signory sponsored the lottery in 1715, only to suppress it after eleven years and re-establish it finally in 1734. Like lotteries in other parts of Italy, it was more or less the same as trying to forecast the first three horses in a race: you picked three numbers which, if they came in the draw of five in the order you had named, brought in five thousand times your stake money. In Rome the lottery absorbed the greater part of the time and attention of the Holy Father's subjects, and though Venetians were less completely dedicated they still took enormous pains to find three lucky numbers and arrange them into *terni*. Each individual had his own pet formula and wore himself out trying to prove it with mystical figures. Dreams were a prime source of valuable hints and implications were to be wrung from the most ordinary occurrences of daily life.

But lagoon-folk trusted less than did most Italians to their personal powers of divination. There were lottery booths all over the town, lit up invitingly at night, and people preferred to take the advice of the ticket sellers there. A dog who toured the *campi* fishing numbers out of a basket also inspired great faith, though apparently no one paused to wonder why the ticketmen, or the dog's scarecrow of a master, who were so kindly marketing the means to fame and fortune, seemed never a penny better off.

If anybody actually won, the whole neighbourhood went mad. Gasparo Gozzi describes the explosion of rejoicing in the courtyard of Ca' Barozzi when a mattress-maker's wife had won the lottery. All the residents came tumbling down the steps, there were hugs and tears, an apple-woman tore her apron to ribbons, another kicked her slippers over her head and danced in her bare feet; a gondolier seized the opportunity to throw a pretty girl up in the air, catch her and throw her up again, and they all gabbled tales of treasure. Not the sort of thing that happened very often, but it served to show the possibilities and caused a run on the ticket booths next day. Yet Venetians did not, on the whole, delude themselves with dreams for very long. They were too enthralled in the present moment to live for seven mortal days in hopes of a draw at the end of the week.

CHAPTER FOUR

LOVE AND WOMEN

The Council of Ten, in debate on December 10, 1776, denounced in the following terms the conduct of females in Venice:

'The way the times are going, together with the great and universal alteration in manners whose full effect is with us now, demonstrate, to our profound and justifiable grief, the inevitable result of the free and licentious life our women lead. This was, and ever will be, the chief cause of the decline and ruin of the Republic.'

A forceful introduction, prelude to nothing but a ban on women going into theatres masked, and this feeble measure was all the less likely to stave off the ruin of the Republic for being one hundred per cent ignored. The Ten might call for 'rigorous execution' of the regulations, but too often their vigilance was unequal to the task of practical enforcement. Law in Venice, as we have seen, was more than elsewhere ineffective against social custom.

It was generally acknowledged, all the same, that Venetian ladies, or at any rate a vast number of them, behaved very badly, and it may be that their misbehaviour reflected upon the honour and dignity of the state just as the Inquisitors said it did. The fact also remains that it was not the least of Venetian attractions in the eye of the foreign visitor.

Decline of moral standards, love of display and the eternal Carnival had all contributed to the emancipation of women, but the final touch was a dress-reform at the beginning of the century. Until that time ladies had always worn *zoccoli*, high wooden clogs that tipped the feet forward; the higher they were the more elegant they were supposed to be. *Zoccoli* were originally meant for protection in the muddy streets and became such symbols of luxury that

136

precious stones were sometimes used instead of nails in making them. The wearers achieved a long, tall look but were practically debarred from walking, being unable to keep their balance or move about unless upheld by a servant on either side. So circumstanced, it was never very easy to slip away to an assignation or take a furtive gondola to some undiscovered little entrance door, yet the fashion prevailed against sumptuary laws and mockery. It prevailed, that is, until women themselves began to feel the need for greater freedom. Then they adopted *scarpe*, flat slippers of thin leather or of gold or silver brocade, and revolution was accomplished. The new woman appeared, at her natural height, independent of supporters, with movements unhampered and ready for anything. The Doge Contarini had foreseen this with distressing clarity. Hearing someone remark that the little slippers were convenient, he intoned, 'Too convenient; much, much too convenient'.

The women of Venice, from mistress to maidservant, had an apparently well-merited reputation as the best-looking in Europe. Outside blood has altered the pattern now and to see what they were like it is better to study contemporary portraits than their modern representatives. The pictured beauties, despite the dark, brilliant eyes, are not of the same southern type to which the men so often belonged. Their hair is dyed, of course, and their radiant complexions may be only make-up, but they are slim and slenderly built. Their features lack the almost architectural regularity of the Greeks, but are clear-cut, with noses boldly arched; and the *smorfia*, that not quite haughty, not quite come-hither smile, brings the whole face to life. The hair was either worn loose to the shoulders or, more usually, in a chignon held with silver pins, and admiration seems to have been concentrated on the point where neck and shoulders join. Descriptions are rapturous: 'there was never such willowy elegance, such rounded delicacy, as theirs when they turned and bowed and raised their heads, nothing more delicate and lovely than those necks. You thought of swans and doves.'

Women of the middle class dressed more or less as did their opposite numbers in France, imitating the mode of the patricians while avoiding its sometimes very odd extremes. The little slippers and the *tabarro* were fashionable for all. So, too, was the *zendale* which, though late on the scene, was very popular from the 1770s onward, hailed as a crying scandal by a spy of the Ten: the chief scandal being, of course, that women had made something attractive out of what began as a jealous device to shield oriental wives from observation.[81] The thick black wrapping of the original *zendale*, an unpleasing garment that swathed its wearer, shapeless and invisible from head to foot, had been rejected long ago and the model that came into fashion around 1770 had an exactly opposite effect. Now it was a flimsy veil edged with fine lace, covering head and bosom. Knotted at the waist, its two ends floating gaily, it did less to protect modesty than to attract admirers. A pair of bright eyes would shine through the folds just long enough to send their demure hint or coaxing message; the face was revealed for a second at the most flattering angle. Venetian ladies had a whole new repertoire of charming by-play, a new weapon in their already well-stocked armoury.

How did they dress, the women of the Serenissima? Those of the working class wore skirts to their ankles only, sleeves short and bodices low. The apron was a matter for individual taste and often very pretty. They had thin shoes, dancing-slippers almost, and a white veil or brief shawl crossed over the shoulders. Country-women used to carry wide-brimmed hats and tuck a sprig of blossom alluringly behind one ear.

The sumptuary laws have been mentioned more than once as intended to curb the personal luxury which, to the government's way of thinking, 'sapped the citizen's income and so robbed the State'. But whether they curbed the coquetry of the citizen's wife we may beg leave to doubt, for accurate and faithful portraitists show the Venetian belles in a deal of strictly forbidden finery. By rights they should never have worn those long trains, those elaborate collars, pearl-embroidered gloves and silken ribbons. Even stitching and trimming came under the regulations. None but ambassadresses, princesses and female relations of the reigning Doge ranked as *fuori delle pompe* and were allowed to bend the rules a little. Yet still the rich materials, with ornamentation of silver and gold, were worn beneath the graceful, bright-hued *tabarrino* reaching to the knee, and the French *andrienne* introduced by the Duchess of Modena was popular until the end of the Republic, despite its train and the expensive *cascate*, or lace ruffles, on the sleeves.[82]

Small silver and golden fans had indeed been laid aside when officially prohibited, to be replaced by larger ones, studded with pearls and diamonds on their tortoiseshell spokes and decorated by the finest painters to be found in Venice. But the change was due more to coincidence than any desire to obey the regulations, and made solely and simply because the big fan had become a necessary aid to flirtation and was now used to signal encouragement, threat or promise, and as cover for the smile or tender sigh.

The women in fact were expert as ever at making the best of themselves and went on dressing exactly as they pleased. The Dogaressa herself, exposed to continual preaching as she was, paid absolutely no attention and the *magistrati alle pompe*, who decided all the do's and don'ts, took their duties lightly. Nobody, indeed, was serious about the sumptuary laws, neither those who made them nor the *provveditori* responsible for seeing they were carried out. It had been obvious for a long time that the more severe they were the less notice was taken of them, and the most stringent were the first to go. The law forbidding women to wear anything but black, for example, had been a dead letter for three decades when it was finally cancelled in 1732.

Officialdom had one small success in preventing the circulation of French designs and fashion-papers, which it impounded at the frontiers. Since France dictated dress, hairstyles, accessories and feminine adornment to Europe at large, this left the ladies of Venice with a mortifying year, or even two, to wait before they could do what Paris told them. But if we may believe Goldoni they still contrived to change their fashions radically and often and the dress-makers, just as nowadays, waited to the last moment before revealing what was going to happen next. Their secrets were kept until Ascension Day, when the *Piavola de Franza* was shown in the Merceria and the whole town went to see. Whatever this mannequin doll was wearing became the mode, no matter how exaggerated, and inspired all the hats and gowns. The imitators were never servile. They kept the true Venetian touch and some of their ideas spread to foreign countries; 'Polish' dresses from Venice, for instance, were eagerly adopted in Paris long after they lost favour by the lagoon. Yet one extraordinary and never-broken rule obtained: in this city, with its gorgeous native fabrics, all the women who cared for clothes insisted on imported French material. Goldoni has a scene in his *Femmine Puntigliose* in which a dress is refused because the stuff it is made of comes from Venice.

The law might forbid the small accessory elegances, but there were still plenty of them to be found, copied from French models if not actually brought in from France. Exquisite haberdashery and fancy goods were sold from little trays in the Piazza by a selection of gay, vivacious girls who were said to have more than one string to their bow. Certainly they brought a dash of gallantry to the transactions. Their business, whatever it was, did remarkably well and the *confidenti* informed against them in vain. One agent reported that a 'a French Madame', as he calls her,

> '. . . is said to have been the first to parade round the square with a portable case of salves, balms and assorted trinkets, and they say she drove an excellent trade. Increasing numbers have followed her example, peddlers cluttering the arcades of the Old and New Procuratie night and day – and some of them with more than their wares to sell. They go into the coffee-houses, there to engage in ribald conversation and behave no better than common courtesans.'

Some of the trinket-vendors even opened shops, among them another Frenchwoman nicknamed *la Sansona* – Samson – whose peculiar activities also kept a secret agent busy.[83]

Venetian women, unlike their French contemporaries, were extremely fussy about personal cleanliness and fond of taking baths. Bath-water was scented with musk, myrrh or mint, and they used all sorts of creams afterwards to whiten the hands, soften the skin or give a rosy tint to their long fingernails. At night they had a sort of face-pack made from strips of veal soaked in milk.

A fashionable woman passed seven hours a day at her toilette, according to Molmenti, much of the time with the hairdresser who attended her at home and had the delicate task of applying a large range of complicated dyes to ensure the correct dark golden shade of Venetian blonde. Turning this desirable colour had been something of a trial in her grandmother's time, when one had to spend long intervals out in the sun or in front of the fire with one's hair draped over the brim of a crownless hat known as a *solana*. A chronicler in the sixteenth century speaks of ladies 'planted and taking root' out on the balcony; Lucrezia Borgia took several weeks travelling from Rome to Ferrara because she could move only on alternate days; on the others she was fully occupied getting her hair dry. Dyes were improved since then and hairdressing was less tedious, but still the sessions were long enough. It was a prodigious undertaking to build up the curls, the fruit, the flowers and all the bits and pieces of a modish coiffure. A satirist spoke of women re-

sembling greengrocers with trays on their heads. They were slower
in taking to wigs than were the men, but by 1797 were keeping 850
wigmakers in business on ever larger and larger creations, counterparts of those piled-up towers of ringlets and feathers and artificial
birds that were the pride and joy of Versailles. The wigs would
dwindle at Carnival time, however, for the fetching tricorne hat
that went so well with the *bautta* did not sit happily on a great scaf-
fold of hair bristling with long pins.

It was the hairdresser, too, who put paint on his employer's
face and even on her breasts, for gowns were worn so low that it was
a wonder some of them stayed up at all. But make-up was never
excessive. Preferably, it was invisible, and here the naturally glowing complexions of Venetian women were an enormous help.
Rouge, so overdone in France, was sternly outlawed, and any Pari-
sienne who went on using it as though she were at home would
quickly realise that it was frowned upon. On pain of being shunned
in society she would also have to give up the strong scents that were
fashionable in her own country.

Another task for the hairdresser was that of fixing the patches
without which no lady in Europe would have felt complete. In
Venice the patches never spoke the language of politics, as they did
in England, but only the language of love. The *sfrontata*, worn on
the nose, implied a certain degree of forwardness, as one might guess
from its name. A patch at the eye-corner was a *passionata*; the *civetta*,
or coquette, was placed in a dimple, and most brazen of all was an
assassina, at the corner of the mouth.

Hours with the hairdresser were hours of recreation. He knew
the latest gossip, hummed the newest tune and was handy at need
with notes and errands in a love affair. From him a woman had few
secrets; he was her confidant and might be her intimate friend, if
passably presentable. A hairdresser of whom Albergati wrote[84]
has this to say for himself: 'From now on our profession really de-
serves general applause. Some of the ladies don't mind making love
with us and of course they have a ready-made, watertight excuse for
seeing us every day – we have simply come to do their hair.' And
when Figaro is not making love on his own account he can always be
of use to someone else: 'then there are ladies who like us to act
as personal secretaries or take messages, and they give us showers of
presents and the benefit of their protection'. A poet named Savioli,
on the other hand, a Bolognese like Albergati, saw the calling in a

more moral, modest light and wrote of the hairdresser as a careful guardian, not only of powder and perfumery, but of honour too.

With the first part of the day devoted to dressing and beauty treatment, the ladies of Venice reserved the late afternoon, the evening and often the entire night for enjoying themselves. Their pleasures were many and various and all alike in one respect – their setting was never at home. As marriage came to mean less, home, too, grew less important. Women received very seldom, save at the *conversazioni*, and the convention that decreed such functions decreed also that they be few and far between. Friends kept in touch by leaving small engraved cards, often embellished with erotic drawings. A palace was not a home any more, it had become a museum, a kind of family monument. 'There are two hundred sumptuous rooms in the Foscarini palace,' we are told, 'and not a single corner or an armchair you can sit in, in case you damage the carving.'

The new climate of moral ease and freedom would have been unthinkable at the end of the previous century. The Frenchman la Haye[85] had found that wives in Venice were treated by their husbands like slaves, 'hidden away from every living soul'. Another is still complaining that the ladies were unseen nearly twenty years later, and that one could hardly guess what sort of lives they led – all anyone knows about are their endless hours on the rooftops, bleaching their hair. One never meets them anywhere. Memoirs and private letters are silent, there are none of those personal records that would have been so fascinating. Charles Yriarte, writing in the 1870s about Marc Antonio Barbarigo, could not even discover in the course of detailed research whether the Republic had allowed an ambassador to take his wife abroad with him. A woman's days, according to Molmenti, were pleasant and 'full of repose', which is as much as to say that she lived like a recluse. The only glimpse we can catch of her is, occasionally, on canvas, when she is painted sitting on a balcony as somebody sings on the water below.

But the moral, social and material changes of the *Settecento* altered her whole world. Now nothing could keep her at home. Not her husband, too busy with his own amusements to stay there long himself; nor the task of educating her children, who were handed over to paid tutors or put into convents; and certainly not the reprimands of the Inquisitors of State, which she treated with derision. Eager and carefree and gay, she took one light step into a waiting gondola and vanished among the network of canals, not to be seen again until the next day's dawn. No one knew where she went to save the gondolier and he never gave her away. Her husband, if by any chance he happened to worry about it, could prise no information out of his own servant. The man who broke that rule would be expelled from the gondoliers' brotherhood and even, if the cause of serious trouble, drowned.

And where were they off to when they disappeared, these charming, newly-emancipated slaves? They could scarcely have been keeping rash or amorous appointments the whole of the time, but all the hallowed old restrictions had been discarded with their high clogs and they went wherever pleasure beckoned – under arcades and into gardens, among the thronging maskers in the Piazza di San Marco, and when the coffee-houses were forbidden them in 1776 they went to the *casini* instead. Many had private *casini* of their own where they could meet as they wished and where their pastimes were not always innocuous. Other resorts, too, being open to anyone in visor and masquerade dress, were more or less public and a fine field for adventure. Eventually the tales of wholesale encounter came to the ears of the Ten and such places were shut up, though the proprietors might bear illustrious names. Some of the noblest wives in Venice were temporarily shut up too, confined to their palaces for having allowed the *casini* to be put to improper use.

For improper use, of course, the gondola was always irresistible. Unseen, a couple might drift about the shadowy canals, or out as far as the Lido island where the courtesans, and they only, would bathe and the young men join them in notably uninhibited beach-parties. Leisured onlookers were absolutely enthralled by the lascivious scenes – according to an Inquisitorial spy, the truly terrible scenes – that afforded them unfailing entertainment there.

It was after the play in the evening that Venetian ladies went floating off, heaven knew where, until the early hours. Some were then shameless enough to show themselves in the mixed company at the Erbaria with those who had spent the night gambling or making love. Casanova, who was often there, fulminates about it rather unconvincingly:

'The popularity of that gathering at the Erberia indicates how far a national character can change. Our forbears kept everybody guessing in love and politics alike, but we have to make all as clear as day. If a man goes there with a woman it is to reduce his friends to envy by showing off his luck; and if alone, he is prowling round in hopes, or trying to make somebody jealous. The women are only there to be seen and to be ostentatiously unembarrassed. They could hardly be trying to attract admiration in the state they are in – as though they have all agreed to appear looking like wrecks to give people something to talk about. As for the men upon whose arms they lean, their careless manner and general nonchalance are calculated to convey boredom after the event and imply triumphant responsibility for their companions' disarray.'

II LOVE AND THE 'CAVALIERE SERVENTE'

A society so bent on pleasure, and whose women had such freedom, would have been fatally disorganised if love had conquered all; and women were so obliging as to regard love as a habit merely, that had nothing to do with passion. 'Where will you find nowadays those violent, unforgettable passions aroused by a woman glimpsed behind a dark veil and wooed at a window once a month?' enquires Chiari in one of his plays. Times were changed indeed and love was all caprice and fantasy. No throbbing hearts, no deep and true affections any more. Venetian courtship, Venetian libertinage, were touched with irony – shallow, placid, sunny, tricked out with songs and flights of fancy. Love was something ephemeral, ready to melt away at the first hint of storm.

We should not imagine that the women were without exception immoral. Domenico Martinelli, a writer who did not readily make excuses, defended them in the seventeenth century against the foreigners who 'talk as though there were nothing to choose between them; but, *per lo sangue di Diana*, they are not all alike'. The prudent women folk of the artisan and business classes were, it has been noted, unusually well behaved, and we hear of patrician ladies, too, who were models of virtue. Yet they must have been out of the ordinary for us to hear of them at all, and most were very dissolute indeed. Reaction against their former state, little better than that of harem women, made them eager profligates, impatient of the wiles and strategems of old-fashioned infidelity.

They put up the feeblest token resistance, in their new-found freedom, against the besieging hordes of would-be seducers. Mottoes of an encouraging nature, usually in French, were worked on their garters in letters of gold, and though they cried 'Hands off!' when anyone pinched them in a crowd, they had no objection to caresses of a less impetuous kind. Caterina Barbarigo summed up their attitude to love in her loaded farewell to the Abbé de Bernis on his departure from Venice: 'I shall be constant to you always, M. l'Ambassadeur, and never faithful.'

Others besides Caterina could have put it as neatly, for these ladies were quick-witted despite their scrappy convent education. Knowing nothing, they understood everything. Their letters might have been scrawled by kitchenmaids, but they could concoct delightful verse when they wanted to, apposite, with a wicked slant to it, tinged with melancholy and laced with childlike candour. Some were real scholars, such as Isabella Teotoki Albrizzi, who sat to Mme Vigée-Lebrun and has been compared to Mme Récamier; and she was not the only one. A young girl with brains had every opportunity to meet clever people and develop her gifts. Venetian society resembled that of contemporary France, an unpedantic school where many of the women were said 'to have learned all there is to know without any lessons at all'.

The wholesale moral unrestraint put marital faithfulness out of the picture. In patrician circles married couples compromised, each playing a suitable part when they met at christenings, burials or official entertainments, and otherwise leading separate lives. Should husband and wife by chance be thrown together at a gambling-hell or worse, they pretended they were strangers.

Nor did the guidance of a family serve to anchor them to hearth and home. Fathers never concerned themselves in any case, and mothers delegated their responsibility to servants. Apart from the regulation parade visit in full dress every morning, the children (who paraded in full dress from the day they could toddle round and defy the sumptuary laws in lace- and gold-trimmed jackets) never saw their parents.

But if his upbringing were thus neglected, a son nevertheless received a great deal of formal instruction. A boy's first governess taught him to read by the novel means of letters printed on playing-cards. At seven he was either given a tutor, usually a Jesuit priest, or sent to one of the ten schools in Venice run by that Order before its suppression in 1773. The Jesuits offered no more than a solid grounding in Latin and conventional subjects, but the secular clergy who succeeded them enlarged the curriculum, which by the end of the century included the study of practical economics. After school came university, and the young noble would also attend on some elderly senator who taught him politics, the art of public speaking and the right way to draw up memoranda. Often he accompanied one of the ambassadors abroad to learn something of courts and foreign customs.

All this was for likely candidates only. The youth who showed no taste for study was provided with a mistress when he was sixteen and, like his father before him, plunged at once into low life and concentrated on dressing exquisitely.

Educating a girl was very little trouble. Girls came out of the convent only for marriage, which was an arrangement with no love or feeling in it, and to launch without delay into the social whirl. Wedded bliss was hardly to be expected for two people who met for the first time at the signing of the contract; and it was rarely achieved, since complete independence was the rule for both. This at least meant that women were not driven to reason as did their sisters in Rome who, according to Pope Benedict XIV, had a startling theory that 'you have to get married, so you can enjoy the blessings of widowhood some day'.

But many of them sighed for greater freedom still, and since their husbands were often of the same mind divorce was frequent, and easy to obtain. All either party need do was to lay a petition before the Council of Ten. This was never rejected, though the woman had to retire to a convent until the hearing was over, supposedly seeing no one but her lawyer and her parents. Too rigid control, however, was not to be looked for in the convents of Venice.

The Patriarchal Curia heard no evidence, made no investigation and did not delay its verdict. It was enough that the defendant should not dispute the arguments of the other side, and no one enquired whether these were true or invented for the occasion, as generally they were. The couple could take their choice among fourteen canonical grounds for annulment and the most popular, even when children existed, was impotence. Impotence was extraordinarily adaptable. It might be *erga omnes* or it might strike only in one special set of circumstances – the result of antipathy occurring,

perhaps, after years of happy, fruitful union. It was thus a very ser-
viceable argument and could apply to almost anyone.

But if the parties disagreed about the case it went before the ecclesiastical authorities, who were by no means so speedy. Their courts
were said to be open to pressure and to lend an ear to false statement, lying oath and every sort of influence. Also, being, as Casanova once reported to the Council of Ten, inclined to look on marriage as a form of punishment, they were prone to annul it without
too close an examination of relevant facts. Yet they had to be used,
for divorce was no concern of civil justice. 'In so far as marriage is a
contract it is matter for the civil law; a civil court might fittingly
hear and judge proceedings for annulment and so check a scandal
that is an indelible stain upon the religion and honour of our city.'
This, too, is Casanova, who took a strong moral line on the question
in his secret agent days.

The barristers practising in the ecclesiastical courts were considered little better than the judges who presided there. They abused
the confidence of female clients, it was said, pushing them into
divorces whether they would or no, and giving up a case half-way
through, when all the available money had gone on free meals and
retainers; they were also charged with diverting the course of justice
by 'unlawful means'. Altogether, an examination of divorce petitions in the Venetian archives throws a cruel light on marriage in
those days – revealing documents from which Molmenti compiled
a list of plaintiffs' accusations. He found the 'unfortunate' wife
complaining of brutality, of forced marriage, the squandering of her
dowry and, of course, of impotence; or she might be seeking freedom
from her husband's creditors. A man most often cites the frivolous
habits of his wife as hindering his career, her extravagance, her
attempts to seize the family fortune, or desertion of his hearth and
home. Jealousy is seldom mentioned.

Weddings in Venice, even in noble families, were not the glamorous
occasions they were in other lands; the sumptuary laws had seen to
that. The girl would have come from her convent a few weeks or
days before. To give at least a loverlike gloss to the affair the young
man would walk by her window every morning, when she returned
a polite greeting. A large company of guests gathered in the largest
room of her father's house. In her silver brocade she entered with the
Master of Ceremonies, knelt for her parents' blessing, put her hand

in that of her betrothed and the priest married them. A modest
kiss was then exchanged and the party began.

Not a soul present, including the relations, ever for one moment
imagined that the union they witnessed was a matter of conscience
for the couple involved. Feelings did not enter into it. Age and taste
were very seldom matched. Getting married was something you did
to ensure that your name and property descended to the next generation, and bride and bridegroom were quite prepared to see it
like that from the outset. Lasting fidelity was a notion that never
occurred to them and if, as occasionally happened, a man married
a girl he was actually in love with, he did not often stay in love
for ever. It was best when the pair drifted apart very soon and went
their separate ways, without concern or hurt.

This parting was the signal for the entrance of a third person, the
cavaliere servente or *cicisbeo*, to balance the ménage. Cicisbeism had
come to Italy with the Spanish gentlemen attached to the Borgias.
It greatly flourished in Venice, where the atmosphere suited it
perfectly, though here the middle and lower orders did not always
adopt it, as they did elsewhere. A *cavaliere servente*, or sometimes
several *cavalieri*, was, or were, only for the woman of quality or the
rich burgher-wife. No lady's establishment could possibly be without one. His job, this modern Galahad, was to pay her every punctilious attention, surrounding her with forethought and little kind-
nesses; to advise her and see that neither she nor anyone else did
anything that might upset her; to fend off all annoyance, find her
things to do, and generally see the sun shone. He squired her in
public, gave her his hand at receptions and stood whispering in her
ear – the Italian for whisper is *bisbigliere*, a possible origin of the
word *cicisbeo*. There he was, a second self, from her rising in the
morning, a ceremony which he frequently attended, until she retired at night: moments of togetherness in which he rendered his
most delicate attentions, 'tying a ribbon or lacing a bodice, pulling
up a garter or smoothing the wrinkles from the top of her chemise'.
And who shall say whether these tempting liberties led no farther?
It is hard to believe that the poor man did no more than gratify the
lady's whims, festoon himself with fans and prayerbooks, lend her
money and tell her what to wear. He had every opportunity to be
alone with her, even at night, if only in a gondola; and the secluded
gondola was the lovers' sanctuary, ever inviolate. If he failed to
profit by it he was no true son of Venice.

One who entertained no doubts on the vexed question was the Président de Brosses, the ironical Burgundian magistrate. Observing the attendant gentlemen embracing their charges, with not a hair's breadth between them so far as he could see, he maintained, in his racy Gallic style, that they were 'ten times more married to them than their husbands were'. The English traveller Samuel Sharp, too, has some trenchant notes.[86] He took the view that most women marry for the sake of living with a *cavaliere servente*, an individual whose mere existence leads to degradation and debauch, with no husband sure of having fathered his own children. Life by the lagoon suggests to him unending Paphian rites and the worst excesses of Antiquity. Cicisbeism, one gathers, was nothing more or less than public concubinage.

And other visitors, with varying degrees of protest and sincerity, expressed their disapproval, arguing that straw and tinder could not fail to end in flame. They were all dismissed by the inhabitants as gross-natured persons, impervious to the charms of subtlety. For everyone in Venice agreed to agree that no *cicisbeo* looked for anything but friendship from his lady. *Cavaliere* meant *gentleman*; no husband was going to make a fool of himself by jealousy. And everyone in Venice furthermore enquired how, in such open and accepted liaisons, there could be anything to hide?

Lalande, the French traveller, believed that a *cavaliere servente* did more good than harm for female virtue, and the fact that he was often named in the marriage contract argued that *serventismo* was a wholesome institution: family and fiancé would hardly stand by and let a girl ensure herself a lover under their very eyes. The chosen *cicisbeo* was usually a steady sort of man, of the same age and rank as the husband – a relation, a friend in reduced circumstances, or someone likely to be useful in politics or generous with money. Whatever he was, he inspired trust and was confidently referred to as *amico della casa*. Some there may have been who betrayed this hopeful title, but many others played their rôle most honourably.

That they did so was perhaps due more to their chivalrous spirit and a sense of duty than to any great capacity for resistence on the part of the ladies. There are abundant tales of chaste denial, but how can we ever know what went on in the *casino*, the *felze* or the alcove? The remarks of the lawyer Giuseppe Antonio Costatini, who in 1794 published a work entitled *Critical, Jocose, Moral, Scientific and Learned Letters*, leave us none the wiser. Costatini was rather conceited, and fond of proclaiming how immoral cicisbeism was. 'Make me believe that donkeys fly, but you won't persuade me that hale and hearty people of opposite sexes can concentrate on one another like that, for years at a time, and never think of going any further.' When he himself became a *cavaliere servente* and was about to test his theory, he was, as it happened, foiled, though only (he says), because a maid arrived at the wrong moment. This is all as difficult to believe as it is to dismiss, and indeed no recital on the subject seems quite sincere or quite objective. We never get a clear statement.

At most, a few anecdotes in memoirs shed some light on the *cavaliere*'s zeal and on the support he might look for from a husband. Properly to do all that was expected of him he needed the attributes that Ugo Foscolo[87] once enumerated – those of a male model, an up-to-the-minute reader of fiction, a supplier of oddments and hair-dressing equipment, a finished master of the bow and the dance, cheerful payer-over of large gambling losses, encyclopedia of frivolities and man with nothing else to do. His daylong employment as auxiliary husband meant being in helpful attendance from the time the lady got up to the time she went to bed, and was no sinecure. His purse was at her command when her last penny went at the card-table, and he must be forearmed for every crisis with absolutely anything she might require. Mme du Boccage, for instance, who wished to do the right thing and had chosen a nice *cavaliere servente* for her stay in Venice, was out paying calls one day when she realised, to her horror, that she had forgotten the vital engraved visiting cards; but her efficient man at once produced some from his pocket and, when she marvelled at his splendid prevision, said it was 'part of the job'.

Often the *cicisbeo* ordered the meals, so that nothing was served in a lady's house that she would not enjoy. He also sat at her side, feeding her titbits by hand. It was he who controlled the staff. 'Who's supposed to make these people obey me and show some respect if it isn't you, I should like to know?' demands a wife in a play by Goldoni, rounding indignantly on her *cavaliere servente* when one of her husband's lackeys is rude.

As for the husband, he fell in with the whole ambiguous arrangement, which he had generally helped to organise and, at all events, upheld. At the slightest sign of of a quarrel between wife and *cicisbeo* he hastened to make peace. To him the latter complained if the lady seemed chilly, from him came every effort to return her to the prescribed path. It was sheer catastrophe for him if the other grew weary and left, for the *cavaliere* saw to all the minor tasks he neither could nor would perform in person, and with him went the domestic peace and quiet a Venetian husband prized. No married woman could expect from her lord the tender cherishing that kept her happy and, even had he wanted to, he could not have given it. People would have laughed. Only among those of low degree was such behaviour possible, and even they were not too eager. No upper-class couple would dream of showing affection in public and a man had to live up to the widely-held belief that husbands knew nothing about love. If he were seen to arrive with his wife at a reception or sit with her at the play, there would be murmurs about apron-strings; he would be shamed for ever. The artificial morality of Venice condemned all serious minded, settled types as dolts and simpletons, far inferior to those who pursued the course of gallantry in the gay world.

A man in any case had something more to do than domestic escort duty. He must fulfil the obligations of his birth, see to his business affairs and his own pleasures, and act as *cavaliere servente* at another address. He was accordingly delighted that a third party should lavish on his wife the care and attention he was himself bestowing on someone else's. 'Good heavens!' – Goldoni again, in a scene in which a lady's reputation has been attacked – 'how can it hurt her reputation to say Rodrigo serves her? I serve Donna Virginia, you serve my wife. Where's the harm in that?'

On greeting a gentleman one always asked after the lady he served and nobody's husband was silly enough to worry about bosom cordialities and semi-surrender when the loverlike relationship was so open and above-board. It was all too good of the *cavaliere*, his rewards were justly earned. And were the esteemed proxy detected in some glance or gesture that overstepped the bounds a little, nobody's husband would court ridicule by taking any notice. He would, in fact, be first to stand up for the *cicisbeo* if a rival threatened and the two of them made common cause against the intruder, though usually without success. The ladies of Venice were practised hands at avoiding the curtailment of liberty and neither husband nor serving gentleman was going to turn them from their dedicated, delicious career. Nor, of course, were the Inquisitors of State, who rarely intervened in such cases, though informers frequently suggested that they should. Details of one of these ludicrous problems come down to us in a report of Casanova, who was not unversed in tangles of the kind:

'The wife of Sanfermo, a woman of amorous disposition, who was brought up at the Mendicanti, is in love with the Noble Gentleman Minio. Her husband does not approve, wishing her to be escorted always by the Noble Gentleman Alvise Renier, son of Bernardino; and he, though she fails to appreciate him, is currently her attendant. The Noble Gentleman Renier is aware of her secret correspondence with the other man and joins in a chorus of lamentation with Sanfermo who, unable to make her obey him, considers he has a justifiable grievance against the Noble Gentleman Minio. The latter cannot resolve to leave the Noble Gentleman Renier and the husband in peace, for he loves the lady and is loved by her. The situation may well have serious repercussions and might repay Your Excellencies' wise consideration.'

Like so many others, the report went unheeded. The supreme court of Venice could not have got through the work had it embarked on this kind of thing. Women never did settle down. Proverbially, they were as hard to control as a bag of fleas. Their love was ardent and tender, but it was also giddy, unstable and impermanent. They were strangers equally to fatal passion and to high romance; anguish and ordinary decency were both unknown. They neither went mad for love nor did anything particularly horrifying and yet their intrigues, if they never sprang from ungovernable, blind lubricity, could be something more than a superficial game of hearts. But the deeper feelings were not for them a source of agony, existing as we have said, merely to bestow an extra grace and radiance.

Great ladies, and good society in general, were not alone in doing as they pleased in this indulgent atmosphere. Profligacy spread among the lower ranks as well, where money was, of course, more openly involved and proved an effective means of seduction. A rich man's casual presents made him a Croesus in the eyes of a woman of the people, and all sorts of arrangements were possible: somebody was always on hand to see to the details. A husband would see no harm in leaving his wife to finance the housekeeping by a discreetly conducted, convenient affair, and two more Venetian proverbs cast their gleam upon such cynical compliance. 'Horns are like teeth,' says one, 'the first lot hurt and after that you use them to eat with'; and the other, 'Better wear the brute's horns than take the brunt of the charge'.

To avoid these misfortunes the working man often remained single and changed his doxy as the fancy took him, while those, says Misson, 'who are not rich enough to keep a Miss for their own use, join with Two or Three Friends; and this plurality, which would in other places be insupportable, does in this place serve only to tie the Knot of Friendship firmer between Companions in the same Fortune'.

Also known among the lower classes was a form of concubinage that amounted to unofficial marriage, with the ceremony deferred until the man was on his deathbed. He would have promised to marry his woman then in order that their children might be legal heirs, and if he could, he did so. Whether he managed it or not, however, he had a most biddable consort in the meantime, for she was 'in daily fear of being turn'd off' and literally never sure of anything up to the last minute.

III COURTESANS

Finally, the huge army of courtesans. Venetian prostitutes were for centuries a European legend and many a traveller must have arrived privately determined to discover whether all one heard were true. This was the only city that regarded them as necessary and made things pleasant for them. Risen herself like Venus from the waves she was, it was generally agreed, quite right to show goodwill towards those who served the goddess.

Their special reputation went back to the days when the many-minded men of the Renaissance, all of them humanists more or less, felt the need for women who understood what they were talking about, or who gave the impression, at least, of doing so. Love, and transient love in particular, was to them a form of mental stimulus, with a deal of mind and learned discourse in it, and for generations their harlots had a bloom, a refinement of speech and temper, to suit this intellectual attitude. The beautiful clothes were carefully thought out, extravagance and taste went hand in hand. Educated, even erudite, *sages au parler* as Brantôme called them, these women led a life so very courtly that the word courtesan no longer applied to them and they were known instead as *donne del buon tempo*. Their profession was *l'onorato mestiere*, the honourable trade and, far from being disgraced, they were esteemed for following it. The patricians contended for their favours, they queened it at banquets and assemblies and even on public occasions it was usual to show them 'admiration and respect'. Mind equalled body in their catalogue of attractions, so that it cost as much to engage them in conversation as it did to bring that conversation to its logical end. Artists had to pay them more to take their clothes off and be painted than to take their clothes off.

They were still treated like queens in the seventeenth century, before the married women escaped from their secluded prison-life. The courtesans alone studied the arts of love, the government protected them against deception and unfair advantage and they could safely flout the sumptuary laws. They were possibly less well informed than their predecessors of a hundred years before, but they learned their wit and manners from men of breeding and the most gifted artists of their time.

But social custom changed and their monopoly slipped from them. When the *zentildonne*, too, became emancipated and plunged eagerly into the lists on equal terms, the hitherto privileged caste lost ground. Soon the noble or the great magistrate gained as much kudos from a mistress with the blood of Procurators in her veins as from any fashionable courtesan; and it was the patrician ladies, as they devoted themselves to love, who shed lustre upon Venice, because of them that she was acknowledged capital of sensual delights.

And yet, despite this relative falling-off, courtesans in the eighteenth century had all their accustomed charm and coaxing ways, their poise and their straightforward business sense. There is a song that tells how skilful and correct they were:

> *Sanno usar con gli amanti arte e drittura:*
> *Prodighe a quelli dan tutto il cuor loro*
> *E si tirano a se l'argento e l'oro*

> They'ld give you the whole of their hearts away,
> And nothing but silver and gold to pay.

And they were all truly admirable, says Charles de Brosses, in point of good behaviour; a fine body of women.

Prostitution, then, was still very much alive, but it had changed with the type engaged in it. The competition of aristocratic amateurs had put an end to the unchallenged reign of the great courtesan, and now only actresses and especially adept members of the sisterhood shone with anything like the old radiance. Most, it seems, were tarts at set prices. They were comely and willing, but that was all. Misson describes them, like tulips in their gowns of red and yellow, bosoms half-naked, 'their Faces painted a Foot deep, and always a Nosegay above their Ears', standing in groups outside their houses or leaning from the windows, each with a bare arm trailing over the sill.

They were to be seen thus, however, only in the special streets where they were supposed to stay, far from the centre of Venice. There was no hint of bias or ostracism in this, merely of consideration for those who wished to avoid contact. The law safeguarded liberty, even to the libertine, but it wished to preserve order, and only if you caused no public scandal could you do as you liked. The girls obeyed such excellent regulations just so far as these proved professionally helpful, living cheerfully in the designated streets because people could find them there, but emerging as and when they chose. They made church-doors the most notorious spots in the whole town and gathered after dark round the twinkling vigil-lights of the street Madonnas. They mingled freely with the Carnival crowds and there were many inns where they were always at home, and the enthusiastic customer could make a night of it, from hostelry to hostelry. Only respectable women appear to have taken any notice of the order of 1776 about keeping out of coffee-houses; the rest, relieved of so much competition, rushed in to pick up clients on the forbidden ground. 'Prostitutes are there in plenty,' reports a secret agent, 'some masked, some in gowns and *zendalî*. They are going in all the time, coming out with one man or another, and off to a nearby courtyard or into the alleyways round the Ridotto.'

The pimps for whom these girls worked had the expressive nickname of *mangiamarroni*, or chestnut-eaters – chestnuts, be it understood, that others pulled out of the fire. A low lot, though they thought themselves despised unjustly. 'Our offence,' so one of them maintained, 'is no more than to live with our mistresses and not to be jealous of friends who happen to find them attractive and who enjoy their favours with our blessing.' Some of the pandars, however, acted as subordinates to the overlords of the trade and these secret bosses, as they would be called today, were persons of substance and repute. Police reports name important bankers like Giuseppe Berganti as being involved.

Lalande says that prostitutes catered only for the dregs of the population, adding that monks and priests were independent of them. (He rests this bald and thought-provoking statement solely on the case of a Lenten preacher who felt obliged to import a wench of his own for the visit to Venice.) Montesquieu says the whores were 'mercenary enough to discourage the most resolute', and not very beautiful, what was more; though it seems he never met the cream of the calling. But there were in fact girls to suit all tastes, with an army of go-betweens to help the customer make up his mind. By 1750 there were so many pandars in the field that the government was driven to arrest over 500 of them, and their enterprise was altogether notable. Stepping outside normal professional bounds, they undertook negotiations with women of the middle class and decent workmen's wives; it was not unknown for them to put his own wife's name before an enquiring husband. By and large, it was better to rely on the gondoliers, who charged less and made more trustworthy arrangements.

Not all the daughters of the game had come to it out of depravity or spinelessness. The working classes were always in the market to sell a pretty girl to some rich family needing a good, safe mistress for a son of the right age. Friends and neighbours called with congratulations on such a bargain as though for a proper wedding and it was a careful mother's duty to find a protector for her daughter. One writer says that nine out of ten harlots had been pushed into keeping by their mothers, and Misson mentions the remarkable sight of a woman bartering her child away by the month or year for a certain sum and vowing 'by God and upon her Salvation' that she could not let her go for less. In 1781 the mother of a dancer, finding the girl was hanging fire, put her in a lottery, tickets a sequin each, virginity guaranteed. Often, if no better prospect offered, parents urged a spell on the streets with the laudable aim of earning a dowry to ensure an honest marriage. This explains why there were so many short-term prostitutes, and why so many had an aura of decency and rectitude.

When Jean-Jacques Rousseau was in Venice in 1743 he was extremely anxious not to appear *troppo coglione*, too foolish, and, having decided that this was 'no place to keep away from loose women', paid regular visits to two of them, both personable, entertaining and, in their own way, sensible. One was the lovely Zulietta, whom he considered a masterwork of Nature, 'as good and generous as she is kind and beautiful'. But she found him a less than fiery lover and sent him off with the sarcastic advice to leave the girls alone and concentrate on mathematics. The philosopher, 'at the same time frozen and transported', had prefaced his inept perfor- mance with an unconscionably long and thorough-paced harangue on that favourite theme of French Romantics after him, the mystical reverence due to the fallen woman. This was a shock and a sur- prise to poor Zulietta, who was only twenty, with less exalted notions of her honour; and in a bower of bliss like Venice his lack of abandon was certainly most unusual.

Beyond, and ranking, as it were, above the common street-girls was another category of courtesans who cultivated no obvious wiles and were scarcely to be told from ordinary women of the middle class. Zulietta must have been one of these, her appearance giving little clue to what she was. Once the *zendaletto* became the general wear, the harlot was no longer distinguishable and, as we know, Angiolo Tamiazzo said in 1774 that all *persone divote* thought it scandalous. And doubtless some were scandalised, on moral grounds, but it would indeed be interesting to know how many were more truly indignant at having made a bad mistake: it must have been inglorious to a degree to think you had seduced a canty little house- wife and find yourself entangled with a clever professional. But it was by now impossible to divine exactly who was what and the shrewdest were as easily deceived as anybody else. Not even French ambassadors could trust their own eyes, as witness this recital of one of the *confidenti*:

'There is, too, a courtesan named Zanetta, living in the Calle delle Post at Rialto, and she, I learned, is panic-stricken about the French ambassador[88] who had paid her to take him, at six or seven in the evening, to the public gardens, to the end where the best-dressed and most contriving of the prostitutes are found. She didn't say who he was, just a gentleman from Germany, and they took him for an all-night ride in a gondola to a part of Venice, she said, where they would not be recognised. The purpose of the expedition, however, had been beyond mistake – Zanetta got five lire in every sequin earned. And she told him that one was a Venetian lady, another a shopkeeper's daughter, a third a citi- zen's wife – in short that all of them came from good and well- conducted families.'

Nor was this the limit of dissembling, for courtesans would

pass themselves off as ladies of the highest birth and breeding. Their houses were beautifully appointed, their managers unprincipled, and whores whom anyone could buy were introduced to rich foreigners under patronymics lifted from the Golden Book. Sebastiano Poli was one such manager, a notorious pimp, says the spy who shadowed him, organising a kind of seraglio of prostitutes in the palace of an affluent Englishman and telling him they were all persons of fashion. A woman using a great name and noted for the crowded receptions she gave was found, when the agent Andrioli got into one of them, to be conducting a public brothel among the refined conversation. And prices matched pretensions. The same agent told how a Dalmatian named Giorgio Bradamonte, tendering four ducats to the same pseudo-patrician, was haughtily informed that it was 'far too little to pay for a lady'. Touting grew so blatant that no man of prosperous appearance could take five steps in the Piazza without being offered a rendezvous with Lady This or Lady That – wives of Procuratori and *cavalieri* – and getting a common harlot if he fell into the trap. Here again a husband might easily hear the name of his own wife used by a tart to justify the price she asked.

All the top members of the profession, too, played a game of assumed respectability. It increased the profits and they played it very well. On the score that 'it was best to get to know people first', nothing was to be had of them until a second meeting, which meant, as Brosses noted bitterly, that you paid them twice for one working session. Those who sought a really choice clientèle went to enormous trouble to seem other than they were, living at palatial addresses, wearing the clothes patrician women wore, walking about with two pages in front of them and a *postiglione* behind. The negotiations of the Président de Brosses with one of their number demonstrate the skill and coolness with which they conducted their affairs.

'I sent my gondolier yesterday to fix things up with the famous Bagatina, but when I went to her house at the appointed time she was not in. The maid told me she had gone out with a female friend to the *conversazione* of Signore Someone-or-other, left her excuses and would I come back tomorrow? While this tale was going on I inspected the huge, magnificent apartment, decorated I thought, in a style far and away above the lady's station. I accordingly asked the girl whether my man had not come on my behalf to see La Bagatina? Oh, yes, he had been there, certainly, but her mistress was not La Bagatina; her name was Abbati Marcheze, and she was the wife of a Venetian nobleman.

' "But what in the world did your mistress think I was here for, then?" I enquired.

' "She thought you must have a letter of introduction. You can leave it with me, Signore, or come again tomorrow, just as you prefer."

'At this point I had the gondolier up. He stuck to his version, she to hers. She called him a rogue and a thief and I was ushered out with many curtseys, undecided as to whether to call next day and see what in fact was going on. In the end, I determined to risk it. So today I went back, and there was a big, nicely-rounded woman of thirty-five or so, with a ladylike air. Carried herself well, superbly dressed and dripping with jewellery. She advanced, looking grave and asked what I wanted. I knew what I wanted all right, the only trouble was how to phrase it. I delivered some unintelligible compliment in my usual dreadful Italian. After a moment she realised the cause of my hesitation and very sensibly resolved it by shedding her false name and her false propriety together. She even seemed somewhat surprised at what I paid her, but how could one press too paltry an offering into a hand that glittered with diamonds?'

It was partly the fault of the ladies of Venice if native and foreigner were so easily deluded, for many were silly or shameless enough to dress and behave in a way that left little to choose between them and the trollops who imitated them; the fact is evident in one of the innumerable decrees published by the Senate in its never-accomplished hope of sorting them out again. Some, moreover, practised the profession themselves, and with such scanty concealment that spies denounced them to the Ten, commenting how deplorable it was 'that a foreigner can go home and boast he has had a Venetian lady for money'. Angiolo Tamiazzo, keen as ever on July 20, 1776, found a noble woman roaming the streets at night, 'looking for someone to go home with'. Others, such as Cecilia Minio, reported by one of his colleagues in October three years later, lured men into deserted *calli* for 'dishonest purposes'. These may have been extreme examples, but yet another informer might well have been thinking of a whole monstrous regiment when he rather consequentially announced that the supreme authority would, if fully appraised, 'take steps to regulate their scandalous goings-on'. Maria Querini Benzon comes at once to mind, the renowned beauty whom Longhi painted, whose conversation Stendhal admired and who, with all the gifts and charms a woman ever had, made no bones about the fact they were for sale.[89]

But whatever their moral standards, some of the courtesans were blessed with real wit and others with irreproachable middle-class convictions. Obviously their particular contribution to the Revel of the Earth was not exactly an improving one, but it was part and parcel of the attraction, an essential ingredient in the magic. The Serenissima, therefore, never failed to protect them. In the sight of her law they were always a special case and because of her kindness Venice was an Eden for them, a precinct, it has been said, 'where neither those who bit the apple nor those who proffered it need suffer pangs of conscience'.

Giacomo Casanova de
Seingalt

13   Ceiling of the Camera dei
Pagliacci (Villa Tiepolo),
painted by Tiepolo

14 Venetian woman wearing the *zendale*

CHAPTER FIVE

RELIGION

I 'VENETIANS FIRST AND CHRISTIANS AFTERWARDS'

There was no town in the peninsula where religion bore less on public or on private life than Venice, crowded with resplendent churches though it was. People reared in the pursuit of pleasure were unlikely, in the nature of things, to tend to any very pronounced spirituality and Venetians looked no farther than their present hour. Taine was to compare them aptly to the inhabitants of declining Thebes, 'who clubbed together to feast away their fortunes, each in turn leaving the survivors the remnants of his share'. Relations between church and state were, moreover, managed in such a way that the priesthood, so powerful in the kingdoms and dukedoms of Italy and paramount in Papal territory, was here severely limited.

Not that the Serenissima was hostile to religion. On the contrary, she saw her rôle as that of a Christian rampart, steadfast against the infidel. Her censorship. if no very fierce guardian of orthodoxy, discouraged subversion and weeded out anti-religious writing. But one could not blink the fact that, while upholding the doctrines of the church, she never allowed the clergy to poach beyond the due limits of the spiritual domain.

This meant in practice that priests and monks might shepherd their flocks as they chose but that their freedom was limited, like that of other citizens, by a jealous government that clung to the ancient maxim of *prima di tutto Veneziani, poi Christiani*. To preserve the state was the prime consideration and the church submitted to a degree of control unthinkable elsewhere. The Republic laid claim to a quasi-religious character itself and the part played by the Doge in the great ceremonies was almost that of a priest. Every feast of the church was combined with some political celebration, and it was no coincidence that the Wedding of the Adriatic took place on Ascension Day. Over the years the state in its piety had sought for holy relics and sacrificed much to acquire them, but the rejoicing that greeted their discovery had always been official, the affair not of prelates but of the lords of the Republic. Relics still received their official veneration from the Doge.

In every particular the *Dominante* maintained this supremacy. The church was protected, but under eagle-eyed supervision, and kept out of politics, so there was evolved a whole body of law and precedent aimed at the subordination of the hierarchy. Patriarch and bishops were appointed by the Senate, whose choice was merely confirmed by the Roman Curia, and ring and crozier bestowed by a Venetian dignitary. Parish priests, deacons and sub-deacons were elected, like beadles, by the parish. No ecclesiastic, even of noble birth, might hold public office, and his misdoings were judged and punished by the civil courts along with those of ordinary folk; the ecclesiastical courts were confined to strictly religious matters and had little to do with laymen save in annulment cases. The Inquisition, too, existed in Venice as elsewhere, but its claws were pared and it was practically ineffective. 'It might not have been there at all,' said Charles de Brosses. Its court had to meet in the presence of three members of the government, one of whom would rise and walk out the moment any Venetian citizen was mentioned, thereby making it impossible to proceed to judge-ment. The state also kept a firm hand on the finances of the church, whose books were closely examined and which might receive only the interest on legacies and gifts, and that for a limited period. If there were any question of tax-relief, nothing she had previously owned was every allowed to qualify. She might neither build nor restore without first obtaining permission, though in practice this was always granted, so long as no subscriptions were required.

Being so determined to brook no interference, the Republic, though never querying the Pope's authority, was at perpetual odds with the Holy See for one reason or another. Some of these differences had taken a serious turn in the past and Venice had lain under Papal interdict five times. Always her response was vigorous – convents closed, religious festivals wiped from the calendar, the publication of any communication from Rome, interdict included, forbidden in her territories. By the eighteenth century both sides had relinquished such dramatic gestures, but their late-learned discretion did not yet preclude the waging of cold war. A Venetian had only to obtain some job or benefice from the Vatican to lose all right to a share in the government at home, along with any office he might happen to hold.

Since written attack on the Papal court was tolerated, not to say welcomed, in Venice, the Curia naturally returned the compliment. No ambassador sent to Rome from the Serenissima was ever made a cardinal, and there was marked reluctance to admit any Venetian to the Sacred College, whatever his merits. They could not all be kept out, however, and there was a Rezzonico cardinal who became Pope as Clement XIII in 1758, when his countrymen remarked, 'It's a long time since we had any hats, but at last we've got the man who makes them.' Clement was mindful of his origins and, though the basic political doctrines of the Republic went unmodified, relations with Rome improved during the eleven years of his reign.

One method by which Venice discouraged possible infringements was by regulating recruitment into the church in such a way that no ecclesiastical proletariat arose. No one, for instance, might become a secular priest who did not possess a minimum amount of money; without it he had to content himself with being a monk. And she gave her secular clergy privileges far beyond those normally countenanced by Rome. The least of them could go about like bishops in purple stockings, or like cardinals in sashes of scarlet. But they were kept rigidly within the bounds of their profession and it was noted that 'churchmen have no chance of intrigue here'. Not even the secrets and private opinions they learned in the course of domestic visiting could profit them at all. As Count Giuseppe Gorani[90] points out, one of the advantages of Venice in his time was that government spies knew so much anyway that you had nothing to fear from what other enquirers might unearth.

The private life of the clergy could detain us for hours if all the contemporary gossip and journalism were to be trusted, but it is well to take the scandal with a grain of salt, remembering that there were in Venice monks devoted to austerity, strict theologians and priests true to the purest evangelical spirit of their charge. No category of Venetians, however hedged about with moral law, was likely, on the other hand, entirely to escape the tempting activity going on so merrily all around them in that pleasure-seeking atmosphere; and so it followed that monks might be corrupt, *abati* worldly-minded. Chaplains and confessors did indeed instigate, and often take full advantage of, shocking laxity in convents where so many nuns were such reluctant inmates. Rumour is sufficiently confirmed by the unattended senatorial decrees that priests of canonical age are alone eligible to serve as convent chaplains.

But if some priests gave the secret agents plenty of material because of dissipation, others caused alarm by their intemperate zeal. Pulpit-thunder against sinful ways not only made the hearers blench, it disquieted the Council of Ten, quick to construe such speeches as insult to the government. The holy men were blamed, too, for being over-peremptory in their demands for alms. A spy once reported a priest named Lorenzi as having prayed, 'Oh, Lord, make all those here this morning give all the money they are carrying', and that his congregation, duly bludgeoned by this stern petition, emerged from their devotions without a ducat between them. But then, all sermons ended on the note of patriotic appeal – You, too, will be aiding our Republic – that no Venetian could resist.

The parishes were known each by the name of the titular saint of the parish church and each, whatever its social level, had a character of its own, to be fostered if good and improved when otherwise. That of San Samuele, for instance, was distinctly otherwise, a painful reputation summed up in withering popular verse:

> Contrada piccola, grande bordel;
> Senza ponti, cattive campane,
> Omini becchi e donne putane.

> Small as it is, San Samuele
>   Is one great brothel behind the doors;
> Canals unbridged and the bells all jangled,
>   The men all cuckolds and the women whores.

This is the church where Casanova was baptised, later receiving the tonsure and the four minor orders here; and though the bells may have been tuneless their tower remains, a charming specimen of an old Venetian campanile.

Save for San Marco and one or two more, all the churches of Venice in the eighteenth century were, or seemed to be, spanking new. Most were, of course, very old,[91] but they were newly brimming with the turmoil and show and amplitude of the baroque. The frantic striving for theatrical effect had furnished them with barley-sugar columns and bright, coloured stucco-work; their ceilings shone like very heaven, while below consorted the droves of gilded figures, voluptuous angel-forms and bouncing *amorini*. Many churches came to resemble ballrooms and often the Madonna seemed to be standing in a boudoir rather than a chapel; and if this does not suit all tastes, there are nevertheless some lovely things to see. The rose and azure frescoes overhead may be by Tiepolo or his first teacher, Lazzarini; the walls glow with canvases by Veronese, Titian or Tintoretto. Every oratory is a museum fit for a king and a surplus of wonderful pictures hangs in every sacristy. San Sebastiano springs at once to mind, the church that is both a Veronese exhibition and the artist's burial-place.[92]

Whatever one thinks about baroque art, it must be admitted that it is marvellously right for Venice. It suited the climate and the way of life and went beautifully with the church music – that playhouse music that the Goncourts said might have been conducted by the wand of Harlequin. The melodies were often quite unsacred, but in those gala surroundings there seemed nothing odd in worshipping one's Maker to the strains of a gavotte. There was at this period some holy or historical celebration almost every day, when a five-hour Mass was interspersed with musical fantasias repeated again and again after lengthy lead-in passages. As many as four hundred instrumentalists might be required, divided into several orchestras. Six such bands were mustered on occasion in San Marco, and always the congregation listened devoutly as they played.

But there were other times when all was chaos, in spite of the notices reminding people of how to behave in church. (And unbelievable some of them are. One in the Salute read, 'In honour of God and His holy nature, please do not spit on the floor!' Or the faithful might be urged to put nothing but coin in the collection, for the preacher went round with it himself and love-letters were apt to turn up among the ducats and sequins if he were a handsome man with an attractive voice.) All the abundant evidence we have appears to indicate that nobody bothered much. Competition was active for the best places, so that outcries and clamour over the seating arrangements frequently drowned the buzz of private conversation. Friend hailed friend across the benches. There was no keeping still, or any regard for the fact that this was a house of God with a service going on. Only at the elevation of the Host all present dropped to their knees in an access of devotion. A deep and sudden silence fell and the greatest sceptics were then as quick as anyone to admonish those who failed to comply. Lalande tells of an English peer who remained on his feet and how a Venetian senator protested at once at this indecent singularity.

'But I don't believe in transubstantiation,' says the Englishman, only there for the sightseeing.

'Oh, neither do I, for heaven's sake,' is the reply, 'but you get down on the floor like me or take yourself outside.' As soon as the moment was over the rumpus surged rudely back, the quizzing of ladies, and even romping with dogs, proceeding as before.

Much is to be learned from the Inquisitorial spies about 'scandalous assembly' in the churches. On June 28, 1771, we read, 'the church of San Salvatore is being defiled by the mixed crowds of women who go there, not to hear Mass, but to be seen and be accosted. Godfearing persons frequently remark that this church has turned into a brothel.' (So perhaps Casanova's parish was not the only one in a terrible mess.) In cases of flagrant irreverence the *confidenti* did not hesitate to name names, often citing nobles and even priests, and in their ardour occasionally denounced the police for joining in the outrages they were supposed to be stamping out. This kind of thing, says the spy Pasini, went on inside St Mark's where 'the *sbirri* of Missiir Grande and the Vizio himself [his assistant chief of police] lurk in quiet corners and talk to the dissolute women. I feel in duty bound to call the attention of Your Excellencies to the complaints of the pious, who are rightly horrified; and with great respect I kiss Your revered robes.'

Certainly many Venetians went to church out of habit, or to see the show, or because it was a promising social opportunity; but just as certainly most were there to catch their glimpse of eternal bliss, their foretaste of the paradise to come. They were not, it was understood, too eager to hear about repentance. Lent was not a season of mortification with them and Goldoni reports them as sitting down to 'every fish that Garda or the Adriatic could produce'. And yet it would be wrong to say they knew no true devotion. In the midst of sensuality and debauch, wrote the Baron de Pöllnitz,[93] 'God is as perfectly served as He is anywhere else.' It was, however, the highly idiosyncratic service of people as little given to the immaterial as they could possibly be, for whom a spiritualised religion would, almost literally, have lacked sufficient body. 'They have to touch and see and feel their faith,' a priest of Venice told Dupaty.[94] 'so naturally superstition enters into it.'

This was the need that lay behind their cult of relics and their passion for the saints, with St Mark, as was to be expected, coming first. Venetians relied on his protection, considering it fair exchange for the fine church they had built him, but did not pester him with run-of-the-mill petitions. He was kept in reserve for more important things, having his hands quite full enough in any case, and lesser saints would do as well. Of these there was a large crowd already and more could always be invented, from hindsight and hearsay, and bolstered up with dubious relics of one sort or another; a number of churches dedicated to people who had never been canonised at all ranked among the peculiarities of Venice. Care was taken to bring before a saint only such problems as he was really qualified to solve, and to present them in due and proper form, while worshippers would haggle and barter with heaven rather as the Sicilians do, who roundly curse the holy ones if the looked-for miracles are denied.

But always the chief popular devotion went to Mary the Mother of God, greatest of the powers above. Every shop had its small shrine for the Madonna; at every street-corner, at the approach to every bridge, there was the Virgin in her lace trimmings and necklace of glass beads, and often when the lamp or candle was lit at dusk a group would stand around her praying. The most poignant of these Madonnas were out in the lagoon, hung on the guiding-stakes that marked the channels, in pious and fitting homage among the waters to the guardian Star of the Sea.

This reverence for saint and Virgin had, however, remarkably little influence on the Venetian in his normal, day-to-day career. For him obedience to Holy Church and her requirements abolished the terrors of the Last Judgement. His priest was ever-ready to absolve all sins. What was the point, therefore, in letting fear or scruple come between him and his inclinations? Without a cloud on his conscience a man confessed to having a mistress, rose from his knees and went to visit her. (In exactly the same way, she would have been confessing about him.) The whore, lighting her Saturday candle to the Madonna, considered herself thoroughly purified.

Lightheartedly, then, the children of Venice embraced the delights of life with their eyes shut and never a care for the final reckoning. Invocation of the saints, frequent confession and regular attendance at Mass would, they were persuaded, see them through. They knelt at the Angelus bell, for good measure, and crossed themselves a great deal, and having taken these precautions thought and acted as though this transitory world, like those famous provisional arrangements, would go on and on for ever.

II THE CONVENTS

Though some Venetian girls might experience true religious vocation, they rarely came from noble families. There it was family decision alone that sent one or more unmarried daughters to the convent, and they went because of the unwritten law entitling the eldest-born to first consideration. Ethical or worldly advantage weighed more in the nun-making than any thought of saving money, for a well-born novice would enjoy a whole preliminary series of balls and banquets, setting at naught the sumptuary laws in her splendid attire, while her parents spent the equivalent of a handsome dowry on music, food and fine wax candles.

There would still be a dowry to pay, of course. The delle Vergini convent, under ducal patronage and reserved for ladies of the highest patrician rank, demanded a very large one, and other aristocratic establishments were not far behind. Contemporary records show over three million ducats going this way in the second half of the century. Nor did family responsibility end there, since a young nun needed a suitable allowance for pocket-money and maintenance, and something with which to soften the convent rules and make her life agreeable.

For it was the lack of restriction that sent girls into religion unprotesting. The old saying still held good that women entered the cloister to escape the stringency at home. They went, if not by force, at least by force of convention, without vocation, and certainly never intended to bid farewell to the lenient uses of the outside world. No sackcloth and ashes for them, no fasting.

The question of what to wear they settled, in each Order, by free adaptation. Elegant short gowns showed a flash of ankle and were flatteringly cut. No actress displayed more bosom than a nun in her silk-embroidered bodice. She was perfectly bewitching, with the delicate white veil coming to a point on her forehead and the flowers at her breast, and very much appreciated; and her version of the religious habit helped, there was no doubt, to advance her popularity. The nuns, wrote René Guerdan, had the devil's own beauty, if they lacked the beauty of holiness.

Nuns they might be, but they were still women of their world who kept up with the gossip of the town, its details and its tittle-tattle. To the convent parlours came social butterflies with time to kill, and ardent young men, and nowhere, even in the most outspoken circles, would they exchange more racy talk. Admirers might import an orchestra for a ball, there were dinner parties, masquerades and concert-giving. In some nunneries *bassetto* was played with great enthusiasm. Pietro Longhi's famous picture in the Correr Museum of visiting-day at San Zaccaria perfectly catches the atmosphere. It is that of a fashionable salon, which is what a convent parlour was, with the nuns for ornament and attraction.

They were all amiability and pretty wit and elegance, qualities to which the serious minded succumbed as readily as did gentlemen on pleasure bent. The convents harboured the most brilliant coteries of the time and every visitor of note would hope to be invited. In them was forged what a modern historian has called a magic chain, 'so long, so firm and so far-reaching as to embrace everyone from governing magistrate to commoner, and no one could get on without it'. Weighty conversation was heard in convent parlours, quarrels were smoothed over there and favours and employments handed out, but they were also exhilarating centres of pastime, banter and ultra-civilised exchange, and everything else to make them what they are credibly said to have been: enchanting.

Religious houses, then, especially those for noble ladies, were never short of amusing occupation, and if the pious refuge tended to become a place of entertainment, a similar state of things was not unknown in other lands. Venice merely produced a more graceful variation, with prettier nuns, so it was claimed, and better music. There was, however, the greater and more damaging difference that here licence spread outwards from the convent to give scandal in the town, instead of the other way round. Any nun could count on four or five lay sisters to help in her escapades, and confessors, too, might lend a hand. The Ten were forced to remove the *abate* Galogero from the convent of Santa Clara in 1758 for having issued everybody with duplicate keys. With or without keys – and lay sisters could always think of something – the young ladies got out whenever they liked, frequented balls and gambling-dens and were up to their necks in mischief. When Carnival came round their lovers collected them in gondolas and, donning masks, they passed the evening merrily and stayed abroad until the small hours if they were so disposed. Cicisbeism, too, had invaded the precincts; any presentable nun, we hear, had her *cavaliere servente*. Occasionally the inevitable happened – the pregnant nun, the secret birth, the rumour passed off as 'calumny'. That this licentiousness was an accepted thing is apparent from a casual aside of the Président de Brosses, who says the first people he would think of would be the *religieuses* were he making a long stay in Venice.

Of course, not all the nunneries stand convicted. If half of them blandly closed their eyes to what was going on, there were at least sixteen or eighteen enclaves of sanctity properly managed. Nevertheless, and without taking too literally what Casanova has to say, there are other contemporaries whom we must believe. These, even when they are not trying to blacken the picture, tell us a good deal about the general laxity[95] and government spies corroborate their evidence. Swamped with secret information, the Council of Ten threatened with prison, and even death, the unduly lenient chaplain, the too-kindly abbess and over-spirited nun. As ever, its decrees accomplished nothing, and when it tried to enforce them its agents were received with showers of stones. Once in the sixteenth century the nuns of Santa Caterina retreated before them to the bell-tower, rang the alarm and terrified the town, and such resistance had the support of the most influential nobles: sedate and important figures who very often had their own reasons for wishing to keep things as they were, and showed small scruple in taking advantage of the situation.

In face of mutiny and undercurrent the Ten gave up the struggle and acted only in cases it could not ignore; and even these it handled with a sort of disillusioned mildness, with remonstrances that intimidated no one. Tamely it required Mothers Superior to 'see to the behaviour of their charges', and its hollow reproofs had so little effect that when a new Papal representative arrived in 1739 more than one abbess entered her candidate for the post of Nuncio's Mistress.

Several times we hear of a French ambassador mixed up in convent scandal. Casanova is our sole authority for the tale of the Abbé de Bernis and the nun of San Giacomo, but he is unlikely to have made the whole thing up; and whatever the truth of that affair, there are papers to prove the intrigue of the Marquis de Froulay with the lovely patrician Maria da Riva, an unwillingly-professed nun at San Lorenzo. M. de Froulay had met her in the convent parlour and fallen madly in love with her, as she with him, and they made their liaison so obvious that the Inquisitori tried to stop it be means to which Froulay took exception. He complained to his government. Sharp notes were exchanged between Paris and the Serenissima and the Ten, refusing to heed the French Chancellor and Foreign Minister, ordered the removal of Maria da Riva to a convent in Ferrara, from which she later eloped with a colonel. This colonel she married and, according to Casanova, spent the rest of her days in Parma, scorned by all. As for the Marquis de Froulay, he died, heartbroken at the separation and the wreck of his career. At Venice they said he was out of his mind. A little setback in a little love affair? In that irresponsible city madness was the only explanation that occurred to them for taking the thing so seriously.

CHAPTER SIX

ARTISTIC AND INTELLECTUAL LIFE

I THE ATHENS OF ITALY

Although Venice, unlike Florence, produced no Dante or Machiavelli of her own, her intellectual life was never stagnant. The soil was not one in which great works could flourish easily, with politics forbidden and the ban of silence applied by extension to any sphere in which the government might like to intervene, but her best minds were active and awake. The Masque of Italy bade fair to be the Athens, too.

An enormous output of published material testifies to her interests in the eighteenth century; she was a town of printers, booksellers and journalists. More books were printed here than in any other Italian centre and in much larger editions, so that they cost less and more people read them. The price of publishing was half what it was in Paris and the finished book a handsomer article. Two licences were required, one by which binding, paper and printing standards were regulated, one to guarantee the contents as inoffensive to church and state; and since, as far as the church was concerned, the state was notoriously casual much was condemned in Rome might be approved in Venice. All in all, readers were able to enjoy the work of over two hundred authors in the fifty years before the fall of the Republic.

There were also many translations, especially from the French. Enterprising printers, among whom Albrizzi and Pitteri were the most important, had all the major French books on their lists. The whole of Montesquieu and Voltaire and most of Maupertius and Helvétius were either published in Italian or reissued in French, as was the Encyclopedia itself. Venice could even print, with the leave and encouragement of authority, books that were never openly on sale in Paris, for the Riformatori degli Studi di Padova, the University commissioners who did the censoring for the Council of Ten, never functioned as fanatical wardens of public opinion. With only one of the *philosophes* would Venice have no truck, and that was Jean-Jacques Rousseau, for he had left few agreeable memories behind and had since castigated the laws of the Serenissima as 'framed for wicked men'. This unfriendly criticism aroused marked hostility in the State Inquisitors, as did all the other pernicious sentiments with which they found his writings 'brimming over'. His books were widely read in Venice notwithstanding, together with most others that failed to obtain a licence. There was a large and thriving black market about which Casanova used to relay reports, and prohibition was sidestepped so easily that everyone had access to forbidden works.

Bookshops, numerous as they were, were not the only places that sold books. The trays and stalls were full of them, and they were peddled in every street and campo by vendors who accosted all solitary strollers with their fanciful patter: the devotional volume they pressed upon the grave and godly man was most probably an essay on witchcraft in a deceptive binding, and the hopeful seeker after sensation got something heavy and historical instead of the dirty book that all the whispering had led him to expect.

But the taste for intellectual fare was widespread in Venice and serious literature sold well. It was a liking acquired in the colleges and seminaries run by the church – the largest of which, at Santa Maria della Salute, had Casanova for a pupil – where the teaching was excellent and there were stiff examinations to be passed at the various stages leading to the University. Padua itself was a breeding-ground for intellectuals and it meant something to have been there. The young man introduced as, 'from Padua, where he was a student', could count on approval and esteem. Padua University (known as Il Bo from an old inn of that name, the Ox, whose site it partly occupied) was treated with much consideration by the Most Serene Republic, which for its sake had forgone the right, bestowed by Pope Paul II in 1465, to found a University at home. It was not the only source of higher education, for there were colleges in Venice, including one established by the Procuranza, but these were restricted to one or two faculties, whereas Il Bo comprised all the recognised disciplines – natural science, physics, medicine, philosophy, grammar, theology and law. Casanova, who would rather have read medicine, was a turbulent law-student at Padua.

He was not alone in taking advantage of the freedom there allowed.

The students' disorderly behaviour must have been the real reason that the Signory kept them away from Venice herself. They had the most extravagant rights and privileges, even a sort of diplomatic immunity which encouraged their lawlessness and which they would go to the most violent lengths to maintain and extend. Affray and actual rioting were nothing out of the ordinary and Casanova remembers armed bands of students once killing several *sbirri*, driving off the rest and taking over the town. They were never punished – the University might have found its numbers declining – and authority in Venice passed its innocuous, unregarded measures 'for the regulation of student-promotion and examinations'.

The amorous propensities of the young gentlemen caused upheavals of another kind. No trim and pretty woman under middle age was ever safe from them, and Goldoni says that Padua looked upon its student population as it would upon garrison officers – 'the men abhorred them and the women made them welcome'. The culprits had ample leisure, too, with no compulsory lectures to attend, and here again Goldoni sets the scene: 'we took a distant view of the University and went to ground in the most hospitable houses we could find'.

In spite of all, however, a solid and extensive education was available for those who were willing to work. Professors were well paid, and distinguished men were glad to teach at Padua, where they could split the very high examination fees, always disguised as advance payment but in practice never refunded. 'It is like the theatre,' Goldoni explains, 'no money back after the rise of the curtain.'

Five years at Padua and the youth, having sowed his wild oats and gained a fair fund of knowledge, had a long, instructive trip abroad before he settled down at home. Often, without losing the relish for mundane delights, he continued to feed his mind with scholarship, and many a serene patrician in his sweeping robes was a humanist of the old Renaissance stamp. The roll is long of those who kept up intellectual pursuits of a high order while filling the greatest offices of state. Paolo Renier could recite Homer by heart and translated Plato into Venetian dialect. Francesco Foscari and Francesco Pesaro paid for the printing of important books, and not a few of the nobles followed their example. 'The charms of Latin and the humanities, of agriculture and the law, occupied a whole Pleiad of happy men,' says Monnier. Some founded botanical gardens – the Farsetti gardens were the most representative in Europe – or held academies in their palaces.[96] They welcomed the learned and the interested amateur alike to their famous libraries, while libraries in the convents of SS Giovanni e Paolo, of San Francesco, of the Minorites, San Sebastiano, San Domenico and Sant' Antonio were open to the public. (The fashion of the time was for parchment bindings with brightly-coloured decoration on the backs and edges, and the convent of San Giorgio Maggiore possessed some that made Casotti[97] think of a flowerbed, 'a joy to look at.') Because of her intellectuals, the humanist tradition of Venice never died out. She had gifted children still, able to create and to command attention, through whom, even in her dotage, she could summon back the glorious days.

II JOURNALISM, POETRY, ACADEMIES

In Venice, the first city in the world to have a newspaper, the spice of literary life was provided by gazettes, for something above and beyond the recital of rumour was needed to satisfy a public that loved to chew over in detail all that happened. The *gazetta* was orginally an old copper coin worth two *soldi*, price of the printed sheets that blossomed on every corner like the flowers in May. And the proliferation of gazettes in eighteenth-century Venice is indeed extraordinary. They multiplied overnight and were always the work of one man or one small group. Should the paymaster become bored or leave Venice or the group disintegrate, the paper disappeared, but another sprang up immediately to take its place.

Most of the gazettes were printed in dialect. Only in Florence and Rome did spoken and written Italian coincide. Italian, or Tuscan as it was called, would have sounded all wrong here, where Venetian was used in Senate and court-room, and where law and statecraft could only gain by the nervous, brilliant quality of the speechmaking in that clear, soft, easy idiom with the rich vocabulary and the vivid turns of phrase. But it was a language that had developed out of the basically cheerful native character and was therefore better suited to wit and frivolity than to ponderous argument, so that many writers, and all teachers, usually employed Tuscan. The gazettes availed themselves of either as seemed appropriate to the subject in hand and the theatre did the same, the *Commedia dell'arte* companies acting in Venetian while serious plays were given in Italian.

Goldoni, with his theatrical reforms, retained the use of dialect and in it wrote the greatest of his comedies.

The gazettes were produced by literary men and scholars, often clever and nearly all of them witty, who wove entertainment from a miscellany of ordinary events – and we must bear in mind the fact that ordinary events in Venice tended to have a built-in touch of fantasia to begin with. A gay party had perhaps settled down to picnic on the Riva degli Schiavoni, toasting the passers-by and offering them drinks; a deceived husband was at large, urging everyone he could get hold of to utter a curse on light-minded females; or robbers had recited to their victim a full, legal explanation of what they were up to, and why. There were endless diverting incidents and the local news was like a joke-book, covering every aspect of Venetian life from wild dissipation to tranquil domesticity, the sublime and the ridiculous sandwiched in together. A ducal ceremony, the entrance of an ambassador or a church dedication is followed by the details of someone's operation or of a couple of women fighting. There were helpful hints on how to make ratafia and the latest way of grafting trees, while news of a private character was prominently displayed: the *abate* Chiari's lawyer-uncle has died and left him a tidy fortune; the genteel young widow, address below in full, fervently desires to remarry. The For Sale and Wanted items are beyond belief, a lunatic, unimaginable medley of Venetian supply and demand.

Higher things, however, were not overlooked. New plays are announced and criticised, new books from home and abroad reviewed with long summaries, like those of a modern digest. Art and literature received as much space as practical topics, with commerce and the *Commedia dell'arte* treated at equal length. The bravura essays were varied and fanciful as they could possibly be, on subjects ranging from Petrarch's poetry to things like 'Why Should Love always be Depicted as a Child?' and 'How Great was Alexander the Great?'

Venice swarmed with ready-witted individuals with a wad of manuscript or a page of satire always ready in their pockets. There were encyclopedists and drawing-room poetasters; there were compilers and reporters and a host of gifted beings who could adopt the first style you cared to name and turn out ethics or politics, epigrams or bawdry as required. Prose and verse poured from them in a never-ending stream. They were writing a play on the paper across their knees, they were improvising the words of an opera over the coffee cups. They had theories on absolutely everything, about the moon's atmosphere and the inhabitants of Tierra del Fuego. Some of them collaborated on twelve amazing volumes purporting to be a survey of the terrestrial globe, its past, present and future. It was child's play for them to produce a wealth of articles, grave or gay, for the gazettes, and impossible to name them all, or even to distinguish a few among so many. Besides, despite the huge flow of words, they were not particularly good. One only, Gasparo Gozzi, made a living by his pen and only Carlo Gozzi has a place in literature, but both of these were notable figures.

Carlo Gozzi wrote for every newspaper that was published in his day and especially for the *Gazzetta Veneta*, the *Mondo Morale* and the *Osservatore* which, perhaps for that very reason, were the most popular and longest-lived. His essays reflect his many-faceted personality, he created a whole new kind of drama and left an enthralling autobiography, the *Memorie Inutili*,[98] but it was the journalism that best called out his whimsical gifts and highly individual way of seeing things. Venice might quiver and sparkle around him and alter from one day to the next, but here was a man who stoutly refused to keep up with the times. Born in 1723, he made short work of his patrimony, then did some soldiering; he had dealt in lace and Cyprus wine, he had sold hen-coops. These various avocations, however, left him with many hours to fill and he cultivated the company of actresses, not only for the pleasure of it but to teach them things like spelling and decency. 'I gave them French books that they could manage to read and translate, and wrote imaginary letters for them on everyday topiçs and made them write properly thought-out replies.'

All this did not prevent a reputation for misanthropy. Caterina Tron said he was a bear.[99] He lived alone, a poor and cranky bachelor, and waged his war on affectation, writing chiefly to relieve his spleen and out of the constant need to be attacking someone or other. He was also a poet and frequented literary circles, although he hated them. Carlo Gozzi spared no one, not his sister-in-law, whom he dismissed as 'a romantic and fanciful poetess', not the *abate* Chiari, 'the most fatuous writer of the century'. He was to produce whole volumes against the drama of Goldoni and the *philosophes* bored him to death, for he had a horror of people with a system. Voltaire, Helvétius and Rousseau put him in a fury;

imposters, all of them. Detesting new ways, he was faithful to the old, and to the old drama whole simple purpose had been to amuse an audience. A dissenter from modern decadence, he loved an older Venice, too, 'timeless and unalterable'; his vision was of a day before 'women turned into men and men into women and both of them to monkeys'. His refuge was in dreams. Poetry, pleasure and wisdom seemed to him rooted in fairytale and the plays he wrote were based on fairy stories.

The best work of his brother Gasparo is all in the gazettes, for Gasparo, the 'useless, charming poet', was a journalist to his fingertips, ready for any task or subject. Literary critics say his talent was for the ephemeral paragraph, his vehicle the odd sheet of paper.

The Gozzi family had once been rich but fell on hard times owing to the laziness of its members and their incorrigible habit of doing only what amused them. Their great shared enthusiasm happened to be poetry and all were versifiers – the paralysed father, the mother with her exalted notions, nine fancy-ridden brothers and sisters; even the wife whom Gasparo had taken to himself 'in a fit of abstraction', although she was ten years his senior, because she dedicated an ode to him.[100] Their tumbledown house was a sort of poets' refuge. On their stairs you met every brand of oddity, lackeys and moneylenders, lawyers, unsuccessful authors, old women clutching shopping-baskets, savants and epigrammatic friends in search of a square meal. And in this crack-brained turmoil Gasparo Gozzi wrote. Around him the establishment was beset with writs, dispute and processes at law; they were no concern of his as he sat there writing on every subject under the sun. He wrote for the classroom and the theatre and above all for the newspapers; he wrote love-poetry, satirical poetry and rhyme for special occasions. This poetry and writing, into which he plunged with such self-forgetful, all-consuming passion, became in the end his occupation in good earnest and he was the only man in Venice with a decent income from his pen. In time no one could give a fête without a cantata by Gasparo Gozzi, or make a speech at a Procurator's nomination unless Gasparo Gozzi wrote it. 'There was never a wedding among our noble families,' says Carlo, 'or the reception of a nun, the elevation of a Doge, Procurator or Grand Chancellor, but my brother had to produce some panegyric or selection of verse.'

Gasparo was borne to these heights by his natural gifts, but the

Doge Marco Foscarini helped his career by making him Soprinten-
dente of the presses and general overseer of the book-trade, as well
as poet laureate of the Republic. But though the latter post brought
him a hundred sequins for the shortest effusion, his brother says
that money flew away the minute he laid hands on it, and he never
could grow rich.

It would have been understandable had the Gozzi brothers been
diverted from frivolous pursuits, the one by his official functions
and the other by fundamental distaste for humankind, yet both
belonged to the least restrained and quite the most unusual academy
in Venice. This was the *Granelleschi*, or Balls Academy, with its
badge of a pair of testicles.[101] The Balls Academy was founded as a
rather laboured joke by some young poets, in mock-honour of a
verbose priest and versifier named Guiseppe Sacchellari. Its
supposed aims were to mock at pendantry and revive the unadorned
and sober style of former times, but this large and laudable programme was undertaken in no very serious spirit. The *Granelleschi*
had their recorders and published their transactions, but little is
known about them beyond the jollity in questionable taste that went
on at the meetings. We have Carlo Gozzi's assurance that Sacchellari
was a *raro imbecille*, and as *Arcigranellone* or President – Chief Big
Ball, or Arch Nitwit if you took the other meaning of the word – he
was traditionally the butt of practical jokes. He got boiling hot tea in
summer when the others had refreshing ices, and in winter they
reversed the situation and gave him iced water as they sipped their
steaming coffee. They made him answer stupid questions, improvise
sonnets and sit there crowned with radishes. Only when all this
began to pall did the academicians, under grotesque academic
names, think of expounding Dante or reading productions of their
own, which were seldom free of the faults they criticised in those of
other people.

Also purely burlesque was an academy devoted to the writing of
macaronic verse, with all the words disguised in pseudo-Latin form.
The *Meccanici*, whose rule was foul language and obscenity, had a
fashionable membership of truly rude mechanicals. The *Accademia
degli Infecondi* justified its name by admitting only those able to
prove they had never written a word. When these clubs were in
any way serious they were mere mutual admiration societies, or
passed the time debating idiotic points. 'If Venus had another
child,' they liked to wonder, 'what god would he turn out to be?'

One might enter these brotherhoods on the strength of a single ode, but, like news-sheets, academies dissolved and disappeared at the whim of groups who often meant well but lacked perseverance and staying power. Many of the preposterous names are on record: the *Venturosi* (Lucky Ones), the *Angustoli* (with their Distresses), the *Imperfetti* (Defectives), the *Imperturbabili* (Imperturbable), the *Infermi* (Unwell), the *Silenti* (Speechless) and *Adorni* (Embellished). There was an academy of *Apologi*, dedicated to Fables, and another of *Abbagliati*, or Dazzled Ones, but none of them made much mark in the world. Public sessions were allowed so long as no women were present, but this regulation, designed to prevent all scandal, proved just one more rule for breaking, When the *Accademia degli Ardenti* went so far as to let some of their accommodation to a young and lovely milliner and to patronise the cloakroom in her part of the premises, she was denounced to the Ten on account of the 'immodest and disgraceful happenings' that ensued. Her ardour was evidently too much for the club, despite its name.

Most members of academies, like most people from aristocrat to porter and gondolier, were poets. On all sides the odes and sonnets deluged down. Births, deaths or anniversaries, there was no occasion which did not provoke them. Authors addressed themselves to the stars on any trivial subject; the legs of every third-rate ballerina were hymned in burning rhyme; not a bride went to the altar nor a nun to the convent without her hamperful of tributes. Solemn verse extolled the newly-elected magistrate and the new parish priest was hailed with trusting lines upon his godly virtues. If anyone fell ill he was comforted with sonnets, and stayed with sonnets on recovery; if he died, the family was overwhelmed with sonnets. And the whole vast output of inflated metaphor contained hardly a line of more than average merit.

The sad truth was that no real poet had ever sprung from this most poetical of cities. There had been dabblers in the seventeenth century, nothing more, and subject-matter was increasingly thin-drawn and feeble now. 'A mole or a beauty-patch, a spaniel, a mouse or a pet bird, the curl of a wig, a fan or a chocolate-spoon or the Procuratessa Mocenigo's slipper,' of such things, Molmenti tells us, the poets preferred to write for the amusement of pretty women and elegant *cavalieri*. Goldoni himself offered a poem to the French ambassador's dog. This sort of poetic puerility was indeed the bane of the lightweight *Settecento* here, when history 'fragmented into anecdotes' and aspiring grandeur provoked uneasiness. It was the day of the diminutive. Not for nothing did it favour the form 'Tiepoletto' when referring to Tiepolo.

It is scarcely necessary to add that poets got few pickings. You had to be Gasparo Gozzi to exist by your efforts. The pages of verse were passed gratis from hand to hand, with nothing for the author but an occasional cup of coffee or glass of wine from an admirer. If he wrote a poem on commission and were then lucky enough to be paid, the rate was very low. Carlo Gozzi calculated that a cobbler earned more every time he made a stitch than a poet did for a line of verse.

Nor did other writers fare much better. Translation was paid at three lire a sheet; the distinguished man who put Chamber's Dictionary and Conyers Middleton's *Life of Cicero* into Italian received no more. A successful comedy might bring the playwright thirty sequins, a tragedy forty.

The solution seemed to lie in dedications. Dedicate a book to some exalted personnage and he might give his patronage in return. Yet this, too, often proved a mirage and barely worth mentioning, for dedications were not repaid in good hard cash. At best, there were a few small gifts. From the distinguished men to whom he dedicated his collected plays Goldoni collected no more than a watch, a gold box, a silver chocolate service and four pairs of lace ruffles. His memoirs make bitter allusion to the wretched state of writers in Venice. In France they might expect pensions and favours from the King, while here they drew tiny profits from their books and could only 'moan and groan' in apathy. Most fortunate were those who managed to become private tutors, secretaries or librarians, or who found humble places in great households as little more than hangers-on at their employers' beck and call: if not allowed in the drawing-room they stayed in the kitchen and blended with the rest of the servants. Some, failing to secure a bread-and-butter occupation, starved to death like Domenico Lalli (1679–1741), of whom it was said that he was born rich and died a poet.

Obviously the rich poet had to be a priest or nobleman. And yet the spirit, blowing where it listed, often lit upon the *servitori di barca,* many of whom composed their own songs, and the patrician gondola might speed its pair of poets, master and boatman together, over the flashing water. Among these gifted gondoliers, two, named

Bianchi and Sibillato, were judged to have true lyric fire and each enjoyed a triumphant time in the salons and some very flattering friendships as a result.[102]

III THEATRE

There had been numerous theatres in Venice from the seventeenth century onwards, mounted on trestles out of doors or sketchily fitted up in any available hall, but the *Settecento* saw the first spacious stone buildings where plays could be properly presented. Seven already existed when more were forbidden by a law of November 10, 1757. Each bore the name of the parish where it stood – San Benedetto, San Luca, Sant' Angelo, San Giovanni, San Cassiano, San Moisè and San Samuele, the latter the scene of Casanova's violin-playing before he embarked on a career that took him sensationally far beyond the bounds of the world of music. Four of these theatres gave opera, the others drama.

Seven large and well-filled public playhouses were a lot for a town of 130,000 inhabitants at a time when Paris itself had only three. Many palaces, too, had private theatres; there were street-theatres for the Carnival and travelling puppet-shows, all evidence of how much plays and music meant to the Venetians. Actor, singer and musician provided a livelihood for countless stage-hands and designers, men to light the candles, hawk the tickets, copy the scores and coach the cast; and there were all the mothers and hair-dressers and shoemakers, to say nothing of the father-confessors, the official protectors and the secret admirers in attendance on the actresses. Such was the spell of the theatre, moreover, that people entirely unconnected with it would study its arts as though expecting a summons to take the boards at a moment's notice. They were the glorious dreamers, to be seen in genre pictures of the street-life of the city; the hopeful, never-to-be-heard-of authors reading their pieces to disengaged actresses who listen over their knitting, the never-to-be-called-on actors stretched in comfortable chairs outside their houses, going over their scenes. No courtyard was without its resident who played a small part once in some one-night perform-ance and claimed to be a Thespian ever after.

Such illusions were willingly upheld by friend and aquaintance, for society as a whole found theatre-folk glamorous in the extreme. They were welcomed with open arms in noble mansions and cossetted by aristocratic ladies, to the great alarm of the Inquisitori, who were always trying to warn the aristocratic gentlemen. One of the Ten, who might have spared himself the trouble, bade the actors 'remember you are persons whom God abhors, tolerated by the Prince only for the sake of those who enjoy your sinful antics'. But Venetians adored actors and were not to be put off. Over women singers, whom they adored most of all, they went into ecstasies. *Venetiis anno Todi* lived in their calendar as the year of the Portuguese idol Luisa Todi, much as *annus victoriae navalis* had marked Lepanto two centuries before – and what star or pop-goddess could claim that sort of compliment today?

Plainly the theatre, that 'liberating dream of an ancient and artistic race', held a supreme position in all hearts. And the audience did more than take their places and applaud, for a drama would be discussed in every corner of the town and every unlettered gondolier have something to say on the subject. The Republic, relieved till Doomsday of political unrest, was time and again in uproar over purely theatrical intrigue and dispute, split into irreconcilable camps by playhouse rivalry. The hiring of a ballerina could become a state concern with the Ten and the foreign embassies involved, and loom large in the chancelleries of Europe. When the Marquis de Montaigu wrote to the minister in Paris on February 1, 1774, the dancer in question was wanted for Potsdam, for the theatre of Frederick the Great:

'The problem of the Barberini is not settled yet. That girl – her head's like feathers, let alone her feet – assured the Spanish ambassador and me that she would fulfil her engagement, and then notified the King of Prussia's envoy he would have to petition the Senate if he wanted her to go, willingly or otherwise. As she is a subject of the Queen of Hungary [i.e. Maria Theresa] Her Majesty's resident has also been to see her, in hopes to please the King of Prussia by making her stick to her contract. From a slightly different angle, there are two Englishmen implicated as well, both of them Members of Parliament, which puts the Senate in a tricky position.'

Another factor was the touchiness of players, their on-and-off ways and unpredictable requirements. We know what quarrels Goldoni had with the capricious Teodora Medebac, so long his favourite leading lady; how she would throw up a part on the spur of the moment and take to her bed with convulsions so violent that witchcraft seemed the only feasible explanation and exorcism and relics were applied; and how, as soon as a substitute was named, back she came in perfect health to send the usurper packing and promptly concentrate on convulsions once again, grimacing horribly. No one could foretell on any given morning whether she would or would not feel disposed to act that night, but Goldoni adopts a philosophic attitude and obviously such trantrums were not uncommon in the theatre world. 'I held my tongue,' he says; 'these little touches of temperament are only to be expected when someone is free to do as she likes and refuses to listen to reason.'

The actual theatres belonged to various patrician owners who let them out to managers on the very simple basis of taking all the entrance money. But entrance money did not pay for seats, which were bought separately from a man who passed among the audience while the play was going on. Usually, it seems, he had little trouble or argument, though occasionally some sharp character might try to slip him a bad coin under cover of the poor light. This is what Casanova had been doing when he had his explanations with the Ten – awkwardly enough for someone who was working for them as an informer at the time.

The lessee rented the boxes to individual holders and could run a gaming-room in the building. This was the most important point of his agreement, for a theatre without its gambling profits would show a heavy loss and running costs were high, even without many expensive modern items. There was none of our publicity, for instance, nor floods of posters, even at the theatre doors. Two small bills, one at Rialto and the other in the Piazza, were all that announced the daily programmes until town criers took over the task at the end of the century. Theatres were open every day, not excepting Fridays, when they were closed in the rest of Italy, and managerial economy resulted in what we should find most inadequate lighting arrangements, candles bing confined to the stage and the auditorium plunged in gloom on the plea that fire risk was thus reduced.

As for copyright, it was neither respected nor protected, and the dramatist was at the mercy of the manager, contracting his work in advance, by the year, for low fixed rates. Goldoni, who once provided his employer with sixteen three-act plays in a single season, was given nothing extra for them. 'Not a penny over the year's salary, nothing at all,' he protested. 'Plenty of praise, plenty of compliments and never the hint of a bonus. Angry as I was, I kept quiet, but one needs more than glory to live on.' Some of the actor-managers even claimed royalties when 'their' plays came out in book form and this fate, too, Goldoni suffered. Worse, he was to discover that no fewer than fifteen unauthorised editions of his comedies had been published by 1760, and very badly printed, which upset him more. We may easily believe his lament that he was urged by honour and paid in fame for the special care and labour he put into his work. Anyone in the same line of business would have agreed with him that the playwright's share of the takings was barely worth collecting.

It is doubtful whether actors did much better. Those whom the public took to its heart were well, if grudgingly, rewarded by impresarios who could not do without them, for then as now the star was the main attraction. It was the popular actor, the *castrato* with the seraph-voice, who pulled the audience in; such magnets must be paid, and grossly overpaid often enough, for they usually demanded more than they were worth. There was a respectable living for competent players of the second rank, but lamentably few to earn it, and some highly peculiar casting emphasised the fact from time to time. On one occasion Goldoni found his heroine, or *prima amorosa*, though a good actress, well stricken in years, 'the second lead a clumsy beauty with vulgar manners and the Columbine a fetching, fresh brunette on the point of having a baby'.

Talent-spotting performances were held where a beginner might show his paces in a variety of parts, but they seldom brought any startling gifts to light. The plays chosen were so full of characters that dozens of actors could flounder on and off without making much impression. Goldoni declares that there were not two good soubrettes among the forty or fifty he could name. There existed in fact, a sort of theatrical commonalty, miserably paid and devoted with touching persistence to the stage. And of course the humblest actor who really and truly acted had always a certain aura. The audience might not get on its feet to applaud him, but at least when he got home the neighbours thought he was marvellous.

The interior fittings of a theatre were, as we have noted, paid for by an illiberal owner and not over-lavish, but the heavy stage expenses fell on the lessee. He had to provide complicated machinery and new ingenious settings for every piece – some means, for instance, of swift and smooth descent from operatic heaven to earth. Most operas called for extravagant mounting and all managers saw that they got it, and that the large cast was splendidly attired. for every cast was large. It had to be: no audience would have sat through anything for which the stage was not completely packed, if only with extras who never opened their mouths.

But the worst of all was the constant search for new plays. Not only tradition, but the law of diminishing returns imposed this burden, for it was nothing unusual to have to let the gondoliers in free to fill the house after a very few performances. A run of two weeks was a huge success. Goldoni says of his *Il Cavaliere e la Dama* that it 'was hailed enthusiastically and lasted fifteen nights'. *La Vedova Scaltra* with its twenty-five showings in 1748 constituted a triumph without precedent. Plays had always to be new and revivals were unknown, though the management was not necessarily free to chose the programme. When an audience started shouting '*Questa! questa!*' when the next night's title was announced at curtain-fall they wanted a repeat of what they had just seen, and it would be a foolish impresario who disappointed them.

And yet, in spite of everything, theatrical enterprises paid. Nobody made a fortune, but out-and-out ruin was rare and success would balance failure on the whole, especially as the price of seats went up when a play did well – as much as four times for some of Goldoni's pieces. This was done unofficially, on the black market: the government could not conceivably have countenanced such a proceeding.

Not until a later period would Venetian playhouses show anything like the brilliant interior decoration of contemporary establishments in other parts of Europe. Here a theatre looked bare and its amenities were few. The pit was furnished, insufficiently, with wooden benches. Lighting, save on the stage, was sparse or non-existent, as was any provision for hygiene. Before the play, peddlars went along the rows with fruit, cold meat, fritters and wine, and the pit, having eaten and drunk, indulged without discomposure in what one writer euphemistically calls 'the consequent activities': it is certain he was not thinking only of the peel and apple-cores and sticky paper thrown carelessly about. The show lasted four or five hours; nature, after all this intake, made her imperious demands and where people sat there they fulfilled them, ignoring the special space they were supposed to use, just between the front benches and the stage. What with this, the reeking tallow from the footlights and the smell of food and wine spilled in the din and confusion, it is small wonder that the whole place stank.

Yet the ears were, if possible, more dreadfully assaulted than the nostrils. A Venetian ambassador playgoing in Paris was amazed to find himself able to hear the actors rather than the audience, and reported that French theatres (by which he meant the boxes) were 'very different from ours; here one comes to listen and not, as at home, to talk'. And the pit at home was even worse, bawling and calling out remarks and insults, and falling on occasion to fisticuffs; while the box-holders had only to turn from their diversion of gossip to that of spitting or of throwing candle-ends into the melée below for the benches to retaliate and things grow rowdier still.

But theatres were open only during the free-for-all of Carnival, so that the universal masking accounted for much of the licence. Many of the theatre-goers would be young folk more interested in acting out their own carnival characters than in watching the play, and their efforts to stand out from the crowd struck one visiting Frenchman as so singular and so shocking that only those who had seen them, he thought, could possibly believe the tale.

The boxes were somewhat better behaved because they functioned mainly as social meeting-places where women liked to chat, linger over their ices and hear what their gallants had to say. And a box was always the perfect setting in which to show off dresses and jewels. The Inquisitori thundered in vain from time to time against immodest toilettes, and kept repeating that the proper wear in public was the *tabarro* and *bautta*; there is no case on record of any lady's having paid them any more heed than usual.

People of quality hired their boxes by the season. M. de Montaigu had a box at each of the theatres and, says Rousseau, would announce over dinner which he intended to occupy that evening, leaving the others free for the embassy staff. But multiple box-holders were not usually so generous and the business of sub-letting increased with the limitation of the playhouses. Of the famous beauty Cecilia Zeno Tron, Caterina's sister-in-law, who overcharged the Duke of Courland, the wits of Venice said she was asking more for her box than ever she did for herself. Quite right, was her rejoinder, *perché i miei favori non li vendo, li regalo* – my favours are given, they are not for sale; and she was, by reputation, never niggardly.

As many as four tiers of boxes might rise one above another, and Row Four, where the occupants, male and female, ignored the stage and followed their own disorderly devices, had a very bad name. Casanova, much concerned, in his guise of vigilant guardian of decency, with the 'right and pure conduct' of the citizens and playing the saintly informant, drew the attention of authority to scandals at the San Cassiano. There, he averred, things were going on in the fourth row of the *palchi* which, if they had to happen at all, were best to happen in the dark.

The performance itself invited interruption at many points and the pit knew no half-measures between clapping and cursing furiously. An actor might evoke such a storm of jeers that he had to be replaced there and then; or the audience might divide for and against him until neither party could be heard for hissing and applause, farmyard imitations and general hullaballoo. Upon the wretched players there fell a hail of sometimes horrid objects, all launched with malice aforethought, for the cooked pears, the oranges and inevitable fritters were bought at the door for use as instant ammunition. Some of the battles would begin with inter-theatre rivalry, as in the open war between the Sant' Angelo, where Chiari's plays were given, and the San Luca which employed Goldoni and stood for an entirely different kind of drama; or, more often, they revolved round actors and spread from the theatre to the world outside. On November 19, 1760, the secret agent Medri stated that

' . . . all the dancers and musicians of the San Moisè and San Benedetto theatres, together with many noblemen, including . . . the protectors of two of the San Moisè dancers, are in league against those of the Teatro Sant' Angelo. The men all put similar multi-coloured cockades in their hats, the women in their dresses, and wear them constantly, in and out of the theatre and when going about masked.'

Those who really wanted to hear a word or a note were forced into the heroic course of sitting somewhere in the front rows nearest the stage, where they were exposed to more than their fair share of orange-peel, tomatoes and soft-stewed fruit. Any disturbance, more-over, continued so long as the contestants had strength. Arrange-ments for stopping it did not exist. No police were on duty save the occasional government spy, impenetrably disguised and under orders not to declare himself unless things grew desperate; and this perhaps was wise, in view of what happened in January 1774, when Favretti Felice came into the open to reprove a *castrato* from Bologna. His action triggered off a stream of high-pitched threats of dire obscenity against all and sundry, from the devoted *fante* up to and including the Holy Ghost, though no untoward result is actually recorded.

Often enough, though, all went smoothly. Ballet especially commanded rapt regard because the costumes were worn with a studied negligence ensuring the revelation of much they were supposed to hide. The council of Ten stopped all this, rather tardily, in 1793, but they had previously shown great indulgence to the ballerinas, who led brazen lives and many of whom were obvious prostitutes. So sought after were these girls, and so expensive, that several young men would often club amicably together to keep one, though marrying her was out of the question. Any inappropriate entanglement would be broken up ruthlessly by the Ten, and the case of the dancer Carlina was by no means unique. Molmenti, quoting from the *Annotazioni degli inquisitori dello Stato* for 1765, says she was permanently banished from the territory of Venice for having brought some patrician's son to the 'monstrous resolve' of marriage.

But if a ballet company could root its audience to the spot by mere force of its physical attractions, others found it harder to gain attention. Even without faction-fights or arguments over the performance the house was restless at a play or opera, if only because the noise was part of its enjoyment. The normally mirthful Venetians were more hilarious than ever at a comedy, laughing long before it began and giving way as it unfolded to what is described as 'disorderly and unrestrained merriment, and exclamations of all kinds'.

There was plenty to laugh at, even in the tragedies, for the actors kept doing their best to amuse. The mobled queen might at any moment tuck up her skirts and break into the *furlana*, or trill some cheerful local ditty that had nothing to do with the play. These interludes were essential if tragedy was to be listened to at all, for the Venetian could not abide anguish, even on the stage. As soon as the curtain fell he liked to recall the slain with hearty cries of *Bravi i morti!* and, the niceties of dramatic convention being quite beyond him, regarded all the characters as real people. If he saw anyone in danger he yelled a warning. Goethe once heard an audience who, at the sight of a tyrant giving his son a sword with which to kill his wife, insisted that he take it back again. It would have made havoc of the plot, but there was deadlock until the son, advancing to the footlights, entreated them in all humility to wait and see, assuring them on his honour that things would come right in the end. A dramatist would himself add a light touch as often as not, to reconcile the public, and French tragedies were amended without scruple 'to suit the national taste'. Arlecchino and Pantaleone went cavorting through the action of Corneille. Imagination boggles.

The Président de Brosses noted an 'unbelievable infatuation' with music everywhere in Venice, and this despite the fact that the favourite theatrical pieces were never opera, but comedy. Yet neither the *Commedia dell'arte* nor the comedy or manners and character sponsored and so brilliantly written by Goldoni could oust the airs of Cimarosa, make them less devoutly listened to or curtail the endless, wild applause with which the singers were acknowledged: Lalande says that a duet from Scarlatti's *Clemenzia di Tito* evoked howls, rather than shouts, of appreciation. What the public really loved, however, were the glorious melodies and celestial *cantilene* that sent Rousseau into transports. Works with long passages of recitative were not so much admired and avoided as a rule, and Venetian likes and dislikes were altogether different from those of Paris. A Venetian visitor to the French capital once annoyed his neighbour by enquiring, '*Signore, quando si canta?*' 'When does the singing start?' was the indignant response. 'Can't you hear them at it? They've been singing for the last four hours, man.' 'I beg your pardon,' said the other – Casanova himself in all likelihood – but we should call that droning where I come from'.

Perpetual novelty was demanded, with opera as with plays. Last year's music, says the Président, made no impact at the box-office and Dr Burney adds that a piece once heard is as stale as last year's almanach.[103] Music was not worth the trouble of printing, there was so much of it, and yet these short-lived works included some of the finest compositions of the eighteenth century, such as Handel's *Agrippina* of 1709, Gluck's *Ipermestra* of 1742, Jomelli's *Merope* of 1747, *Il Convito di Pietra*, by Cimarosa, Pergolese's *La Serva Padrona* and Piccini's *Grizelda*, of 1793. Not even the giants, Vivaldi and Scarlatti, were accorded revivals.

It was very expensive to put on opera and, with so few performances given in Venice itself, managers got their money back in the mainland towns. Carlo Gozzi has a vivid, lively sketch that shows a touring company on the quayside, ready to set out:

'Two boats moored and waiting to take singers, dancers and musicians, big trunks, little trunks, suitcases, portmanteaux, bags and baskets, hampers, panniers, small boxes and anything else the inventive packer can think of to put things in for travelling. . . . One by one the kings and queens arrived, the princes and princesses, the orchestra and *corps de ballet* from every town and country, speaking every language known since the tower of Babel. . . . Here a young singer indulged in a passionate exchange with her lover, whispering in his ear though her hawk-eyed mamma was standing at her side. . . . There a musician was pestering a ballerina and being shooed away for his pains. . . . "Dancing's the thing," I head one of the dancers cry. "A breath of fresh air won't affect our legs, even if we lost our voices." . . . "Oh, Adriano!" exclaimed someone else, "pick up that bundle oₓ yours and get it on board. Sabina's dog's just cocked his leg all over it and those two hounds of Emirena's look like being next. . . .'

IV COMEDY

For three hundred years the truly national institution of the *Commedia dell'arte* had prevailed in Venice as in the rest of Italy. It was a theatre of improvisation. The manager would assemble his actors, briefly outline the plot, distribute and indicate their parts. He then bade them remember that such-and-such a town was supposed to be setting, that such-and-such a house belonged to so-and-so, and consigned them to the stage. They acted the piece in their own words, as wit and invention might suggest, and practically wrote it as they went along.

The characters were set and invariable, fixed by tradition time out of mind. First came the two old men, the sincere and simple Pantaleone and the Dottore, a caricature of erudition who never stopped talking. The pair of them, though always ready to revive in the company of young ladies, cough and spit without pause and are predestined victims of the fantasticated serving-men, cunning Brighella and gullible Arlecchino, who play them terrible tricks. Peasants, pedants, villains and sharks come and go as and when required. There are artful ladies'-maids (*servette*, or soubrettes) and simpletons like Captain Spavento who never wears a shirt because

the hair on his chest bristles with everlasting fury and might tear
it to bits. They all flourished away together with their repartees
and proverbs, songs and nonsense stories, introducing stock tirades
on every suitable cue. These came down from generation to generation of the players and relied for effect on sheer irrelevance.[104] For
the rest the whole company, actors, singers and dancers, followed
their prodigal imaginations through a whirligig of byplay, horseplay,
theatrical business and parody. They set about one another with
canes, kicked each others' backsides and roared with laughter in
the hurly-burly. They were all engaged in the work of creation and
out of their rioting fancy the play was brewed, red-hot, never the
same twice running, but fast, alive, spontaneous.

The public loved the *Commedia dell'arte* for they found there, night
after night, an exaggerated picture-with-a-story of the lives they
led all day. This was the common talk, these were the daily gesticula-
tions, shouts and singing of the lawyer and the man he argued
against, of water-seller and gondolier. It was their own wrangling
and vehemence, their own cursing and good temper they saw in
that faithful interpretation of lower-class manners and circumstance.
There on the stage was their street at home and all that happened
there they recognised from personal experience. Actors and audience
fused into one and the preposterous play assumed reality, for in it
was the spirit of a people ever ready for life and amusement, were
it only the amusement of laughing at themselves.

This improvised comedy was still alive in the eighteenth century,
though it had evidently nearly run its course. The artificial lay-
figures were frozen in the old, hackneyed situations, without light
or shadow; they made nothing of mankind's diversity and many-
sidedness, and this at a time when interest was first aroused in the
inner workings of human nature. The quality of the actors, too, was
falling off. Good players grew harder and harder to find and most
were barnstormers with too many mannerisms and too little
experience. They had no sort of intellectual appeal, relying for
their laughs on attack and buffoonery, clowning and rigmarole,
and had so few new jokes that Goldoni in his *Teatro Comico*, half-play,
half-manifesto of 1751, complains that you knew what Arlecchino
was going to say long before he said it. If comedy were to survive,
something new was needed.

And this was when Goldoni intervened, with his theories of
drama. His kind of comedy was written, and well written. It pre-

15   Venetian masks, after
an engraving by Jean David

16   Morning Habit of a
Lady of Venice in 1750

17. Scene of the Grand Canal of a Gondola

18   The Arsenal

19   The Piazzetta
by Canaletto

20 S. Maria de la Salute, by Francesco Guardi

sented natural human life and real domesticity; its aim was the portrayal of manners and the study of character. The people on his stage were flesh and blood, leading the lives that everybody led, speaking the unexaggerated language everybody used.

He came into the world with a passion for the theatre, acted at the age of four and wrote a play when he was eight. In an adventurous career he had been a diplomatic attaché and a consul, gone bankrupt and reached the verge of becoming a monk. A count of one hundred and forty-nine comedies, ten tragedies and eighty-three operas was made by his biographer Charles Rabany,[105] who never claimed it was complete. There is even a play with an all-male cast, 'suitable for garrison theatricals', commissioned by a college of Jesuits. He wrote something of everything, verse and prose, dialect and Italian, good and bad, but the best invariably derives from his native city, for his inspiration flagged when he sought material farther afield. He has his weaknesses – a lack of depth, perhaps, and of pronounced moral content – but he stands head and shoulders above his fellow Venetians, not only the greatest among them but one of the greatest comic authors who ever lived. He does not attain the scope and reach of Molière, for he creates no unforgettable types and ignores philosophical and social issues. He simply brings a whole warm and vivid world to life, full of *cicisbei* and flirtatious women, of periwigged pundits and alluring, unquenchable maidservants warbling and fluting through the plot: a universe given over to laughter and enjoyment. Nobody ever approached his art of spinning a play out of nothing, of assembling the beautifully dovetailed scenes and buoyant sparkling dialogue into a masterpiece. His comedies have been likened to the early music of Mozart, and it is a fair comparison.

All Goldoni's work was directed towards reform of the theatre. He wanted to bring life on to the stage, life with its antic turns and complications, quite other and much funner than those of the *Commedia dell'arte*. He replaced the old conventions with plain truth, artificiality with naturalism, and started by doing away with the masks. Static through joy and sadness, anger or good humour, these fixed, immoveable faces had impeded the traditional comedy. An actor might gesticulate, alter his stance or vary his inflections, but the strongly-marked features and broad characterisation of the mask remained, putting subtleties of expression out of his power. Goldoni's other great new departure was, of course, the provision of a text with plentiful stage directions and no room for invention; the company no longer made up the words.

Within this novel dramatic framework he was to display an all-pervading comic gift, a gift he never lost and was always first to relish. No playwright was ever more fertile of plot and incident, nowhere are plays so brimful of fresh, sane, open laughter. It is heard even in the sketches he produced as potboilers and in which, earthy as they are and meant for the groundlings, he carefully cuts down the burlesque, unruly elements of the *Commedia dell'arte*. His traditional characters, recognisable still, were modified. Dunces were a shade brighter, the pranks a little cleverer and more refined. Arlecchino was no longer the dolt ordering a coffin and planning to attend his own funeral because someone told him he was dead; rather, he develops the mild brand of mischief that endeared him to French audiences when they, in time, met the new Goldoni version of a harlequin.

Despite their wide differences, there were other points of resemblance between the Comedy of the Craft and the comedy of character that was Goldoni's shining achievement. He, too, often resorted to clowning and commonplace, for the fact of the matter was that he, too, was an improviser. His were written scripts but written in a week. If he took a fortnight it was because he had to compose five full acts, all of them in verse, as, for instance, with *Il Festino*. 'I sent it to be copied act by act as it was finished, and the players learned their parts as they arrived. It was billed the fourteenth day after I began it, and produced the next.' He threw *La Casa Nova* together in seventy-two hours in 1760 and the sixteen-play season of 1750–51 included some of his best work.

But speed like this was bound to leave its mark. His contemporary Bachaumont[106] thought the plays were like scenarios, with sketched-in incidents, inconsequent dialogue and endings hastily cobbled up after sudden, unaccountable reverse turns, as though the author were in too much of a hurry, repeating things and contradicting himself. It was the insatiable theatre that imposed this breakneck pace, but Goldoni could have worked no other way, for his bubbling genius and comic invention were urgent within him and he was obeying his own volatile temperament. Always the quickest, latest thought beckoned his attention. 'I am what I am,' he said, 'and worth what I am worth.' Take him or leave him.

He had enormous difficulty, nevertheless, in getting the public, especially the intellectual public, to take him and it is surprising that many who criticised him were men of taste and judgement. Giuseppe Baretti accuses him of having deafened the ears and corrupted the understanding of the common playgoer. According to others he wrote in a silly-sounding mixture of words lifted from all the dialects of Italy; his ideas were trivial and he made incredible mistakes over law, ethics, medicine, anatomy and 'geometry', whatever they meant by that. Chief grievance was that actors should be forced to reel off words they learned by heart, debased in the process to mere echoes, 'incapable of speech had no one spoken first'.

The chosen champion of the old comedy, the abysmal *abate* Chiari, is still remembered as a sort of nether point in Italian literature. Pompous, turgid and inflated, as Carlo Gozzi said, he was for years at open odds with Goldoni and the world of letters rang with their warfare. The thrilling controversy swept the town, conducted with great energy on both sides, and invigorated the whole population. Chiari and Goldoni and their relative merits were the theme in salon, street and shop and in the very fishmarket, while the number of epigrams coined in the course of battle broke all records, filling a stout volume in 1754 alone. Casanova, with his finger in this as every other pie, had the grace to support Goldoni and paid dearly when the vengeful *abate* put him in a novel – a vinegary portrait but, it is to be feared, not far short of the truth.[107]

Goldoni cherished a theory that credit and decency would return to the drama if one of the playhouses in Venice were to cater, at higher prices, for the more intelligent audience. Cheap seats, he said, were the bane of the theatre, He could persuade nobody to agree with this Utopian view, however, and had to resign himself to the verdict of the untutored. His fame spread all over Europe and was especially high in France, but his comedy of character never entirely carried the day at home, where the public would have had to be re-educated from the beginning to appreciate it. Under pressure of Chiari's attack he made concessions to the popular taste, but merely wrote several poor plays as a result, and falsified his position. In 1762, disheartened by the clashes in Venice, he went to Paris to work for the Comédie Italienne, and was still living in France on a royal pension when the Revolution broke out. This of course ruined him. He died on February 6, 1793, the very day before Marie-Joseph Chénier, poet brother of the poet André Chénier, persuaded the Convention to renew the income granted him by Louis XVI.

Prominent in the Goldoni–Chiari affair was Carlo Gozzi. That endearing eccentric abhorred both parties equally. He accused Chiari of pandering to the low taste of the times with the mixture of pathos and vulgarity in his far-fetched tales, all full of elaborate disguises, eloping nuns and floods of moonlight; and he looked with no kinder eye upon Goldoni's wished-for return to naturalism. He himself stayed resolutely out of fashion, took the purely fantastic for his province and made a late debut as a dramatist with *L'Amore delle tre melarance*, a play based on an old nursery tale. He thus fathered a theatrical genre much admired by German Romantics such as Hoffmann, Schiller (who borrowed the plot of *Turandot*) and Wagner (who was indebted to *La Donna Serpente* for *Die Feen*.) Carlo Gozzi told lovely fairy-stories. His princesses are all spell-bound, his kings from packs of playing-cards. He spirits the hearer away to the Magic Isles, to 'the land where the bluebird lives and anything can happen'. For a while the Venetians were enchanted to see their childhood visions come true again in plays so steeped in marvel and mystery, but neither the Magic Isles nor the domestic drama of Goldoni could win them from the *commedia dell'arte* in the end. That was their nonesuch, that their very own, and they never really deserted it.

V MUSIC

Music, said Sansovino long before, had at Venice *la sua propria sede*, and the city of rippling water and rosy palaces was indeed as much the abode of music as of love. In church and theatre, out of doors and in the concert-room, there was music, in the *Settecento*, everywhere.

In the street it took its simplest and assuredly its most poetic form: everybody sang. The workman carolled along to work and the fishmonger among the fish. The gondolier as he waited for passengers sang, sang when he found them, sang better than ever as he rowed them away. Song spilled from the shop doorway and from windows overhead and any lonely promenader was certainly humming to himself. 'Harmony prevails in every part,' Dr Burney wrote, 'If two of the common people walk together arm in arm, they are always singing, and seem to converse in song.' Acoustics made the feeblest voice distinct and clear on the canals, where each note and variation was distinguishable. And no one ever sang unheard, for there was no getting away from the sound, we are told, if you were anywhere in earshot. The melody drew near and passed, faded in the distance and was followed by another.

The endless succession of song consisted of airs from oratorio and opera as well as ballads of sentiment and romance. The aria begun as a solo always finished in a harmony of accompanying voices. At night the boatmen sang their snatches of Tasso from one to another, each taking up the verse from somewhere in the dark. Fishermen's wives at the water's edge sang bits of Ariosto, and husbands and lovers out in the lagoon sang back to them, continuing the lines: a lament without melancholy, Goethe said, and their distant, alternating voices were moving to hear. Song regulated the whole rhythm of Venetian life, the mother-tongue and native expression of the labouring class. All they felt and thought came out as *mattinate* and barcarolles.

They had no monopoly of music, however, for it was equally dear to the patricians. Theatre boxes above the crowded pit were full of noble music lovers, who also entertained their friends in palace, *casino* and country house with intimate concerts, gatherings dignified with the name of 'academies'. 'Hardly an evening goes by,' reports the Burgundian Président, 'but there is an academy somewhere, and sometimes two or three are announced for the same date.' It was an accepted thing for people to come in gondolas when there was a concert anywhere on the Grand Canal, and listen under the palace windows.

Just as the musical public was drawn from all walks of life, so were some of the academies grander than others. The Gritti or Labia families might offer the first performance of some famous opera, but in humbler circles the concerts, though less brilliant, were held more often. Many an ordinary bourgeois had his music-room with harpsichord, violin and 'cello, sheet-music and scores, where a handful of enthusiasts came, at his invitation, to play. One of the ladies would strum a barcarolle, an old *abate* would sit down to accompany her, and a Venetian academy was straightaway in being. 'It costs so little,' said Jean-Jacques Rousseau, 'that there is no point in going without music, if you happen to like it.' He hired a harpsichord himself, and for a trifle assembled four or five instru-mentalists to play him passages that had struck him at the opera.

He had been very prejudiced against Italian music on arrival, but came to feel for it 'the passion it arouses in those best qualified to judge'; and adds, 'listening to the barcarolles, I realised that I had never heard real singing before'.

The lower echelons who were not invited to academies had the music of all the impromptu orchestras in the Piazza to enjoy, and did so, it seemed to Dr Burney, in a perfect swoon of delight. He thought that in Venice you needed a hundred ears, as Argus had a hundred eyes. Life, in fact, was saturated with music. It alone could express the all-pervading high spirits. The Serenissima, regarding it as the noblest exercise of the mind, gave it protection and encouragement, and had been known to treat it as an affair of state.

Like painting, music is indeed one of the contributary glories of the Republic and all kinds of odd privileges were attached to it. The priesthood, for instance, was not denied to the many religious who were *accomodati per la musica* – castrated, in other words, for the sake of the high, silvery voices which, Dupaty said, so ravished the ear and so appalled the sensitive nature. This was a deliberate flouting of canon law, which required priests to be whole men, and the accepted excuse was that the dulcet singing put the worshipper in a receptive frame of mind. Certainly the holy capons, as Stendhal called them, were chiefly responsible for the beguiling sweetness of sacred music, but generally speaking they were less in favour here than was the case at Rome, where actresses were not allowed. Venice had magnificent women singers for opera rôles and *castrati* were usually engaged only at private concerts. For their very occasional theatre appearances they were forbidden to use female dress, and so lost the chance to display their ambiguous charms to interested gentlemen, of whom there were many. But a *castrato* voice was always a terrific draw and some of the singers gained tremendous reputation. There was one named Peschierrotti to whom, in 1730, the whole town appealed to sing the Christmas Mass in San Marco.

The world of music had a population of its own, of precentors and organists and solo players, serving their art as others served their God. A galaxy of gifted composers – Marcello, Lotti, Galuppi and the rest – purveyed oratorios and operas by the hundred to a voracious public that constantly demanded something new. Vivaldi stands supreme among them for the breadth and variety of his genius, incredibly writing his fresh and lovely music in that period of moral chaos; music that has been likened to a spring of flowing water, that was his Paradise Regained as the world went to pieces. But true art will remain unaffected by exterior circumstance and both music and painting are still sane and vigorous as the Republic falls into decay. Not only does declining Venice produce her crop of remarkable composers, but she attracts the most famous then alive elsewhere. It is here that Handel, Gluck, Piccini and Paisiello wrote some of their most delectable operas. Cimarosa comes here to die, Mozart to celebrate the Carnival. The whole unceasing festival, moreover, conspired to praise and pet musicians. Charles de Brosses deplored the extravagant adulation, but all successful concerts ended with everybody present, Venetian and visitor alike, in collective and invariable delirium.

Best attended of any were the concerts at the *conservatori* attached to the four big hospitals, the Pietà, the Ospedaletto, the Incurabili and the Mendicanti. Here illegitimate or orphan girls, and some whose parents could not afford to keep them, were educated and provided by the state with dowries when they left for marriage or the convent. These *scuole* concentrated on the discovery of musical talent and the inmates, cloistered like nuns (for what that was worth), and studying hard under experienced masters, emerged as fine singers or executants, some to fame and fortune. It was a great question, round about 1740, whether la Chiaretta from the Pietà or Anna Maria from the Ospedaletto were the best violinist in Italy. As to the leading singer, all were agreed that was la Zabaletta of the Incurabili, and to mention anyone else in the same breath, says the Président, was as good as asking the populace to set upon you. All Venice adored these girls. Every boatman on the water and every citizen in the street called them by their Christian names. They were everybody's children, daughters and darlings of the city, and their talents fully merited the devotion they received.

The visitors yearned over them with the rest. Goethe was infatuated and Rousseau, quite carried away, vowed that never had he imagined anything so voluptuous, so touching, as their music. 'The art and taste, the beauty of the voices and the fine execution – everything about these delicious concerts produces an effect which I defy any man born to resist, little as it has to do with the dresses that are worn.'

Rousseau may have felt that the standard of costume did not match the non-sacred character of much of the programme. Many foreigners were shocked at what the young performers sang and played in church and chapel, and their choice was indeed calculated to bewilder the ascetic soul. In the ordinary way, when Venice went to church it could have danced to most of the music there, which differed little from what was heard at the theatre; but the *scuole* went farther still and regaled the audience with the most frivolous madrigals and opera tunes they could find, all among the *Stabat Mater's* and *Salve Regina's*. Saints at their concerts resembled dramatic heroines, though their admirers questioned whether the very angels could match the heavenly sweetness of their tones.

Every hospital had its speciality. The Pietà went in for orchestral, the Mendicanti for vocal music. Concerts, unlike opera, were listened to with deep attention and not a sound was heard unless, at a moment of culminating pathos, some lady went thudding in a dead faint to the floor. Each hospital, too, had its furious partisans; feeling ran so high that when Alvise Pisani managed to assemble stars from all four *conservatori* to perform in the same cantata for the King of Sweden he was credited with a diplomatic triumph and Francesco Guardi again commemorated the event.

The grille that separated these orphans from the world was very insubstantial. Often they were summoned to sing and play in palaces on the Grand Canal or at the spendid summer villas, and it could happen, in those exquisite surroundings, in the moonlit nights that they inspired the love they sang about: many of them became the mistresses, and some the wives, of noblemen. It was quite usual, we are told, for members of the audience to fall in love and to resolve on matrimony, and when the performers were pretty it was more usual than not. Often their physical attractions equalled their musical gifts and were well set off by their white dresses and the sprig of pomegranite tucked behind the ear. A large expanse of bosom naturally gratified M. le Président, who swore to his friend Blancey that nothing could be nicer.[108] The less susceptible Rousseau, too, was numbered with the adorers, on the grounds that the performers were transfigured by the music, music that was, in his opinion, unmatched in Italy or anywhere else in the world.

VI PAINTING

Since the day she rose from the ocean, Venice had loved and welcomed art of every kind. She bred sculptors of note, and architects whose skill created a distinctive style, a blending of Roman, Gothic and Oriental, of lightness and magnificence, grandeur and fantasy. But it was through painting, first and always, that she found her most complete expression. Bellini, Carpaccio, Giorgione, Titian, Veronese, Tintoretto had had no rivals and the love of painting, native to a people so devoted to the beauty of form and colour, was undiminished in the eighteenth century. But though the studios were still as full, and artists were cosseted and praised as much as ever, the giants had departed. The old traditions of elegance, line and colouring endured, but a new school had arisen, painting pictures of another sort.

This city, said Charles-Nicolas Cochin in his *Voyage Pittoresque de l'Italie* of 1751, could boast the ablest painters in the land, as good as the best in Europe. And art lovers were quite prepared to by-pass the rest of Europe and call upon Venetians, whose triumphs spread across the continent. Artists from Venice decorated princely and ducal residences, the palaces of kings and of German Electors, and the luxurious burgher-houses of Amsterdam. The Regent Orléans in Paris employed a Venetian and the Prince de Condé another, who later worked for Catherine the Great. Giovanni Segola was court painter at Vienna, Jacopo Amigoni at Madrid. Men like Sebastiano Ricci, Amigoni and Antonio Balestra simply dazzled their contemporaries with the boldness of their decorative schemes and their brilliant, subtle landscapes, and there are many others to note before we come to the great names in that long list: Giovanni Antonio Pellegrini, Antonio Diziani, Bartolomeo Nazari, Pietro Rotari, Jacopo Guarana.

Supreme among them is Giambattista Tiepolo – Tiepolo who brought some of the old glory of Veronese back to the autumn of Venice, a master of miraculous fertility and speed. Count Tessin told the King of Sweden that he could finish a picture in less time than another man took to get his palette ready.[109] He worked with driving, superhuman energy, spreading his daylight clarity over the ceilings of churches. The style may be theatrical and exaggerated on occasion, but the grandeur is constant, as is that pouring, lambent light. It is Venice herself we see on the high wide painted spaces, and in the fair-haired *amorini*, the goddesses and naked women floating in the clouds, have been identified the last troops of the Serenissima, an ultimate storming-party on the ramparts of sensual pleasure.

Tiepolo is followed by a galaxy of lesser painters, though they perhaps rank as such merely because there is no undue load of mystery or message in their work. The new modern spirit had brought a new way of looking at things and they concentrate on externals, turning aside from religious and historical subjects to reality and the common traffic of ordinary life. Their horizons are possibly narrowed a little as a result, but in this artistic decline – if decline it should be called – they bring home to us the beauty, the diversions and the daily round of Venice.

Earliest, and in her lifetime most famous of all, was Rosalba Carriera (1675–1757). She started out designing patterns for the lace-makers but later revived the art of miniature-painting, which brought her more money and commissions than she knew what to do with. The Regent Orléans and his mistresses – or two of them, at any rate – went into ecstasies over the small pastels which, in the opinion of the Goncourts, determined Quentin de La Tour in his profession. The whole feminine aspect of the century is apparent in her work; her sitters, with their pale complexions and air of fatigue, proclaim their indolent world to have been, all unsuspecting, in the throes of nervous prostration.

The normal business of this world is shown us by Pietro Longhi, the supreme chronicler of Venetian existence, whose pictures might be the living illustration of Goldoni's plays. Like another Lancret, a friendly, lively, mischievous Lancret who relished the pageant of the streets and loved to join people gossiping in the back of a shop, in front of a charlatan's booth or privately at home, he distilled from what he saw a vivid social record. Through him we watch the pretty nothings of a woman's day, the wielding of the fan, the side-long glance and secret, meaningful smile. Here is the *zentildonna* at her idle avocations and enjoyment as she pays her visits, sips her chocolate or has her hair done, as she interviews the dressmaker or learns the steps of a dance. On canvas after tiny canvas he portrays the masker, the water-seller and all the little folk of Venice, their antics and activities. The petty chronicle is transformed to art and poetry, interpreting and bringing that delightful, vanished life before our eyes until, in the words of Molmenti, 'we seem to hear the rustle of satin skirts and see the happy, dawdling time'. And not only was Longhi the interpreter of his age; he recalled the great painters who preceded him, and in his treatment of light anticipates the French Impressionists.

Then there are Canaletto, his pupils the Guardi brothers and

Bernardo Bellotto his nephew to give us a faithful likeness of the city as they knew it, the canals and festivals, the changing, colourful street-life, the marble and the water. Stylistic distinctions, not really helpful, have been made between them, but they are all very similar, despite Canaletto's characteristic precision, the more meticulous detail of Bellotto and the freer technique of the two Guardi. There are Guardi pictures in the Louvre that have been accredited to Canaletto in their time, and, since he and Bellotto were long thought to be one and the same and both use the signature 'Canaletto', attributions are often dubious. As for Francesco and Gian Antonio Guardi, they are harder yet to disentangle, and a recent exhibition of 160 of their canvases in Venice left the critics little wiser. They present in fact one of the trickiest problems of ascription ever known. It is difficult at best to tell their pictures apart, and they sometimes worked together. The presence of a third Guardi has also been suggested and a fourth one hinted at, for Domenico their father was himself a painter; and even Tiepolo, whose sister married Gian Antonio, may come into it as well.

Painters often formed these small groups, closely linked by professional or family ties, whose equally close collaborations are all but impossible to sort out, so that many works of the period set the same kind of puzzle. It was common practice for one artist to draw, and another to colour, a picture. Tiepolo is said to have done figure painting for Canaletto; Rosalba's painter-sisters would prepare the backgrounds of her miniatures and lay on the first wash. Altogether this particular corner of art-history is a scene of much confusion, for there are few signatures or dates to guide us and no useful documents survive.

But in these pictures of Canaletto, the Guardi and Bellotto, we can examine Venice minutely, exactly and from all angles; so much so that people have felt that little can have changed, save costume, since the eighteenth century, and that Casanova would be immediately at home in the marvellous city now. Yet in this, I think, they underestimate the magic beneath the surface realism. What we see is in fact the vision of artists looking back across the years to an earlier Venice and painting her as she could still appear to them.

And it was their vision the strangers carried away when the day came to leave the clear lagoon and hazy sky behind. It was wrapped up in their luggage with the *vedute* they all took home to remind them of the setting in which the enchanted month or year had passed. These veiw-paintings were produced for export and went abroad by hundreds, which is why Canaletto and the rest crowd the walls of England, France and Germany and are poorly represented in Venetian galleries. One sees the most popular subjects repeated again and again, and the foreigners aquired their inexpensive souvenirs from men who were never to earn the riches and glory they deserved. The view-painters congregated under the arcades, as painters sit in Paris in the Place du Tertre, all too often assiduously imitating the work and signatures of masters like Francesco Guardi, who sat in their company; not all with equal success, but there were enough good forgeries to have left a trail of enigma to this day.

Meanwhile, collectors all over Europe were striving to buy old pictures from noble Venetians in financial straits and the government, which had always kept a vigilant eye on the artistic treasures of the city, including those in private hands, decided in the end to intervene. All works of art were catalogued and the list kept carefully up to date. A commission was formed to authorise, limit and regulate restoration, deciding whether, how and in what spirit it should be done. Export was forbidden after 1773, but the ban came too late to save the whole heritage of Venice.

Aware also of the decline in painting, the government had set up an academy for young artists and sculptors at San Moisè in 1750, and at about the same date the patricians made the painters free of their private galleries. Some even paid good instructors to maintain minor academies in their palaces at one of which a life-class proved particularly valuable, for models were normally very hard to come by. (It was because of this that the great Venetians almost always paint the same female type: the beauties of Venice, 'more skilled in love than art', were supposedly readier to act as mistresses than models.) San Moisè provided one male or one female model on any given evening and allowed no changing of the pose to suit the students' whim. The studio, being open to all, attracted non-painters and non-sculptors in crowds with low motives.

All painters set great store by the public verdict. They put their finished pictures in the shop windows of the Merceria and studied the subsequent criticism in the gazettes. Sometimes a group would combine for an open-air show in one of the *campi*, and nobles and fried-fritter men strolled among the exhibits together, comparing judgments as they looked. Art knew no social barriers, and everybody came.

Not to be forgotten as recorders of Venetian life were those artists, second to none in spirit and invention, who worked so delicately with burin, Indian ink and water-colour on the profusion of ornamental vignettes. Their abiding theme was the langorous charm of Venice. Every fan, every invitation to a ball or a veil-taking, bore one of their tiny pictures, every lady's visiting-card some small, appropriate drawing – a lilliputian landscape or garden-scene, a posy of flowers or dolls'-house perspective of a street.

The illustration of all the almanacs and obscene books that poured from the presses was another excellent avenue for the native draughtsman with original ideas. This was an art which fascinated foreigners and many who practised it settled profitably in Rome, Florence or Lisbon, or as far afield as San Sebastian. Piranesi's taste was formed and his demanding metier learned in tasks of this kind, and though most of his engravings were produced in Rome he was born in the Veneto and must rank with Tiepolo as the supreme Venetian artist of his century.

Though painting was pre-eminent, this was also a time of excellence in other plastic arts. There were sculptors in Venice whom Théophile Gautier considered to have been the peers of any painter working; it always astounded him that they were not recognised at their true worth, and led him to reflect on what an arbitrary thing is fame. Architecture, too, was vigorous and powerful. Venetian baroque is seen to perfection in the Rezzonico and Gritti palaces and in the Gesuati church, and the original decorative tradition lived on as brilliantly as ever in the work of Massari, Tirali, Domenico Rossi and many more.[110]Nor should we pass over those other fertile craftsmen, makers of the painted furniture, the salvers, and the pretty boxes where women kept the mementos and favours of the masquerade – all objects with the typical grace and gaiety of *Settecento* Venice. And the glassblowers laboured in Murano at their wizardry, ever inventive of new shapes in the irridescent stuff that shimmered with every shifting reflection of the sky and the lagoon. Still, as the art of the Republic, which had borne the stamp of pure delight and pleasure-loving since the Golden Age, sank to mere virtuosity, these minor practitioners could touch the true note of the Carnival world. World without end, or so it seemed. World in a magic spell. World so very near its dissolution.

CHAPTER SEVEN

DEATH OF VENICE

I THE DEATH STRUGGLE

Every quality that once ennobled the Dominant Republic, vigour, courage, and activity itself, had vanished by the last years of the century. Gracious living and delicious ease were all that anyone thought about. Day after day, says Molmenti, was filled with 'balls and concerts and leisurely strolls; with caustic or subtle conversation, with love affairs and intrigue and little arrangements for getting round the regulations; with unbelievable luxury, dazzling receptions and endless Carnival.' The fêtes were more numerous and magnificent than they had ever been, for Venice lost all sense of the value of money when money ceased to flow into her coffers. People spent it like water. Cramming into the *casini*, competing for the services of barbers and wig-makers, they took their cue from a state grown prodigal in its old age. An analysis of expenses for the last ducal election – of money, that is, spent solely on the fads and fancies of the great men gathered in conclave to choose the Doge in 1789 – reveals the grave magistrates as entirely preoccupied with airy nothings. Forty-five lire covers all requirements for rosaries and religious paraphernalia, but the account for candles and sweetmeats came to 47,670 lire, while they got through 41,624 lire's worth of cassia (a useful purgative), and seem to have paid out 63,558 lire in tips. Combs, almanacs, toothpicks, rose-water, carnation-water, lavender essence, vanilla, gold-dust and rouge were also provided at staggering cost.

It is a nice question where all the money came from. By no stretch of imagination could it have been the product of labour, for economic paralysis had its grip on Venice. Andrea Tron reviewed the decline in a speech before the Senate: 'The industries we have inherited from our ancestors as part of our great national patrimony . . . are all decayed; in comparison with what they were, and what they ought to be, they exist no longer,' Many trades had perished for lack of custom, others survived thanks only to tax reliefs and the reduction of assessments. The forges were cold at the Arsenal, the potters' workshops all shut down. The weavers were ruined: the production of textiles, which had reached 28,000 pieces annually in the seventeenth century, was now under 700. Glass-making, so long the staple craft of Venice, was dwindling away. The Jews were blamed, as the supposed directors of industry and finance, but it proved useless to legislate against them. Forbidden to engage in business, and in some cases plundered outright, they took their trade and capital elsewhere. Most removed to Trieste and by the end of the century only some fifteen hundred still remained, living embittered under miserable conditions.

The time had been when the cult of Venice made her common people patriots, but for years and years now they had devoted themselves to festival diversion. They could not possibly subsist on their dead trade and dying industries but, under-employed and wretchedly in want, they flocked with all the old enthusiasm to the free entertainments lavished upon them to cloak the harsh realities. The patricians meanwhile went through life like sleep-walkers, the noble instincts that once drove them atrophied. The days of high adventure were forgotten and their idling was a poor example to a population ready, as ever, to imitate anything they did. They had sunk very far down in the world; 'poverty stared through the rents of gold and purple mantles now', as one historian puts it. The palaces crumbled away, rooms were stripped of treasures one by one. Arthur Young says that few owners did much in the way of decorating any more and fewer still were building. Rather, their beautiful marbles and famous pictures were for sale and Venice was compared to an old whore, reduced to peddling the furniture. Decree after decree forbade the export of works of art, but the government's only sanction was 'public indignation' and there was obviously nothing it could do. The upper classes needed cash. More and more of them were living from hand to mouth. Public indignation was not going to stop them raising money on their valuables and some of them even stood as beggars in the street.

For them, too, patriotism was a thing of the past. Office had become a burden. No one wanted nowadays to be a senator, to be a doge. Government business was conducted to empty benches.

The ranks of the patriciate, that had been so jealously guarded, were open to those who cared to pay. And no one cared to pay. The Libro d'Oro, Goudar said, had turned into a silver cash-book, but there were no applications.

As moral standards everywhere collapsed, the *zentildonne* lent themselves to flagrant prostitution, with pimps offering them to all and sundry on the Piazza. Their husbands lived on the profits of gaming-houses and by letting rooms in their palaces as business-premises to courtesans, a degrading activity duly rebuked by the Signory in 1793. Those who should have set an example, magistrates and dignitaries, were sunk in the general corruption. The very ambassadors took to debauch the moment they arrived.

Politically, all was calm as ever. The disturbing new ideas ascendant in France and in most other parts of Europe had not come to ruffle Venice yet, despite the fact that she was more lenient than many other powers and did little to exclude the works of the Enlightenment. Baretti's review, the *Frustra Letteraria*, was openly subversive, but it and others like it were published unhindered and that unorthodox character could lash out as he chose–rather, as has been said, in the spirit of Voltaire. Freemasonry, too, though usually mentioned with disapproval, was accorded the same tolerance. It came late to Venice, but from mid-century onwards mysterious foregatherings had been remarked whose secrecy and extraordinary appurtenances resembled those of masonic occasions. *Le Donne Curiose* of Goldoni reveals the participants in these dark doings for what in fact they were–peaceable gentlemen of the middle class, bent on mutual aid and conferring together on how best to spread their charity around. Casanova was boasting membership of a lodge in 1744, but it was only boasting. When he really was a mason he had less to say and we know from other sources that he reached high rank. That, however, was much later on and did not preclude his acting at the same time as a spy for the Jesuits. When the first lodge was founded in 1772 by Pietro Grattarol, a secretary of the Senate, the State Inquisitors knew of it at once. They knew all about the rules, the ceremonies, who belonged to it, how they were organised, where they met and their connection with Grand Lodge in London. The *confidenti* discovered it all quite easily, for Venetian freemasons were less reticent than most. The informer Manuzzi had only to express sympathetic interest and they told him all the masonic news. Banquets for new brethren were held openly and without precautions and a spy reports that, looking through a hole in the wall, he was able to identify the members and hear what they were saying: nothing, in his opinion, revolutionary or seditious.

Thus presumed harmless, the lodges were left free to extend their influence, and though there were never more than two in Venice, the Union and the True Light, they welcomed in the Barnabotti, churchmen and people from the university to swell their numbers. Under their aegis there arose at last a party with the declared aim of delivering the state from stagnation and giving her new vigour in accordance with the 'enlightened' principles current in Revolutionary Paris. Jacobinical Venetians cherished strange ideas about the 'liberty' of contemporary France, convinced as they were that every peasant would now receive a pension with which to relapse into an unconstrained and leisured life. The flavour of their demagogic discussions may be caught from the diatribe which Count Sicuro, *ingegnere pubblico* in government service and a regular attendant at Florian's, addressed to his barber on March 30, 1797, all in the familiar second person: 'You've heard about the revolt in Bergamo and Brescia? Same thing will happen here soon, and then you'll lead a lovely life. Another regime, different altogether. You'll earn twice as much as you do now, fewer taxes to pay, less to put up with and no one to order you round. Liberty everywhere, everybody enjoying it in peace and harmony.' Naturally, a spy was listening in.

But the commons showed no marked eagerness to receive this gospel. They were, as the barber replied to Sicuro, born subjects of their Most Serene Republic and asked no better than to die the same. Spurning novelty, they plodded along their own path, undisturbed. And yet a tide of opinion did exist, that rose from the spread of revolutionary thinking among the clergy and lesser nobility; a sea of troubles against which authority had no arms but espionage. The secret police were everywhere, hounding out anyone who spoke of, or who gave the least suspicion of seeming to favour, reform. 'Domiciliary visits,' says Auguste Bailly, 'searches and interrogations made of Venice a veritable spies' capital, with every café, church and gambling-house narrowly watched.'

The Serenissima, which almost alone in Europe had preserved the republican form of government and whose liberalism had been a byword for so long, now set her face against what she recognised for a poisonous and fatal set of notions. The doctrines of revolution gained strength on every side, but to the oligarchy of Venice they were to be treated as aberrations, nothing more.

Nor did there appear to be any good reason for amending a 1,000-year-old constitution merely to keep up with the times. In 1780 the Senators Giorgio Pisani and Carlo Contarini, both Barnabotti nobles, made bold to lay before the Great Council a project for reform which would have restored the ancient power of the Senate, long since lost to the Council of Ten. Not only did they find no support, they were thrown into prison for their pains. Such energy as remained to the governing class was used in opposing to the tide of newfangled ideas that great block of tradition and outmoded, immovable theory, the Venetian Order of Things.

The more farseeing, who realised invasion was sooner or later inevitable, demanded that forces be raised. They were assured in reply that the French Revolutionary government could not last; that nobody could attack across the Alps. And there was the sea, their source of strength and glory; nobody could conquer the sea. Lulled in this nonsense, Venice felt safe from the hurricane that raged in Paris. In any case, what would become of the balance of power without her? And how could regicide France do other than seek alliance with a senior republic? Alliance had been promised in 1795, when the president of the Convention greeted Alvise Querini, the ambassador, with the words, 'France beneath the yoke of despotism could prove wily and thankless, but free, Republican France is a grateful, loyal friend. Go and tell your nation it may count the French nation among its most devoted and disinterested allies.' Slothful, improvident Venice laid these comforting untruths to her heart and the fêtes and festivals were just as gay as ever.

Then the guns began to thunder and the drums began to beat. There may have been some small loss of illusion, but when Francesco Pesaro urged in the Senate that Venice was doomed if she did not arm, nobody took him seriously. She could not arm, contended one of the Savii, without unpopular taxes, and unpopularity carried more risk than any foreign threat. 'I vote that Venice maintain a pacific attitude,' he said, 'make no military preparations and proclaim her fixed intention to live in amity with all the world.' And the majority agreed with him.

But the French Army of Italy, Bonaparte at its head, was coming on by leaps and bounds and the situation was anxious. Austria

on one hand controlled the Tyrolean passes, Bonaparte on the other
advanced towards the mainland territory; and confronted with
these mighty foes Venice reiterated her neutrality and claimed a
neutral's privileges. The Conscript Fathers of the Golden Book
went on imagining that luck or cunning would successfully deliver
them from war, despite the fact that they were feeling its effects
already. A former ambassador wrote on July 16, 1796; 'So far our
possessions are defended by diplomacy, but I fail to see that we can
fence like this much longer.'

The town meanwhile was full of rumour and unrest. One small
faction advocated faith in Austria to whom, more than to any of the
powers, it was important to preserve the inherited dispensation.
But they were overruled in council and the discontented element,
set on reform and further encouraged by the French victory of Casta-
glione on August 5, 1796, at the very frontiers, argued for a French
alliance. Increasingly the name of Bonaparte was heard, and though
some hated him, many were enthusiastic. Was he not the man for
this new hour? But still the nobles clung to the belief in neutrality
as an efficient safeguard, and certainly no one, whether he looked
to Austria or not, and assuredly not if he were in the government,
ever envisaged such a thing as the collapse of Venice herself – the
magical city with Europe in her debt. There were no Cassandra
voices. Any twinge of doubt or apprehension was revealed only to
the closest and most discreet of correspondents. Thus Pietro Pesaro
wrote in the April of 1796 to his confidante and 'loving friend'
Caterina Corner, of the attitude in Rome, where he was ambassador: 'These priests! They want peace with the French but dare not
breathe that nation's name. They want to fight but lack the means.
Nothing, in short, gets done because no one knows what to do, and
when the storm breaks – and it will not be long in coming – let
those who are caught in it beware.'

The population as a whole was as little preoccupied as ever with
what was going on, aware only of what it read in the gazettes or
gathered from the cryptic utterances of worried men. The question
of emancipation seemed nothing to bother about. The government
gave them all a good existence and they were deeply attached to it.
As far as they were concerned, the rulers knew what they were doing
and Venice was of course invulnerable. The joybells rang, they
cast care away and threw themselves into the round of pleasure
with a will: the last Carnival of the Republic was every bit as gay

and animated as any that went before. Among the Lippomani family letters[111] is one of February 22, 1797: 'here we are plunged into the whirl of Carnival, with everybody acting as though nothing were wrong and all were going right. It makes a lively spectacle.' A pit was yawning under the maskers' feet to swallow their irresponsible and charming world, yet no one in the humming Piazza di San Marco seemed aware that this was the last fling. They resembled Virgil's Trojans,

> *Nos delubra deum miseri, quibus ultimus esset*
> *Ille dies, festa velamus fronde per urbem.*

> Unhappy beings we were, come to our last day,
> Decking the temples with garlands as though for a festival.

And this with the enemy battering at their gates.

Disaster was henceforth foreseen, expected, known. Marco Foscarini quoted publicly the famous tag from Livy, 'Things are at the point where the evil and its remedy are alike intolerable.' A secretary of the Ten informed his brother, 'as soon as the smallest force is on us we shall lose our possessions, not just in one campaign, but in a monent'. In this terrifying quandary the whole action of the Republic was to order the closing of all cafés by two o'clock in the morning. The turgid speeches on the glorious past went on, the uncontrollable, frantic revelry went on, and the French arrived at the landward frontiers. This time the end was in sight. There began the tragic dialogue of Venice with Napoleon.

II FINALE

For that taciturn and overbearing man the softer side of life might just as well not have existed. From childhood he was used to poverty and hard work. He commanded a tatterdemalion army. What sort of idea could he possibly form of the Serenissima? He was immune to her centuries-old charm, the good breeding of the antiquated state meant as little to him as did her ancient rights. Her people he dismissed as stupid poltroons, quite unfit for liberty. This republic was a shadow, and once within her territories he scourged them like the plague. Small arms, cannon, commissariat were demanded. A hospital here, fifty tons of flour there. Demanded at once, on pain of wholesale destruction. At the first hint of opposition he blazed into ferocity and menace. 'He recognises no limits to the power of his will,' said Mocenigo.

To this unmannerly general with his threats and exactions, his rudeness and perpetual ill temper, Venice dispatched the most accommodating and courteous of her noblemen, whom he treated with undisguised contempt. As Pietro Pesaro knew, negotiations were a waste of time.

Bonaparte brandished his thunderbolts at an adversary he knew to be unarmed and absolutely unprepared to face him. Her fleet was no longer on a war footing, few of the nine thousand pieces of artillery she still possessed were fit to use and the muskets her soldiers carried were worn out. And even with equipment, what could she have done? The traditional bravery of her people was so diminished that at every distant cannon shot they feared the worst. One of the gazettes reported ladies vanishing 'like a flight of doves' the minute they heard an arquebus going off, and added that the gentlemen vanished with them, too polite to leave them unattended.

From these wretched and defenceless lands of the Veneto Bonaparte at first wished merely to wring the money to pay for his campaigns. 'You are to get all you can out of the Venetian states,' ran his instructions to his Quartermaster-General, Lambert; and an immediate five million francs would be acceptable, to sweeten the Directory in Paris. Soon, however, it dawned on him that Venice would make a fine counter in the political bargaining that was about to begin. France badly wanted the Austrian Netherlands and Austria might well give them up in exchange for expansion in Italy. With this in view, the Directory was prepared to return Lombardy to the Empire, but Bonaparte gave added weight to the offer by throwing Venice in as well.

That was the Republic's death sentence. Now he had only to get her government, by force of arms, to abdicate, and must concoct some pretext for his action. Any means was good enough, any trick would serve, and he even resorted to barefaced provocation, admitting as much in a letter to the Directory of July 20, 1796: 'I am having to work up a quarrel with the Provveditore. I exaggerate the number of our soldiers who are being murdered by the people and make a great fuss about belligerent behaviour, which they never showed when the Austrians had the upper hand.' In his quest for trumped-up disputes he descended to the forgery of documents and declarations. At any cost, he had to have a war.

Faced with these tactics, the Republic could not so much as complain. The slightest murmur would have been fatal. As Mallet du Pin later wrote, 'Venice abandoned all her lawful rights, even that of protest.'[112] She no longer controlled her own territories, but everything that happened there was laid at her door. The requisitions, the violence and outrages multiplied. Bergamo and Brescia revolted from her, egged on by the invading French, whose spokesman soon appeared in Venice to deliver his affronts in the midst of the Easter ceremonies. On Sunday, April 15, 1797, Junot came as delegate from his general, convoked the Senate, sat down on the Doge's throne and accused the assembly of bad faith. Five days after this Bonaparte, without the remotest justification, sent a ship to cruise off the Lido island and defy the port defences. It is clear from all the evidence that he was looking for trouble, for Berthier had outlined such a scheme as long ago as the beginning of March: 'The *Sibylle* can provoke the Venetian fleet, which is bound to attack. They then lay themselves open, and we can retaliate.'

The plan worked perfectly. A French dispatch-boat, the *Libérateur de l'Italie*, arrived before the Lido on April 20th and made for the San Nicolò channel, despite warnings from the fort. The shore batteries fired on her. Had they done no more they would have been within their rights, but unhappily some troops also joined in the attack and the boarding-party killed the captain, Laugier, and five of his sailors. The suicidal, hoped-for act of aggression was at last committed.

Bonaparte exploited it without delay, proclaiming it as the most appalling event of the century. 'I shall be an Attila to the Venetian state, they can take their law from me.' When deputies came from the Senate with explanation and excuse he roughly rejected them: 'I cannot receive you. You and your Senate have shed the blood of Frenchmen and all the gold in Peru would not keep me from avenging it.'

The Serenissima had been able to do nothing all this time but suffer, give in, swallow the insults, maltreatment and abuse. Her only object had been to keep out of trouble and to temporise. She had paid, she had submitted. But now the price was terrible. She must part with her mainland possessions, hand over the city and the Arsenal, amend her government into a 'democracy'. Could she, at the last, rally and defend herself? If she must perish, could she go down fighting?

It was not beyond the bounds of possibility. Unarmed she might be, but there were still a few men-of-war, gunboats and galleys.

There were troops, disorganised, but they could shoot; obsolete cannon, but they could be used. There were enough brave and loyal workers at the Arsenal to crew a fleet and overmatch the yet smaller enemy squadron, ignorant of the channels and at the mercy of the lagoon. But such desperate defenders would need example from above and none, at the vital moment, was forthcoming. Failing in their duty, many of the officers refused to engage their men or ships, while others showed cowardice even more openly by flight or resignation of their posts.

Venice surrendered therefore with no honour and no dignity, at the sacrifice of her pride, her past, and everything that ever made her great. The Ten were disbanded, the Inquisitors removed from office. The Great Council ceased to exist. Authority was yielded up to Bonaparte with the request that he establish what form of government he considered suitable; and this proved to be a kind of Committee of Public Safety, ideal, so he claimed, for bringing the creaking old Republic up to date. And as the grievous confusion went on a cry of *San Marco! San Marco!* was heard in the streets, the ancient slogan of freedom that once resounded on the battlefield. It was the common people of St Mark, the porters and gondoliers and still-faithful Dalmatian soldiery, a body of whom, with cudgels and knives in their hands, raised the venerable lion-standard, broke a few windows and assaulted a few notorious Jacobins. After that their courage gave out and by the time an appeal had gone to the new power to restore order, the trouble was over. The flame sank down of its own accord; Venice was not alive any more. The French who entered on May 15th were the first invaders seen there in all her fourteen hundred years of history.

There were only five thousand of them, coming in forty longboats furnished by the Venetians themselves – boats and pilots without whom they could not have come at all. Under General Baraguay d'Hilliers they occupied the islands, the forts, the Arsenal and the strongpoints. They were in tearing spirits, in contrast with the mourning city – lanky men, scorched with gunpowder, who had marched like machines and fought like devils for eighteen months. Now they were masters of Venice and with them a new age began. The light of heart, the heedless charmers, those who avoided all that was ugly or sad, their time was gone. Carlo Gozzi was to head the last chapter of his memoirs *You Cannot Laugh for Ever*, but Venice had thought you could. It never occurred to her that a grain of

fatality lies at the heart of happiness too easily come by; that the
reckoning is presented sooner or later for our sins; that stern effort,
and not pure gratification, makes the world go round. Most of
those who ministered to her pleasures were to see the joy go out of
life. Rosalba Carriera died blind, Goldoni destitute, Caterina Tron
neglected and forgotten. Gasparo Gozzi tried to drown himself in
the Brenta. At the castle of Dux, in Bohemia, Casanova ended as
the laughing-stock of the servants, who hung his portrait on the
lavatory wall. Others, meanwhile, proof against the collapse and
ruin of illusion, hurled the winged lion to the ground and threw
the Golden Book and the Doge's insignia on to a public bonfire.[113]
Women danced half naked round the Liberty Tree in front of St
Mark's and the columns of the Piazzetta were scrawled all over
with adulation of Bonaparte.

Venice ended at the tragic Peace of Campo Formio. 'The French
Republic consents to His Imperial Majesty's taking possession of
Istria, Dalmatia, the former Venetian islands in the Adriatic, of
Cattaro, Venice, the lagoons, etc.' It dismembered her territory
and made division of her treasures.[114] A republican commander,
speaking Italian as his mother tongue and acting in the name of
what claimed to be a generous nation that advocated the brotherhood of man, put to auction a Catholic power which once defended
Europe from the Turk. It is good to remember that there were
French diplomats who disapproved and that an indignant protest
reached the Directory in Janaury 1798, from their envoy Lallemont:
'I shall not disguise from you how much our conduct towards this
people has increased their already existing hatred of all we are and
all we stand for. We tricked our way into their capital and provinces
and, now we are handing them over to a new master, having robbed
them shamefully.'

But if the French in 1797 were too drunk with victory for the
fall of the Serenissima to seem to them very important, Europe as a
whole took absolutely no notice eighteen years later when the fact
of it was confirmed. Under the treaties of 1815 the kings of the Holy
Alliance, sworn to restore what the revolutionary hurricanes had
swept away, left Venice to the Austrians, and in so doing made
cynical nonsense of the liberation they were talking about. They
perpetrated an ignominious fraud, and no one displayed an atom of
compunction over it.

In the opinion of Taine the Republic relapsed into irreligion, like the small Grecian states before her, through thoughtlessness and amorality. Instead of heroes and great artists, it was the voluptuary and the dilettante who lived in the evening of Venice, with never a glance before or behind; an evening that glowed with all the brilliance of day's end on the lagoon. The sunset faded, night came, dense and melancholy over the dark canals, and images of death and dissolution succeeded those of rapture and felicity; no more sound of bells or laughter, no more songs. Doleful nineteenth-century poets saw her as a vast, magnificent cemetery, and that vision held good until quite recently. Now it is to the magic and tranquillity that we respond, taking our less sombre view of her guarded and unstrident loveliness.

It helps, I think, to know something of the Venice of Tiepolo, Longhi and Goldoni, who lived when the delights of the water-city were at their most entrancing, and knew her when she was most perfectly herself. She may have settled too placidly to her unadventurous decline, yet the passion for beauty never left her and redeemed her from vulgarity and bitterness in her old age. It was more than she could do to muster energy for a struggle at the end, but, genuinely convinced the Carnival was going on for ever, at least she died as she had lived: elegantly, at a fête.

NOTES

1. Philippe Monnier, *Venise au XVIIIe Siècle* (Librairie Académique Perrin, 1923). My text incorporates quotations from this and other valuable sources.

2. The heroine of *La Commediante in Fortuna*, a novel by Pietro Chiari, gives a sketch of Casanova which could serve as a portrait of the epoch of intrigue and adventure that he represents. The *abate* Chiari had few literary gifts, but here hatred for his model winged his words and lent venom to his pen. For once he produced something worth reading and Casanova never forgave him. 'His origins are dubious and presumably irregular. He is a well-made man of darkish complexion, affected manners and unbelievable self-assurance. One of those people who seem to cut a dash in society without anyone's knowing where the lustre comes from or what they do for a living. Living a life of leisure, what's more, with no land, no employment and no capabilities. . . . He is mad about everything from the other side of the Alps, talks of nothing but London and Paris, as if the whole world consisted of those famous capitals. He has actually spent some time there, though what he did and how he fared I cannot say. But London and Paris are always being dragged in as models for his behaviour, dress, and interests, in a word for all his silly fancies. He is a dandy, full of himself, blown up with vanity like a balloon and fussing about like a watermill. He has to be working his way in everywhere, paying court to all the women, grabbing every chance to get his hands on some money or use his conquests as a ladder to social success. He plays the alchemist with misers, the poet with pretty women, and the politician with important people – all things to all men, though to anyone with a grain of sense he only makes himself ridiculous. With a head full of air, and giddy to match, he can be your sworn friend or foe in no time at all.'

Equally biting is the picture found in the many reports sent in to the Council of Ten, for Casanova was constantly under close supervision. Right from the beginning he is said to be 'clever at exploiting people and living at their expense'. A spy named Manuzzi notes how he consorts with persons of scandalous life and assists in their unlawful pleasures. He would entice foreigners into rigged card-games and if anything awkward happened 'offer to say he had been cheating and take all the blame himself'.

3. Guido Piovene, *Voyage en Italie* (Flammarion, 1958).

4. Theodore was the original patron saint of Venice, presiding until the ninth century when, though innocent of all offence, he was demoted by popular demand. The embalmed body of his successor, St Mark, was smuggled from Alexandria in a chest irreverently labelled 'Pork'. The Senate bade San Marco welcome in the words of Christ appearing in his cell, *Pax tibi, Marce, evangeliste meus*, and built the basilica to house the relics. The lion, which plays no part in Venetian history before the fourteenth century, holds the book open at the very words.

5. Of the three columns brought from the Orient in the twelfth century, one fell into the sea at unloading. The others proved impossible to place upright, and the Lombard engineer who finally solved the problem was allowed to run an open-air gambling-house between them as a reward. But he did altogether too well with it, and the execution site was fixed here in order to ruin the establishment.

6. Its lack of uniformity is the result of five fires and the subsequent rebuildings, each in the idiom of its own time.

7. The Procuratie were the buildings used as offices and houses by the nine Procurators of St Mark, three of whom were responsible for the basilica and six for the city on either side of the Grand Canal.

8. Charles de Brosses, 1709–77. He was born at Dijon and became eventually Président of the Parlement of Burgundy. He was a friend of Buffon and Diderot, and quarrelled furiously with Voltaire over a property sale. He was here in 1739, and the *Lettres Familières sur l'Italie* were published long after his death, in 1799; a most rewarding book. His other works include a study of Herculaneum and *Histoire des navigations aux Terres Australes*.

9. Robert Abirached, *Casanova ou la Dissipation* (Grasset, 1961).

10. I.e. the Water Department. The magistrates of the Piovego were responsible for checking the level of the lagoon, and similar matters.

11. See the article by Diego Valeri, 'Venise vue par un Italien', *Revue Hebdomadaire* (June 26, 1936).

12. René Guerdan, *Vie, Grandeurs et Misères de Venise* (Plon, 1951). The reference is to an earlier period, but things must have been much the same, at least in the early years of the eighteenth century.

13. Goldoni's Memoirs were published in three volumes in Paris in 1787 and dedicated to Louis XVI, who subscribed for fifty copies. An English translation, edited by W. A. Drake, was published by Knopf in 1926. The most modern edition is that of the *Mercure de France* (1964).

14. The distinguished astronomer Jérôme Lefrançais de Lalande, whose *Voyage d'un Français en Italie* was first published anonymously in 1768.

15. 1521–86, author of *Venezia, città Nobil^{ma} e Singolare*, and son of the architect Jacopo.

16. Respect for long-hallowed institutions even led the Venetians to reject proposals that might have made life easier. The light boats with five rowers known as galleasses were inconvenient, dangerous and expensive, but the Senate managed to abolish them only after thirty years of argument, in 1769, the main contention of the pro-galleass party having been throughout that anything old ought to be venerated and kept going.

17. These figures were taken from the archives of the Razon Vecchie, or Audit Office, and quoted by Charles Yriarte in *La Vie d'un patricien de Venise* (Rothschild, 1874).

18. Though the senators stood up, hat in hand, to receive ambassadors, he remained seated and covered. Some diplomats considered this too unceremonious and casual by far, and St Petersburgh even made official protests.

19. Various naive and artless customs persisted from earlier centuries among the stately pageantry. Until the end of the Republic the fruitsellers would make their formal visit to the Doge, each with his personal present of a melon. And on Easter Tuesday seventeen women from Poveglio arrived who, before sitting down to a hearty meal, availed themselves of an ancient right and all lined up to kiss him.

20. François Maximilien Misson, ?1650–1722, was a French Protestant who took refuge in England in 1685 and travelled as tutor to the grandson of the first Duke of Ormonde. His *Nouveau Voyage d'Italie, avec un Mémoire contenant des avis utiles à ceux qui voudront faire le mesme voyage* was published at The Hague in 1691 and long read and relied on. All quotations are from the English translation of 1699.

21. See p. 43.

22. *L'espion chinois ou l'envoyé spécial de la cour de Pékin pour examiner l'état présent de*

l'Europe was published at Cologne in 1769. The author, Ange Goudar, was probably French by birth. His sphere was that of crooks and card-sharpers and shady literary men and Casanova's Memoirs show what a nasty character he was.

23. Caterina Dolfin Tron had a pretty wit and once introduced the (highly immoral) Princess of Gonzaga among the Venetian ladies with the words: 'Her family one can answer for, but for her, and for me, and for you, I must disclaim responsibility.'

24. Votes were cast by means of *ballotte*, covered with coloured cloth and marked with the arms of Venice. These were placed in voting-urns carried round the benches by the *ballottini*, who were young orphan or foundling children. *Ballottini* for the Senate were selected by lot in the sacristy of St Mark's.

25. To this the one exception was the embassy at Constantinople, which was in fact a magistrature and came within the sphere of the Great Council. The Bailo, as the ambassador to the Porte was called, rule a whole population of Venetians settled or trading in the Levant.

26. When the Senate was first instituted and had no regular meeting-day, messengers were sent to members' houses to request, *pregare*, their attendance; and so they came to be known always as the *pregadi*.

27. First of these Wise Men of the Terra Ferma was the Savio alla Scrittura, almost an Under-Secretary of State for War, with authority over the commanders of the land and sea forces, who were themselves appointed by the Senate. The second was the Savio Cassier who paid the army and the state pensions and all the bills for fortifications and defence. The Savio alle Ordinanze ordered troop movements and saw to quartering and garrison accommodation, while the two remaining Savii helped as necessary.

28. Two of the Inquisitori were nominated by the Ten themselves and called *i neri*, because of their black robes. The third, *il rosso*, who wore red, was chosen from among the ducal counsellors.

29. Casanova was most probably suspected of being a Freemason, but the spy Manuzzi, who was on his track, could report only that he kept bad company and had various devious projects which indicated plain shifty behaviour rather than any particular magical skill: he would take any fool's money and promise to introduce him in exchange to an Angel of Light. An atheistical poem is also mentioned, but no one managed to produce it. The spy indeed offered little solid justification for the arrest. The Inquisitors were going to find their prisons uncomfortably crammed if they pursued irreligion, false pretensions and debauch, yet all these were imputed to Casanova and were just the things they aimed at suppressing for the general good.

30. 'Human nature,' ran the request, 'ever bent on self-preservation, will make a real effort only when its daily bread is at stake.

'For my unhappy part, I appeal to the Most Serene Prince for some small maintenance, not because I have earned it by discovering anything useful – of that he alone can judge – but in order that a pittance may perhaps indicate that what I shall strive to discover may be useful in the future.

'I implore pardon of Your Excellencies, in your wisdom and mercy. Gratefully, Giacomo Casanova.'

31. Giovanni Comisso has published a selection in his fascinating book, *Agenti Segreti Veneziani nel '700 (1705–97)* (Valentino Bompiani, 1945).

32. The letters N.H. stood for Nobil Homine, used before the names of persons of rank.

33. Charles de Secondat, baron de Montesquieu, 1689–1755, wrote much that was of revolutionary influence. *L'Esprit des Lois*, which accompanied Bonaparte while he was campaigning in Italy, was published in 1748. As for the joke, Lord

Chesterfield has been suggested as the culprit, and it would have been quite in character; but he was not in Venice at the time and was ambassador in Holland when Montesquieu met him, twelve months afterwards.

34. 'I have read both volumes,' he wrote on October 22, 1763, 'and consider it my duty, with all due respect, to draw the attention of the Tribunal to this book, which contains metaphysical discussion, mockery of priests and prelates and of the Sovereign Pontiff; together with material concerning the nobility of Venice, the Doge and a patrician Senator, as well as incidents of an obscene and beastly nature.'

35. A varied career. Claude de Bonneval, 1675–1747, was first a naval, then a military officer in France, then fought against her under Prince Eugène. Austria, Venice and Russia dispensed with his services in turn and he embraced the Moslem faith in 1730, commanding the Sultan's artillery under the name of Achmet Pasha, and governing Roumelia.

36. Casanova mentions the abbé Richard, whose *Description historique et critique de l'Italie* was published in Paris in 1766: 'He is wrong about this state prison, for he does not know what he is talking about and makes mistakes. He says that only a strong man can stand the conditions and survive there for four or five years, which is not true. What are called "the leads" are not gaols but small furnished lock-ups, with barred windows, at the top of the ducal palace, and the inmate is said to be "under the leads" because the roof is covered with sheets of lead over the larch-wood beams. These leaden sheets make the rooms cold in winter and very hot in summertime. But the air is good, you get enough to eat, a decent bed and everything else you need, clothes, and clean laundry when you want it. The Doge's servants look after the rooms and a doctor, a surgeon, an apothecary and a confessor are always on hand.'

37. Robert Abirached, op. cit.

38. Such, too, was the fate of consular agents, whose promised salaries were left unpaid. They were shamefully used, and Goldoni was among the victims. Having accepted the consulship at Genoa, he increased his household and made arrangements to live and entertain in style, only to receive no more by way of payment than an official disclaimer: the Senate was very pleased with him, the government agreed he was entitled to reimbursement; but his predecessor had served for twenty years without a salary; there was a war on in Corsica; and authority felt unable to meet an item for which it had long ceased to admit responsibility.

39. *La Storia di Venezia nella vita privata dalle origini alla caduta della repubblica* (1882). This book was translated into English by Horatio Brown and published by Murray in 1908. Molmenti wrote many works on Venetian history and was one of those who insisted on the Campanile's being rebuilt on exactly the same spot after its fall in 1902.

40. This limit was lowered in the case of the thirty young men chosen by lot on St Barbara's day, December 4th, to become counsellors *alla Barbarella*.

41. Giuseppe Baretti, 1719–89. He visited London in 1751 and later lived there for some years, a friend of Johnson, Goldsmith and Garrick. His *Account of the Manners and Customs of Italy, with observations on the mistakes of some travellers, with regard to that country*, was published in 1768 to refute a book by an English surgeon, Samuel Sharp of Guy's Hospital. See p. 149.

42. *La Ville et la République de Venise*, by Limojon de Saint-Didier, was published at Amsterdam in 1680.

43. When, according to Misson, the fur linining was removed, 'but the Edges, and that part which is turn'd up, remain still furr'd'.

44. The objection to the periwig originated with an Inquisitor who was shocked into bad temper by the sight of young men with long blond locks coming to visit

his wife, when he had distinctly and recently seen that their hair was short and dark.

45. The long beard seen in the pictures by Tintoretto and Titian had disappeared many years before.

46. Auguste Bailly, *La Sérénissime République de Venise* (Fayard, 1958).

47. By the same token, bribery and corruption were employed against ambassadors. Montaigu reports that the Inquisitors set one of his footmen to spy on him. 'I had the man followed and found not only that he was opening my letters, but that he really was an agent and went regularly by night to the Inquisitors of State, who paid him six ducats a month to tell them what went on in my household.' (Dispatch of September 18, 1745.)

48. For ten months in 1743–4 Rousseau was not, as he liked to boast, secretary of the embassy, but one of the secretaries of the ambassador, who had a low opinion of him and sacked him like a servant in the end. His stay in Venice forms one of the dullest parts of the *Confessions*. He seems to have seen nothing of the town and never describes it, though one would have thought it sufficiently unusual to have inspired the earliest descriptive writer in French literature. The inhabitants, too, he ignores, save for the account of his not very glorious visits to second-rate prostitutes. The only crumbs of interest are some details of the frugal embassy life – 'not a corner that a decent man could tolerate, scanty food, dirty linen, pewter plates and iron forks'. Overwhelmed at his confidential position in the world of diplomacy, he concentrates on decrying the ambassador in order to emphasise his own importance.

49. It has been said that these detailed narrations are flights of fancy from first to last and Bernis denies everything in his own memoirs. His house, he says, was run like a monastery and even the government noticed how austere he was, 'as though insensible to female charms in a country where no one thought it a sin to succumb'. But other sources reveal him as 'very amorous by nature and devoting himself to the Venetian ladies' instead of to affairs of state, though he pretended that he worked so hard as to affect his health. There is the tale in Stendhal's *Promenades en Rome* of how he stole Casanova's mistress. The fact remains, however, that we have no trustworthy documentary evidence as to whether Casanova tells the truth or not and a note in the Sirène edition (ed. Raoul Vèze, Paris, 1924–35) sensibly suggests that we wait and see what future research may bring forth.

50. It will surprise no reader of Lady Mary Wortley Montagu to learn that this was her enemy, Sir John Murray, who was in Venice between 1754 and 1766.

51. 1757–1832; a poet in both Italian and the Venetian dialect.

52. To practise at the bar it was necessary to hold a diploma from Padua, but since that university taught only Roman law and nothing but Venetian law was used in Venice, this meant five years of study wasted. Aspirants therefore learned their business at the law-school in Venice and showed themselves in Padua four times a year, to obtain certificates of attendance.

53. A translation of these *Memorie* may be found as an appendix to *The Taste of Angels*, by F. H. Taylor (Hamish Hamilton).

54. Auguste Bailly, op. cit.

55. *Italy; with Sketches of Spain and Portugal*. By the Author of 'Vathek' (1834).

56. Verona wines nowadays are excellent and well worth attention. Misson, after lamenting the 'pall'd disgustful Taste' of the sweet stuff drunk in Venice, adds this horrible note on *garbo*: 'After they have drawn off the pure liquor, they mix Water with the Stalks, that they may squeeze some sharpness from them. 'Tis also mixt with Lime, Allum, etc. which gives it some piquant briskness, but makes it very harsh, besides, this Mixture palls and weakens the wine, which was not very strong before.'

57. Eight lire made one silver ducat, twenty *soldi* made one lira, and twelve

baggalini one *soldo*. The crown was twelve lire and the gold sequin twenty-two. Louis Simond, who published his Italian travels in 1828 and knew Venice at the beginning of the nineteenth century when everything except wages had gone up by almost a quarter since the coming of the French, gives a list of food prices with their equivalent in French money. Bread, beef and mutton were four, twelve and nine sous respectively; rice and macaroni four and seven sous; wine was six sous a bottle and a chicken cost a franc. This was when labourers were earning one and a half francs a day, carpenters and masons three and gondoliers two. His figures confirm the values I have suggested here, remembering that wages did not keep pace with prices.

58. Arthur Young, 1741–1820, the agriculturalist, radical and writer of travel books, was in Italy in 1789.

59. 'I, Giacomo Casanova, humble subject of Your Excellencies, lay myself at the feet of your august tribunal, soliciting your inviolable justice, and deserving death if anything I say is less than true.

'Last night, wearing a mask and *bautta*, I went with a masked lady to the San Luca theatre, where I gave the doorman a sequin and asked for change. The porter took the number of our box and promised to bring it to me there: box C in the second row. Soon he came to say the coin was two grains light and I told him to fetch it, being sure it was full weight. The coin he produced did not look to me like the one I gave him, but rather than make a fuss I told him to come back in an hour and I would give him the twenty *soldi*, since I was expecting someone (who in fact turned up), from whom I could borrow it. He went off, but reappeared almost immediately, saying he did not want to wait. This seemed odd and made me rather suspicious. He then found two other men, one of whom, Bartolo dalla Todesca by name, was ruder to me than my worst enemy could have been if trying to provoke me to some rupture of the law. I told him to send the water-seller to me and that I would be able to let him have his twenty *soldi* straightaway, but he refused and I could hardly leave the lady and go myself. In the end, to stop his insults, I gave him the sequin, but neither he nor his friends ever brought me my change, though I should have had twenty lire and eight *soldi*, even if the coin were light.'

60. These had to some extent replaced the Jesuit schools after the first expulsion of the Order in the seventeenth century.

61. Henri, recently elected to the Polish throne, had become King of France on the death of his brother and was on his way home. Refreshments in the main hall of the Arsenal were followed by a grand concert. They worked on the galley while this was going on and she was ready for launching as he left.

62. Here the Président coins the French *ingannions* from the Italian *ingannare*, to cheat.

63. 'They are acquainted with all the Turns and Windings, says Misson, 'they pretend to know the critical Minutes, and the private Stairs, and to hold Correspondence with the Waiting-Women.'

64. A dirty story about his own sister amused him so much that he fell off his stool, knocked himself out and died as a result.

65. 1712–46; a charmer of European reputation. Lady Mary rearranged her life round him and for years hoped that he would join her abroad, but she had to share his affections with Lord Hervey and Frederick the Great, among others. He was a dilettante scholar and his books include an exposition 'for Ladies' of the theories of Newton.

66. All these examples are quoted by Molmenti or Monnier.

67. *Observations sur l'Italie et sur les Italiens données en 1764, sous le nom de deux gentilhommes suédois* (Paris, 1774).

68. The twenty-four hours were reckoned in a most peculiar fashion all over Italy in the eighteenth century: the day began with the Angelus, midday and midnight varying with the time of year. Clocks and watches were regulated to match.

69. In the National Gallery of Scotland, Edinburgh.

70. Betrothal and marriage became no less expensive, for the various ceremonies were all deterimined by ancient tradition and very costly. Goldoni was forced to flee from Venice and abandon a fiancée who, much as she loved him, would never have forgiven any skimping of the requisite formalities.

71. The name Bucintoro is said to have come from the figure of a centaur on the original barge, the prefix *bu* meaning 'big' in Venetian.

72. This was the disgruntled sovereign who once greeted the Venetian ambassador with 'Tell your Doge that if he goes against my wishes, I shall get him into bed with that wife of his yet'.

73. Quotations from Lady Mary are taken from the collected edition of her letters, published by the Oxford University Press (1965-7), ed. Robert Halsband.

74. These battles were stopped in the latter years of the Republic and had by then lost much of the fierceness that so exhilarated Henri III.

75. It is thus described by Norbert Jonard in *La Vie quotidienne à Venise au XVIIIᵉ siècle* (Hachette, 1965): two teams, known as the Mountain and the Plain, came on to the ground, through large wooden entrances, from opposite sides, each with its standard, blue or red, and wearing loose summer shirts. One end of the field belonged to each team, with an empty space in the middle where the big leather ball was put into play. They all ran after it at top speed and whoever got it was at once set upon by the opposition, who tried to take it from him. His own side rallied to ward them off and give him time to carry it to their end and so win the game, though a hail of blows was exchanged in the process. The only permissible method of attack was to butt as hard as possible with the upper arm. Players were floored on all sides, the ball passed from hand to hand, until at last someone had it for long enough to gain his home ground.

76. His picture is in the Kaiser Friedrich Museum in Berlin. The rhinoceros, as Pietro Longhi painted him, square and solid, may be seen at Ca' Rezzonico.

77. The Eccelso, as the Council of Ten was also called, had wished to forbid the mask except for Carnival, but it was told the nobles who 'stayed at home' would never conform to such a law, and had to change its mind.

78. The pick of the bunch, Molmenti thought, were that of the Pisani at Stra, considered a monument to the glory of Venice; the Malcontenta, built by the Foscari in the sixteenth century; the villa of the Manin family at Passeriano; and those of the Contarini at Piazzola, the Erizzo at Pontelongo, the Baglioni at Massanzano and the Farsetti at Sala.

79. 1750-1825. Another typical figure from the floating population of the time, adventurer and gambler, manager of a theatre and publisher of his own memoirs.

80. Letter to her daughter, Lady Bute, of January 5, 1748. The Duchess of Cleveland had always ridden astride.

81. 'In obedience to your esteemed orders, I have the honour to lay before Your Illustrious Lordships the information I have gathered. It is well known that people used to marvel at the Noble Lady Marina Sagredo Pisani for going out with her maid in the mornings and walking about in a gown and *zendale*. No one is surprised to see a woman so dressed nowadays for many ladies wear the *zendale* every afternoon, not only in the street but in the Piazza and under the Procuratie, when their maids or their *cavalieri serventi* accompany them. Married ladies, singers and dancers are there at the same time, all in their lace *zendali*, so one cannot tell the quality from the harlots. Decent people are disturbed by the

scandal, and this is giving rise to talk against the nobles.' Thus Angiolo Tamiazzo, on November 3, 1774.

82. Mlle de Valois, daughter of the Regent Orléans, married the future Duke of Modena in 1721. The *andrienne* must have been named in honour of the actress Adrienne Lecouvreur.

83. Gian Battista Manuzzi turned in his information on March 17, 1766: 'There is a woman called *la Sansonu* with a shop under the Procuratie Vecchie for balms, scent and knick-nacks. She has been recently in the company of a Milanese whom she says is her husband. She got the name Sansona a few years ago, when appearing as a strong-woman at the fair. Quite young, not bad-looking, tall, with pleasant manners and decent clothes. . . . Today, about the third hour, I observed her in Angelo Sperazin's shop, at the sign of the Sultana under the Procuratie Nuove, laughing and talking with some gentlemen. . . . Angelo Sperazin approves of her, so far as I can see, since he lets her hang about his café for as long as she likes, according as to whether she is having a chat or hawking her wares. This is very blatant, the more so as most people think her comings and goings with balm and other merchandise are cover for something less respectable. A year or two back, everybody knows, she was obviously in want . . . and now she eats and dresses well. This is all since getting acquainted with many noble patricians, with whom she is seen to be on confidential terms.'

84. The Marchese Francesco Albergati Capacelli, 1728–1806. He was a member of Goldoni's circle and himself a prolific playwright. Voltaire dedicated a tragedy to him and he translated Racine's *Phèdre* into Italian.

85. *La Politique civile et militaire des Vénitiens* (1668).

86. In his *Letters from Italy describing the customs and manners of the country in the years 1765 and 1766*. This book, published in 1767, provoked that of Giuseppe Baretti in reply. See p. 69.

87. 1778–1827; poet and novelist. After his early admiration of Napoleon, he opposed him bitterly and came as an exile to England, where he frequented Holland House and knew Byron.

88. This was M. de Froulay.

89. It was she who introduced Byron to Stendhal, as well as to Teresa Guiccioli. Lamberti, who was one of her lovers, wrote for her the famous song, *La Biondina in Gondoleta*, and in later days she danced with Ugo Foscolo round a liberty tree in the Piazza.

90. He was a Milanese, described by Molmenti as 'card-sharper and courageous soldier, shameless libertine and witty writer.'

91. The only churches that belong entirely to the eighteenth century are the Gesuati, San Boldo (1735), the Pietà (1741) and San Biagio (1749). The best baroque church in Venice, the Salute at the mouth of the Grand Canal, dates from 1687.

92. Veronese worked here for several years, having found refuge in the monastery, it is said, after murdering a rival painter.

93. *Lettres et Mémoires* (Frankfurt, 1738).

94. Jean Baptiste Dupaty, *Lettres sur l'Italie* (Paris, 1824).

95. Evidence abounds. The following extract from the *Reisen in verschiedenen Ländern von Europa in den Jahren 1774–5 und 1776* (Leipzig, 1778) is by Pilatti di Tassulo, who was a serious and even a solemn observer. It is quoted in the 1923 Sirène edition of Casanova's Memoirs: 'The nuns, or those of certain convents at least, are cheerful libertines who do no harm at all and as much good as possible. If they fail to keep an enforced vow of chastity it is no fault of theirs, but of the parents who pushed them into the cloister and of the people who thought of such a dreary vow to begin with. Their intrigues are generally love affairs, and they

have such nice natures that those who are past the age for loving are always glad to assist the younger ones, so that really, in one way or another, all are being kind. Nuns from the big convents are for ever going masked to the play or out to meet their lovers on the Piazza. All they have to do is get round the sister-portress, who never says no to those with noble families or powerful friends and admirers. If the Mother Superior sees what is happening she keeps quiet for the same reason, and I speak from more than hearsay on the subject, acquainted as I am with nuns who take the cloistered life very lightly indeed.'

96. Paolo Renier was the last Doge but one, and the Procurator Francesco Pesaro was patron of the famous balloon ascent. There is a Farsetti palace on the Grand Canal and the rococo villa at Santa Maria di Sala is now being restored.

97. *Lettere di Venezia, 1713,* published Prato (1866).

98. Venice, 1797, The *Memorie* were translated into English by John Addington Symonds in 1889; revised and abridged by Philip Horne, an edition of this translation was published by the Oxford University Press in 1962.

99. Caterina Dolfin was born in 1736 and was nearly forty when she married the Procurator Andrea Tron. Her poetry made her famous under the name of Dorina Nonacrina and she played a leading part in the intellectual life of Venice, ruling her poets and artists like a queen and always known as Sua Altezza.

100. She had been remarkably pretty but proved a most unsatisfactory housewife and such a hindrance that Carlo, whose capital she had helped to mismanage, had to retreat elsewhere in order to work in peace.

101. Horatio Brown managed to pass this insignia off, in his translation of Molmenti, as 'an owl with two ears of corn in its claws'.

102. There is some doubt about Bianchi, though, whose songs may have been written by the Doge Grimani, for whom he worked.

103. Charles Burney, Mus.D., was Fanny Burney's father, the friend of Dr Johnson and of Giuseppe Baretti. His book, *The Present State of Music in France and Italy,* was first published in 1771. The two-volume Oxford edition (1959) is edited by Percy Scholes.

104. A typical diatribe, all in one breath, was launched against any youth who happened to deceive his father: 'No son of mine! The cat must have brought you in, you scratch the hand that pets you. No softness anywhere, your mother must have been a tigress. And as for fathering you, I should think it was a mule, the way you lash out when somebody wants to give you something. . . . I hope the cocks start crowing when you want to go to sleep, I hope the dogs gnaw your bones. I hope the cats all claw you and lice devour you, I hope you crawl with them . . .' and so on and so forth.

105. *Carlo Goldoni, le Théâtre et la vie en Italie au XVIIIᵉ siècle* (Paris, 1896).

106. Louis Petit de Bachaumont, 1690–1771, knew Goldoni during the years the latter spent in France, where he did, in fact, furnish scenarios for plays.

107. See note 2.

108. Claude-Charles Bernard de Blancey was a fellow magistrate in Burgundy, one of the fortunate group to whom Brosses addressed his travel-letters.

109. The Tessin family had gone to Sweden from France in the seventeenth century and produced several generations of distinguished architects. This Count Tessin was in Venice in 1736.

110. It was Giorgio Massari who added the debatable top storey to Ca' Rezzonico and built the Gesuati church on the Zattere. Andrea Tirali designed the Valier monument in San Zanipolo, and Rossi built San Stae and dreamed up the green and white marble décor that festoons the Gesuiti.

111. Now in the Querini-Stampalia library in Venice.

112. Jacques Mallet du Pin, 1749–1800, the Swiss journalist who supported and worked for the legitimate cause.

113. Henri III of France had written his name in the Libro d'Oro in 1574, but the exiled Louis XVIII personally ensured it was crossed out again a year before the book was burned – a gesture of protest when the Signory got cold feet and forced him to remove from his refuge in Verona.

114. Among the works of art taken away by the French were the four horses from the basilica. They were set up, harnessed to a chariot, on the Arc de Triomphe du Carrousel, built in 1806 as a monumental entrance to the Tuileries palace. Their intended passenger was a figure of Napoleon in bronze, with sceptre and imperial robes, but he himself rejected this scheme and the empty vehicle occasioned opposition puns about *le char l'attend* and *le charlatan*. Louis XVIII sent the horses back to Venice and the group on the Carrousel is a reproduction.

INDEX